TAKING BACK
OUR LIVES

TAKING BACK OUR LIVES

A CALL TO ACTION FOR THE FEMINIST MOVEMENT

ANN RUSSO

ROUTLEDGE
New York London

Published in 2001 by
Routledge
29 West 35th Street
New York, NY 10001

Published in Great Britain by
Routledge
11 New Fetter Lane
London EC4P 4EE

Routledge is an imprint of the Taylor & Francis Group.

Library of Congress Cataloging-in-Publication Data

Russo, Ann, 1957–
Taking back our lives: a call to action for the feminist movement / by Ann Russo.
p. cm.
Includes bibliographical references and index.
ISBN 0-415-92710-2 — ISBN 0-415-92711-0
1. Abused Women—United States.   2. Sexual abuse victims—United States.
3. Feminism—United States.   I. Title.
HV6626.2.R87 2001
362.82'92'0973—dc21   00-051737

For all the women for whom the answers don't come easy— because of sexism, because of racism, because of sex, because of violence, because of family loyalty, because of sexual shame and stigma, because of denial, because of class exploitation, because of child rape, because of ethnic and racial loyalty, because of homophobia, because of self-hatred, because of sexual coercion, because of sexual repression, because of fear, because of rape and battering, because of compulsory heterosexuality, because of alcoholism and drug addiction, because of misogyny, because of sexual degradation and humiliation, because of self-blame, because of sexual violence, because of repetition, and finally, because life is hard.

For all the women for whom the answers don't come easy— but for whom the search for hope and love, and the struggle for social justice, for autonomy and respect and self-determination, for family and community, for intellectual, physical, sexual, and emotional freedom, for equality and mutuality, for choices, for sexual pleasure, for personal and social dignity, and for bodily integrity, as well as for hope and for collective vision and transformation are absolutely essential, necessary, and urgent.

CONTENTS

ACKNOWLEDGMENTS

This collection of essays comes out of my twenty-five years of involvement in feminist and social justice politics, education, and activism in the United States. Each of the essays is connected to historical events, actions, and organizations of which I have been a part. The ideas are not solely mine, therefore, but the product of history, many conversations and debates, and my own struggle to understand and to change the world. The essays are offered as a contribution to lively and ongoing debates and struggles within the U.S. women's movement; the ideas are part of a process that continues to change and develop as I write.

The essays owe themselves to the many words of the many women I have been in contact with over the years either through conversation or reading. Thus, I thank the thousands of women whose stories of survival, resistance, and struggle inspire me daily. I thank all of the survivors, activists, scholars, advocates, counselors, journalists, writers, poets, and performers who inspire me through their words and actions to speak out, to reflect, to cultivate compassion and respect, to protest, to resist, to educate, to advocate, and to struggle for social and economic justice. I especially thank the many women who have told me their stories, shared their experiences and wisdom, and joined with me in commiserating about and changing the world.

These essays also reflect my involvement in many feminist initiatives and organizations. I cannot name them all, but a few stand out in my mind as integral to the essays in this volume—these include Caucus Coalition, The Regulars, Feminist Forum, and the Common Differences Organizing Committee, all in Champaign, Illinois; White Women Against Racism and Violence Against Women, the Ad Hoc Committee Against Sexual Harassment at the Massachusetts Institute of Technology, the Network for Battered Lesbians, all in Boston, Massachusetts; and Queer White Allies Against Racism of the Color Triangle, Dykes against Oppression, and Advocates for Prostituted Women and Girls in Chicago. Many individual women I know through my involvement in the women's movement contributed to these essays. While it would be impossible to recognize them all, I thank the following for their contribution to my ideas and journey over the last twenty years. I thank Karen Kahn, who as editor of *Sojourner* in the early 1990s, encouraged me to write, who solicited my ideas, and who gave me the opportunity to type *Sojourner* for a few years. I'd also like to thank Rhea Becker, Mary Bertin, Debbie Borkowitz, Rusel Busisiwe-Quaery, Gail Dines, Cynthia Enloe, Laurie Fuller, Beth Leventhal, Pam Loprest, Lindsay McBride, Erica Meiners, Claudine O'Leary, Esther Pandian, Angela Radan, Jo Schwartz, Joni Seager, Chandra Talpade Mohanty, Michelle Van Natta, Cheryl West, Rebecca Widom, Joy Wright, and Susan Yanow for conversations, for critical analysis, and for personal support. I thank as well my colleagues at DePaul University who have encouraged me in this project over the last few years, especially Marixsa Alicea, Laila Farah, Alesia Garcia, Mechtilde Hart, Sandra Jackson, Paul Jaskot, Beth Kelly, Susana Martinez, Heidi Nast, Elsa Saeta, and Tama Weisman. I thank Ora Schub for her encouragement, and Ann Stanford for our many conversations about the link between spirituality and activism. I thank the many students in my classes at the Massachusetts Institute of Technology, Tufts University, Clark University, and DePaul University—they sustain my commitment to education as well as activism through their enthusiasm, anger, and commitment. My sisters and brothers have been on various parts of this journey with me. In particular, I would like to thank Mark for his pursuit of truthtelling and for his encouragement to find some peace in this life; Laura for her optimistic belief in miracles and her commitment to creating possibilities; Michele for her supportive affirmations; Rose for her insistent encouragement that I complete this project; and John for his support.

I am very grateful for the encouragement and support of Ilene Kalish from Routledge whose ideas and suggestions helped shape this collection. I am grateful as well for the support of DePaul University in the forms of a Liberal Arts and Sciences Summer Research Grant and a University Research Council leave that enabled me to complete this project.

I thank Barbara Schulman for her many years of loving friendship, for her political savvy, and for her tremendous support through some very difficult times, and Suzi Hart for the gift of a wonderful friendship and for our many conversations related to spirit, integrity, and solidarity. I am eternally grateful to Lourdes Torres whose love and friendship have sustained me over the years and helped me to build a life for myself that I had not imagined possible; Cyd Jenefsky for years of friendship, love, and hopeful critical engagement in our many struggles to create justice in our personal and social relations and contexts; Barry Shuchter for humor, insight, love, and hope despite the bleakness of human atrocities; and Francesca Royster for her wonderful love and for her hopeful and creative spirit. I am most grateful to Robyn Epstein for helping me with last minute research questions, for her assistance with the documentation, and for her passion for social justice. Thanks to Alba for visiting me everyday in the summer, and for going for walks to the lake. I thank Lourdes, Cyd, Francesca, and Barry especially for seeing me through the final stages of this project. I thank each of them for their incredible gifts of friendship and love; I could not have completed this project without their consistent encouragement, support, and undying humor.

PART I

TRANSFORMING
FEMINIST
THEORIZING

IF NOT NOW, WHEN?:
Contemporary Feminist Movement to End Violence Against Women

I have come to call the work that I do "atrocity work."[1] It reflects the information I take in on a daily basis—news from what I call the war zones of human relations, particularly the wars against women, since they are the ones that seem most taken for granted as natural and normal. As Andrea Dworkin (1988) describes, "I deal with what happens to women in the normal course of women's lives all over this planet: the normal stuff that is abusive, criminal, violating—the point being that it is considered *normal* by the society at large. It is so systematic that it appears that women are not being abused when these commonplace things happen to women because these abuses are so commonplace."[2] The problem of violence against women and children is overwhelming—it is huge, it is complex, and it is painful.

Consider simply the reported level of interpersonal violence against women in the United States. One out of three women in the United States reports that she has experienced some form of sexual abuse; up to 70 percent of rape cases are perpetrated by acquaintances, dates, co-workers, friends, lovers, husbands, employers, doctors, therapists, and/or fathers of women.[3] Women are battered by men in approximately one-half of all heterosexual marriages and partnerships and similarly high rates of domestic violence exist in same-sex relationships.[4] A Justice Department study, "Domestic Violence and Stalking," reports that an estimated one out of every twelve women is stalked during her lifetime, and that there are over 1.4 million victims of stalking annually.[5] Most women living in the United States experience varying levels of sexual, racial, xenophobic, and homophobic harassment in work and educational environments, in prison and mental health institutions, on the streets, and in neighborhoods.[6] For instance, a Human Rights Watch report documents pervasive sexual abuse of women prisoners by male guards in the United States prison system.[7]

Fighting this violence seems like trying to stop a tidal wave, but an invisible one—few seem to notice or care about the onslaught of violence in women's lives. In her poem "What Does It Take?" Cherríe Moraga eloquently writes—

> . . . the deaths of our mothers
> are never that public
> they have happened before
> and we were not informed.
> Women do not coagulate into one
> hero's death; we bleed
> out of many pores, so constant
> that it has come to be seen
> as the way things are.[8]

In my scholarship and activism, I pursue the question of what it will take for folks—friends, families, communities, social institutions—to respond as if all women's lives mattered, to take to the streets not just in mourning but in outrage. Moraga ends her poem:

> What does it take to move me?
> your death
> that I have ignored
> in the deaths of other women?
>
> Isn't the possibility
> of your dying
> enough?[9]

In writing about violence against women, I worry that readers won't feel the urgency that consumes me every day when I hear yet another atrocity story from a close friend, a student, a co-worker, the newspaper, or the evening news. And the violence never simply ends in the incidental moment, because for survivors and those connected with them, these events live on and on and on in our lives. Thus, it is not only the stories from today, this week, this month, but the stories from ten years ago, fifteen years ago, thirty years ago that haunt survivors and our allies, including all those who are trying to stop the onslaught of violence and at the same time heal the wounds.[10] More importantly, it is not simply the isolated individual incidents of violence that women experience that we must consider. The violence in women's lives is part of a daily fabric for many women that involves ongoing daily realities of devaluation, mistreatment, discrimination, harassment, rape, and battery grounded in oppressive systems of sexism, racism, classism, capitalism, xenophobia, heterosexism and homophobia, among others. Most women experience a multitude of assaults from a variety of sources and the impact is a result of this accumulation of incidents in social contexts that ignore, minimize, justify, rationalize, and dismiss women's experience of abuse and violence.[11]

Women's experience of violence is not simply in the immediate incident, but is compounded by the responses of social institutions to mistreatment, discrimination, harassment, and violence that perpetuate and reproduce the violence in women's lives. Women's experience of violence and the social and institutional responses to this violence vary by the identities of victims and perpetrators and the specific historical and social contexts. The victim-blaming, the apathy, the indifference, and sometimes contempt and hostility women face from police, from family members, from teachers, from hospital personnel, and from judges and juries are informed by women's social identities, locations, and histories. The mostly negative responses to women who experience violence are often as hurtful as the incidents because they reinforce the messages that women are to blame, that women deserve to be abused, that women accept oppression, and that women are unworthy of social justice.

This book is a collection of reflective essays about my involvement in the feminist movement to end violence against women in the United States. In it I seek to reflect, challenge, and expand some of the current perspectives on violence against women, particularly those that rely on gender-exclusive frameworks for their analysis and political strategy. What I have to say is ultimately a product of my own background and history as a forty-three-year-old, white, middle-class, lesbian, and feminist who was raised Roman Catholic in the midwestern United States. I am a survivor of child sexual abuse within and outside of my family, and a survivor of rape and sexual abuse as an adult by acquaintances, lovers, and a professor. I am able to speak out and name these abuses so candidly in part because of the existence of the women's movement against violence and because both my parents are deceased. Moreover, the unearned privilege of being white in a white supremacist society, and the privilege of being a professor in Women's Studies at DePaul University, make the speaking less burdensome given that I do not have to face the race and class bigotry and presumptions that often attend such speaking.

For the past twenty years, I have been a political activist and educator addressing sexual violence against women. My ability to survive, and even to thrive, has been a direct result of feminist analysis, politics, and activism—helping me to channel some of my blame, anger, rage, and grief outward, instead of inward. My survival has to do as well with the unearned white middle-class privilege that provided me with access to higher education and to many resources. Significantly, this privilege made it so that my stories, perspectives, and participation were welcomed into predominantly white middle-class feminist organizations. The feminist movement that in many ways saved my life also has been a source of anger, frustration, hurt, anguish, and grief because it has not been the panacea of sister-hood and love that some of us had naively dreamed possible. As much as the movement afforded me a language and a community to recreate myself and change the conditions of my life, I needed to recognize and own the ways that white and middle-class privilege has shaped these conditions. Through my experi-ence in the movement, I have learned about the many ways that feminist initia-tives have often been exclusive and limiting. It is this exclusivity and limitation that I seek to challenge and change through the writing of this book. Mainstream perspectives, mostly emanating from the experiences of white and middle-class and heterosexual women, have often not addressed the multiple and interlocking systems of oppression and privilege that shape all women's lives. The essays in this book reflect the ways I have tried to address the exclusionary, limited, and some-times dangerous politics of the mainstream feminist movement in the United States. My purpose is to contribute to the efforts to expand and transform feminist work for social justice within and outside of the women's movement.

This collection of essays draws upon my experiences in the feminist antivio-lence movement as an educator, scholar, and activist with a focus on interpersonal violence. The essays are based in my involvement in antiracist feminist education and activism over the past twenty years. The voices, perspectives, and challenges of many women inform this work. Such a collection would not be imaginable had it not been for the works of many many writers, activists, and scholars, including Audre Lorde, Cherríe Moraga, Gloria Anzaldúa, Angela Davis, Andrea Dworkin, Kimberlé Crenshaw, Melanie Kaye/Kantrowitz, Aurora Levins Morales, Dorothy Allison, Barbara Smith, Chrystos, Inés Hernandez-Avila, Beth Richie, Emma Perez, Antonia Castañeda, Mari Matsuda, and Adrienne Rich, among many oth-ers. Their words and efforts continue to challenge, enrich, and change my own work. Taking seriously the call to action these writers evoke, I have sought in these essays to address the complexities of violence against women by placing the notion of interlocking oppressions and privilege at the center of the analysis, rather than around the periphery.

U.S. WOMEN'S MOVEMENT AGAINST VIOLENCE AGAINST WOMEN

Violence against women began to gain prominence once again as a major social is-sue in the United States in the 1970s.[12] This was a major breakthrough in public consciousness. Prior to 1970, for instance, most social discourse constructed rape and wife battering as individual women's problems to be borne in silence and shame, except in the cases of interracial rape involving men of color and white women. In the latter case, the socially constructed white supremacist myth of the

Black rapist of "innocent" white womanhood was responsible for justifying the mass lynching of African-American men and for ignoring the systematic rape of women of color and poor women. With the rise of feminism in the late 1960s, and through participation in consciousness-raising groups, women began to politicize women's personal lives. Through this process came the knowledge that pervasive interpersonal and institutional violence shaped woman's lives, and as a result women began to organize to publicize it in an effort to end it. Beginning with the early 1970s speak outs against rape and throughout the intervening years, thousands of women (and increasingly men) have testified to the many forms of interpersonal, public, and state violence against them[13]—including intrafamilial and interpersonal battery and rape;[14] sexual harassment and assault on the street, in the workplace, in educational, medical, and prison institutions;[15] sexual assault, battery, and torture in wars and in the service of colonial domination;[16] incestuous assault and child rape in and outside of families;[17] prostitution, female sexual slavery, pornography, and the international trafficking of women and girls.[18]

Feminists argue that the violence in women's lives must no longer be understood as an individual private experience; instead, it is a systemic problem that is institutionalized throughout the society. Moreover, structural inequalities and the social conditions of women's lives inform and shape the incidence of violence in women's lives, the ways that women experience violence, and the ways that social institutions respond to it. Feminists, for instance, point out that harassment, abuse, rape, battery, and sexual torture contribute to and are informed by histories of patriarchy, capitalism, colonialism, white supremacy, and slavery. Capitalism and private property, compulsory heterosexuality, white supremacy, hierarchical and competitive market systems create current social conditions of poverty and homelessness, endemic mistreatment, abuse, and violence, as well as produce the conditions for women's resistance and struggle against multiple forms of injustice.[19] Feminists politicize the systems of oppression that fuel the interpersonal and institutional violence in women's lives and call for social and political strategies and solutions, rather than individual ones.

The strengths of grassroots feminist theories and activism, to me, are the passionate anger, astute analyses, and resilient resistance of women who have been willing to speak out about the truths of our lives and call for an end to violence against women. Feminist movements created forums for women to tell each other our stories, to get enraged, to develop analyses and theories based on women's experiences, and to collectively engage in political action to change everything— from our individual selves to the entire world. What most compelled me to be involved in these initiatives has not been the rhetoric or even abstract theories, but the rootedness of this research, analysis, and activism in women's daily lives and our struggles for personal dignity and social justice. As Aurora Levins Morales writes:

As each woman in turn spoke about her life and we recognized how much we had in common, we became able to identify the sources of our anger, frustration, and self-doubt in the treatment we had received at the hands of men. Our exhilaration came from the realization that our pain was not after all a character flaw but a direct result of systematic injustice and that our reactions made complete sense. Oppressed communities have created many forms—from support groups to written testimony, from "speak bitterness" sessions to autobiographical anthologies—through which the connections between conditions of oppression and their impact on the oppressed can be made explicit and public.[20]

Over the past thirty years, thousands of women's organizations have grown up to support and empower women who have been hurt by violence and to organize to end violence against women. These organizations provide validation, information and resources, housing, legal and political advocacy, and grassroots and direct-action organizing efforts. Through the 1970s, antirape groups and rape crisis lines formed all over the country; by 1976, 1500 antirape projects and 400 autonomous feminist rape crisis centers existed across the country. Women organized from the grassroots level, and as the organizations grew, they became more institutionalized and thus more dependent on government and foundation funding. Many of the collectives became hierarchical organizations with paid staff whose credentials were increasingly dependent upon professional degrees, and decreasingly related to first-hand knowledge of violence and grassroots activism in the community (although these are not necessarily mutually exclusive). Many of these nonprofit organizations are not that different from mainstream social service agencies and increasingly they have become tied to state and national government policies and institutions.[21]

Some organizations have held out against complete institutionalization. Boston's Transition House, for instance, started in 1975 by two formerly battered women who opened up their apartment to battered women seeking shelter, remains a collectively run battered women's shelter with battered women, lesbians, women of color, working-class, and activist women on staff. Additionally, a number of smaller, less institutionalized, groups continue to form and thrive for various lengths of time. Feminist activism against violence has taken a variety of forms—including direct action protests, civil disobedience, demonstrations, and vigils; speak outs; newsletters and zines; service networks and legal defense organizations; civil and criminal court cases; legislative efforts to change laws and public policies; and peer education and prevention programs. Some women have publicly confronted their perpetrators, pressed criminal charges, and filed civil suits (a method successfully used by some adult incest survivors against their fathers). Profeminist men have initiated groups committed to holding themselves and other men accountable for male violence, and to public education to contribute to ending violence against women. The many accomplishments—while seemingly small in relation to the overwhelming incidence of sexual violence—are a result of thousands of individual and collective actions across the country. All are important in challenging the status quo and all make a difference in some women's lives. One can see an improvement in the way that some individuals, families, communities, and social institutions understand and respond to violence. Yet the institutionalization of the movement in particular, and the increasingly hegemonic ideological cohesion with existing systems of oppression, has led to some serious limitations in scope and breadth.

Most of the institutionalized projects addressing violence against women assume an exclusively gender-based analysis of violence against women. Many feminists, especially those whose perspectives are tied to white, middle-class and/or heterosexist values and orientation, place gender inequality and misogyny (usually defined as men's hatred of women, rather than both men and women's hatred of women) at the center of the analysis of violence against women. Increasingly, mainstream feminist organizations are sometimes indistinguishable from social service agencies and are often closely aligned with the state in monitoring and controlling violence against women. This has led to a movement more focused on individuals and social control mechanisms rather than on broad-based social and institutional transformation. White and middle-class feminists who are often in leadership positions mostly assume that women's common experience of men's sexualized violence has the potential to bring us together to demand fundamental changes in the male-dominant U.S. culture and society. For many feminists, the prevalence of violence against women is testament to its centrality in women's oppression, the horror of it is testament to its urgency and significance in women's lives, and the acceptance of and/or apathy toward violence by most social institutions is testament to its foundation in a patriarchal, male-dominant, misogynistic society.

When faced with the contradictory evidence in women's stories and the multiple perspectives women inevitably articulate, feminist leaders of the most prominent organizations tend to ignore or deny the complexities involved, or to minimize their significance. The multiple identities and experiences of women arising from interlocking oppressions are peripheralized in the face of what is defined as the "common experience" of sexualized violence. For instance, despite the knowledge of the multiple roots of violence, as well as the centrality of racism and classism to how social institutions respond to violence, many feminists continue to articulate an analysis of sexism and misogyny as the primary explanatory framework. Similarly, many feminists resist the evidence of women's discrimination and violence by other women and hold tight to exclusivist theories of male domination. This gender-exclusive framework inhibits the creation of coalitions and alliances across gender, racial, ethnic, sexual identity, class, and national lines to prevent, challenge, and stop broad-based discriminatory violence based in multiple and interlocking systems of oppression and privilege.

Feminist movements face many challenges—personally, collectively, and politically. One major challenge is how to address the complex realities of the violence and its effects, given the ways that sexism, racism, homophobia, classism, xenophobia, and other systems of oppression continue to reproduce violence and inequality. In addition, feminists must continually address the generalized inertia, victim-blaming, and differential treatment embedded in social and institutional responses to the violence in women's lives.

MOVING BEYOND A GENDER-EXCLUSIVE FRAMEWORK

From the start of contemporary feminist organizing against violence against women in the United States, a critical mass of feminists of color and antiracist allies have theorized and politicized the limitations of an exclusive focus on male domination. The work of Angela Davis and bell hooks, among others, has been central to the development of these perspectives.[22] While men's violence against women is connected to gender inequality and misogyny, racial and class hierarchy and sexual stigmatization and criminalization as well as xenophobia are enmeshed with the forms and strategies that sexism and misogyny take.[23] In contrast to a framework that conceptualizes sexism as a separate system of oppression, Patricia Hill Collins suggests that we view "the relations of domination for a particular woman for any given sociohistorical context as being structured via a system of interlocking race, class, and gender oppression." This approach expands "the focus of analysis from merely describing the similarities and differences distinguishing these systems of oppression and focuses greater attention on how they interconnect."[24] Rather than creating a binary oppositional framework, Collins suggests that we embrace "a both/and conceptual stance" that "moves us from additive, separate systems approaches to oppression and toward what I now see as the more fundamental issue of the social relations of domination."[25] Similarly, Morales emphasizes the enmeshment of race, class, sexual orientation, and gender forces in the shaping of all of our lives. She argues that these are not distinct systems; rather, "Each one is wholly dependent on all the others for its existence. For a liberation theory to be useful, it must address the way systems of oppression/privilege saturate each other, are mutually necessary and, in fact, do not exist without one another."[26] The enmeshment of systems of oppression and privilege is evidenced in the incidence of violence, in its effects, and in the ways that specific families, communities, as well as social and legal institutions differentially respond to violence.

Violence against women has multiple interconnected sources, and is not tied exclusively to an isolated system of misogyny and male dominance. Histories of conquest, immigration, and slavery account for women's differential targeting and experience of rape, torture, and murder. Antonia Castañeda and Andy Smith document the colonialist-based rape of American Indian women in the genocidal war against Indians in what is now considered the United States.[27] White supremacist and colonialist ideology constructed American Indian women as racially different from white women in ways that justified the rape of Indian women, while protecting the "purity" of white women. Lucie Hirata examines how Chinese immigration in the nineteenth century involved the "lethal exploitation of Chinese prostitutes both as part of the working class in America and as sacrificial victims for the maintenance of patriarchy in semifeudal China."[28] This history is connected to the ongoing exoticization and sexualization of Asian women in the United States.[29] bell hooks, Angela Davis and Darlene Clark Hine, among others, historicize the harassment, rape, and murder of Black women in the United States and its rootedness in U.S. slavery, white supremacist patriarchy, and capitalism.[30] Each of these authors illuminates the interlocking matrix of oppression as well as resistance shaping the life experiences of women of color in the United States. Joan Nestle, Leslie Feinberg, Gregory Herek and Kevin Berrill, among others, document the institutionalized heterosexism and homophobia in the United States and the ways in which violence—e.g., hate crimes, police brutality, forced psychiatric institutionalization—against lesbians and gay men, queer folks, and transgendered folks, has been justified, rationalized, legitimized, and perpetuated.[31] In each of these cases, the sources of violence as well as resistance are multiple, varied, and interconnected.

These systems of interlocking oppression and privilege account for the ways in which women and men are differentially constructed and treated, as well as the ways that women resist and struggle. Misogyny, racism, classism, heterosexism, and antisemitism, among others, construct the differential contexts of women's lives. The differentiations account for inconsistent and unfair responses to multiple forms of violence against women. The ideological framework of categorical and hierarchical distinctions that shapes social institutions in the United States makes some women's lives (i.e., poor women, women of color, lesbians, disabled women, women in prostitution) seem "less important" than the lives of those defined as "valuable," "innocent," and "pure" women—that is, typically white middle-class and upper-class heterosexual women. Violence against white middle-class heterosexual women often gains significance only when the perpetrators are nonwhite or working-class or in some way perceived as "strangers" or "outsiders" to the women and their so-called identity "group." Similarly, the male perpetrators of violence against women are socially differentiated. Men of color and poor men are more likely to be criminalized for violence whether guilty or not. They are assumed to be violent, whereas white middle-class men are less likely to be held accountable for violence and less likely to be criminalized. These differentiations must be addressed in feminist analysis and activism, otherwise such differentiations, which are grossly unfair and unequal, will simply be perpetuated, and the movement to end violence will ultimately be ineffective and unjust.

RAPE AND RACISM

The enmeshment of racism with sexism is vivid in the social and institutional response to rape. Mainstream feminists have argued that social responses to rape are in part premised on the dichotomous construction of women as virgins and whores. A woman's sexual identity and past sexual history are often central to whether or not her lack of consent is acknowledged and she is believed to be a true victim of rape.[32] This is borne out in the ways that, prior to changes in rape law in the mid-1970s, a woman's past sexual history could disqualify her claim of rape. What is left out of this feminist analysis, however, is women's differential access to a claim of innocence, which is intricately connected to race, class, and sexualized identities.

Women are not treated the same under this system of interlocking oppressions. Antonia Castañeda explains:

> For women of color, the inseparable, interlocking oppressions have produced a conceptualization of our sexuality as promiscuous women who offered their favors to white men. Thus these stereotypes, which abound in the historical and popular literature as well as in all aspects of nineteenth- and twentieth-century popular culture in the United States, include the placid Indian "squaw" who readily gives her sexual favors, the passionate Black or mulatto woman who is always ready and sexually insatiable, the volatile Mexican woman who is fiery eyed and hot blooded, and the languid, opium-dowsed Asian woman whose only occupation is sex.[33]

In contrast to women of color, she argues, "White women are reified as the incarnation of both sexual and racial purity. That reification is bought at the price of the devaluation of women of color."[34] White women are often differentiated from one another along the lines of class and implied sexual experience and stigma. In cases of white on white rape, the reification of white womanhood often is dismantled in the service of protecting white men from accountability for sexual violence against white ("his") women as well as all women.

These racial differentiations between women are central to the way that rape law has been interpreted and developed in this country. As Angela Davis argues, the myth of the Black male rapist historically has been used as a justification for white lynch mobs to murder Black men and terrorize Black communities. It continues to instill racial hatred.[35] At the same time, white men's rape of Black women from slavery to the present continues to be dismissed, ignored, trivialized, and ultimately blamed on Black women on the basis of their purported sexual promiscuity.[36] As Jennifer Wriggins' study of rape law and racism further indicates:

> From slavery to the present time, the rape of Black women has been denied by the legal system. During slavery, the rape of Black women by Black men was legal. The rape of Black women by white men was frequent, legal, and a crucial weapon of white supremacy. After the Civil War, the legal system's continued denial of the rape of Black women was manifested in discriminatory doctrinal rules and judicial language. Today Black women continue to suffer rape in disproportionate numbers, while the criminal justice system still takes the claims of Black rape victims less seriously than the claims of white victims.[37]

This racialized sexism is evident in the 1992 St. John University case where a group of white male student athletes was charged with sexually assaulting a Black West Indian woman. The young white men were members of the university's lacrosse team. The men were acquitted on the basis of her alleged "consent" to multiple sexual assaults. This case is not isolated; rarely are white men held accountable for the rape of women of color, let alone for their rape of white women. White men, especially middle-class men, are rarely seen as criminals; instead, if they are convicted of rape or battery, the violence is seen as tied to an individual pathology rather than to their positionality as white, middle-class men. Instead, white supremacist social discourse in the mainstream media and criminal justice system perpetuates myths and stereotypes about women of color which justify and/or deny sexual violence and about men of color as sexual predators who target innocent white women.

White middle-class women's stories are informed as well by the racist and classist systems from which we derive white middle-class privilege and authority. In listening to the stories of women of color, I often hear stories of institutional and cumulative indifference, hostility, and brutality from the police, from social service workers, and from healthcare systems evolving from a racist and classist as well as sexist system. In contrast, while sexism informs the responses of the police to white middle-class women, white middle-class privilege also informs their responses. An example of the difference is reflected in the story of the brutal rape and assault of Girl X, a young African-American girl, in Cabrini Green, a low-income housing project, in Chicago, Illinois. It took community outcry for the media and the police to respond to this case. The underlying racist and classist in-difference to this young woman was exemplified in a Cook County Public Guardian's response to her life. He was reported to have said, "No one is surprised when an underclass kid is raped or killed. It's not that people don't care, it's that they yawn. Whereas if it's a blond-haired, blue eyed kid, they all go crazy. I've seen it a million times." Such a response is outrageous, and more importantly, it is in-dicative of a broader system of indifference and hostility. Contrast this with the ex-periences described by Susan Estrich and Micaela di Leonardo, both white women raped by African-American men.[38] Both women reported the rapes to the police. The police officers' initial belief in their stories rested in part on the fact that the rapists were Black and they were white. It was a combination of sexism and racism that informed their treatment. If the rapists had been white, and/or a nonstranger, it is much more likely that the police would not have taken the re-ports seriously. The differential treatment of "stranger" rape in comparison to ac-quaintance rape is the focus of Estrich's book, *Real Rape* (1987); unfortunately, she does not pursue the racial implications of her own experience; di Leonardo, on the other hand, offers a critical analysis of these intersections.

In a connected and yet different way, white racist officials in the United States have used the myth of the Black male rapist historically to justify the lynch-ings of Black men; this myth continues to instill racial discrimination and hatred, as evidenced in the ways that the racist media and criminal justice system respond to interracial, "black on white" rape. For example, the white mainstream media's handling of the Central Park gang-rape demonstrates the interlocking connection between rape and racism. The white-middle-class-dominant media orchestrated racial and class bigotry against the young African-American and Latino male sus-pects in the name of "protecting" a white upper-middle-class professional woman; the crime was tied in the media discourse to their racial identification, not their gender, and used to further the interests of racism, not to explore the foundations of rape. This response is very different from the way the media handled the St. John University case, and the cases of white male fraternity gang-rape that involve white men and white women. In these cases, white middle-class men are continu-ally let off the hook so as not to "ruin" their lives by holding them accountable for their crimes.[39] The women in these cases are often portrayed as sexually promis-cuous, thus blameworthy. Sharpley-Whiting offers a critical contrast in her com-parison of the way U.S. media constructed the cases of sexual assault and harassment involving William Kennedy Smith, Michael Tyson, and Clarence Thomas.[40] She writes:

> All three trials [Smith, Tyson, Thomas] alleged sexual misconduct or abuse. However, only the black males dealt with the burdensome stigma

of sexual savagery that racism created and continues to perpetuate. While Tyson . . . was depicted as the quintessential sexual brute and Thomas reportedly had a taste for hardcore pornography, Smith, who had been accused by at least three other women of sexual assault, was presented as a clean-cut American boy by the media. Indeed *Time* deemed Smith 'an unlikely candidate for the rapists' role.' Having all the ingredients of a sensational trial, the televised Bowman/Smith saga nonetheless lacked that racial flavoring which vulgarizes sex, making it all the more tantalizing to the white American psyche. The name Thomas, rather than Senator Robert Packwood, would become synonymous with sexual impropriety in political culture, and Tyson, not Smith, would come to represent the 'poster boy' for date rape.[41]

Years ago, I witnessed firsthand the working of this racist rape mythology when a friend in her 80s was raped in Central Illinois. She was among a group of eleven older white women who were raped over a period of several months. As word spread about the serial rapes, public pressure mounted on the police to identify a rapist. The police sought out whatever similarities they could find to link the cases. The day after the rape, my friend reported to my mother a very sketchy memory of the specific events; but her description of the assailant seemed clear—he was a "clean shaven young white man." In the weeks following the assault, however, her story began to shift as the police worked with her very hazy memory to convince her that it might have been a man that they had in police custody, an African-American man, not a white man. Not surprisingly, the criminal court eventually convicted this man who, as far as I knew from the news reports, had no family or community support in Champaign. He was convicted for two of the rapes, although the police and media publicly linked him to all of the rapes. While my friend's story was not central to the criminal case, her story was connected in the public's mind and eventually in her mind. Her story taught me firsthand how racism operates to criminalize men who may very well be innocent, to evade and protect white male rapists, and to give white women the illusion of protection at the expense of the Black community by perpetuating the myth of the rapist as always/already a Black man. This story directly confirms Angela Davis' analytic history of rape and racism.[42]

Another result of these sexist and racist strategies is that the violence against women (and children) *within* racial and ethnic groups remains invisible and unmarked. However, the relative invisibility depends on the social identities of the victims and perpetrators as well as the contexts. When the white middle-class dominant media reports the interpersonal sexualized violence of white middle-class men against white middle-class women, they construct the stories as individual cases of "sexual misconduct" or "miscommunication" on the part of white mid-dle-class men. In contrast, they portray the white middle-class women in these stories as less than credible and as responsible for the assaults. The stories are rarely connected together into a larger story of the social and systemic nature of men's violence against women. Violence against women of color, poor women, working-class women, lesbians, and prostitutes rarely makes the news, and when it does make the news, the violence is constructed as if it is inevitable and linked to a "culture of poverty," or it is displaced onto the "psychology" of particular eth-nic (read "nonwhite") groups.

WOMEN'S VIOLENCE AGAINST WOMEN

Women's use of violence and misuse of power also complicate mainstream feminist politics. The more women have spoken out about the truths of our lives, the more feminists have needed to recognize and analyze how women are not only victims of violence—rape, battery, abuse (physical, sexual, emotional, verbal), and harassment—but also perpetrators. Women, like men, use violence in the ser-vice of power and control—in lesbian relationships, in the physical and sexual abuse of children, and in other relationships characterized by power and hierarchy · (doctor/patient, therapist/client, teacher/student, employer/employee, prison guard/prisoner). The recognition of women's violence against women and children challenges the attribution of all violence (and therefore power and control) to men and victimization (and therefore powerlessness) to women. Like the response to reports of women's racism, classism, antisemitism, ableism, and homophobia, a good many feminists either deny or minimize women's use of violence. Many ig-nore or minimize the evidence, hold onto theories of male domination to explain women's oppression, and do not include an analysis of women's differential power and privilege in organized efforts to stop violence against women.

The focus on men as the perpetrators of violence and women as the victims may make sense to a certain extent, given the pervasiveness of men's interpersonal violence against women and its connection to the larger context of gender in-equality and societal misogyny. This doesn't make sense once you recognize race, class, age, social status, and other differentiating systems into the analysis of the violence in women's lives. It also doesn't make sense in a society where violence is socially accepted as a method to gain or maintain power and control. This accep-tance is not exclusive to men, women are also culpable. It is fundamentally naïve and false for us to assume that women are somehow immune from using and con-doning aggressive emotional, verbal, physical, and sexual violence to gain or main-tain power and control in personal and social relationships.

But mostly, it doesn't make sense because it *isn't* true. Throughout the time I've been involved in the feminist antiviolence movement, I've known about women's use of power and control strategies, including violence, against women. It's not that women haven't been talking about women's mistreatment, abuse, and violence in our personal lives, but rather that we don't publicly address it in our political theories and actions. For instance, feminists seem reluctant to politicize mothers' abuse of children. This abuse is mostly minimized and/or rationalized. For years I lived with the knowledge that mothers abuse children—my own mother and the mothers of many of my friends, lovers, co-workers, teachers, students, acquaintances, and fellow activists—and yet, it took me years to begin to incorporate this knowledge into my politics. Some of the resistance to recognizing women's violence against their children stems from the feminist struggle to challenge the automatic mother-blaming of psychoanalysis and other patriarchal perspectives that place the responsibility for family problems on mothers.

More importantly, feminists encourage empathic responses to women's use of violence in terms of oppression and powerlessness; this often precludes a documentation and analysis of women's power as mothers, as women in positions of authority, and as privileged by racial, class, religious, and national identifications. This has had an enormous impact on feminist analysis of women's participation in child abuse. For instance, when I became a feminist, I developed an intellectual understanding, and even empathy, for mothers who were abusive and violent (of course in the forefront of my mind and heart, though rarely publicly stated, was my own mother). I attributed mothers' violence to *their* victimization at the hands of their husbands and fathers, and their economic, social, legal, political, and, in relevant cases, their racial, class and ethnic oppression under the larger white male dominated system. I understood my mother's status and behavior in the family and society through this feminist lens. If anything, I tended to feel sorry for her, despite her verbal and physical violence. The challenge remains for feminists to create a social analysis and response to mother's abuse that holds women accountable, and yet doesn't further punish women for situations of oppression.

One thing is for sure, feminist strategies for accountability must not be ones that further instantiate an oppressive and unequal system. In the creation of strategies, feminists need to follow the work of those who examine, document, and critique the social and cultural system in terms of interlocking systems of oppression and privilege. Otherwise, the strategies may further harm many women by being based on the experiences and locations of socially privileged women in the broader society. Strategies must account for multiple and interconnected realities. For instance, I grew up middle-class and my family's "privacy" was protected from public, community, and state intervention. As a result, the abuse was denied, ignored, or downplayed. The "privacy" of white and middle-class privilege shielded my family from state intervention, but this privacy is not afforded to families with less social privilege in this society. White middle-class social service organizations have a history of scrutinizing, punishing, and disempowering women of color and poor women, while ignoring similar issues within the white, middle-class. As Rhea V. Almeida points out, "*Autonomy* (i.e., self-reliance) and *privacy* for white women serve to perpetuate the separation between the public and private domains of their lives. Women of color, however, do not have the same experience. *Public intrusion* into the lives of people of color and working-class people controls their lives in the public arena. It is the modus operandi of social service practice. Furthermore, social service professionals enter this private space with racial biases they do not even notice."[43] These same service agencies would *not* intervene nor be interested in interrogating my white middle-class family. Increased policing and state intervention cannot be the answers to child abuse unless the entrenched racism and classism of these institutions are overhauled. Feminists need to challenge the middle-class biases and assumptions as well as personnel that run social service agencies, and the women who seek services from these organizations must be the leaders in designing needed changes.[44]

In feminist work against violence, many lesbians and bisexual women also have come forward to speak about the realities of woman to woman rape, battering, and other forms of sexual harassment and abuse. And yet battered and formerly battered lesbians and bisexual women face denial and passivity by the feminist antiviolence movement and lesbian and bisexual women's communities. By labeling the problem as male violence, many women assumed that lesbians and bisexual women in relationships with women somehow had a better chance at freedom from coercion and control. Many of us hoped we'd find safety and equality in women's organizations (or at least the potential for safety). Lesbians and bisexual women, however, who are battered and/or raped by their lovers (or whomever) have few resources to find support and advocacy. Because of heterosexism and homophobia, in combination with sexism, racism, classism, and other forms of oppression, many battered and raped lesbians and bisexual women are limited in their options. It is very difficult, if not impossible, in many situations to rely on the police for protection; and only recently have a very few shelters and services scattered across the United States welcomed lesbians and bisexual women.

When confronted with women's violence against women, many feminists argue that it is less about inequality because it involves socially equal partners, and many attribute the interpersonal violence in lesbian relationships to personality or to living in a sexist and homophobic society. Such arguments are problematic for a number of reasons. First, women are not socially equal to one another. Feminists cannot assume consent and mutuality just because the people involved are lesbian and bisexual women. Lesbians and bisexual women face heterosexism and homophobia within and outside of their communities, and our lives and relationships are further shaped by race, class, religion, ethnicity, and national locations and contexts. By denying or minimizing the violence in same-sex relationships, and by not addressing the multiple oppressions informing the experiences of and responses to violence against lesbians and bisexual women, feminists implicitly perpetuate the use of violence to establish power and control in intimate same-sex relationships. Lesbian feminists would not accept these forms of power and control in a heterosexual context. With little to no community accountability, it is the battered lesbians and bisexual women who leave town, who are afraid to go to community events for fear of further abuse, and who suffer in silence and isolation.

Feminists may also tend to defend or excuse women's violence on the grounds that lesbians and bisexual women are oppressed; some trace the propensity toward violence back to difficult childhoods. Similar to justifications about mother's abuse of children, focusing soley on women's oppression as an explanatory framework can deflect attention away from women's active perpetuation of rape and battering. Meanwhile, this approach does not serve to address the needs of the women being raped and battered. The women (whose chances for survival and for a better life are being actively diminished) often get marginalized in these discussions. I have had a difficult time coming to terms with lesbian and bisexual women's violence myself, since I, too, have excused women's treatment of me on the grounds of oppression. What I have learned is that violation and control over anyone in an intimate relationship is not acceptable no matter who is involved. Abuse and battery are wrong and are not mitigated by claims of love and sisterhood. Moreover, just because someone has been abused herself does not give her a right to abuse others. We can neither accept these excuses nor use them as rationales for behavior or reasons not to actively support lesbians who have been raped and battered. At the same time, unless larger contexts of oppressive practices and relations are addressed, such violence will only continue.

For the most part, feminists have not integrated the knowledge of women's violence into our broad-based political theories and activism. This lessens our potential for personal and collective outrage because not all of our experiences are being given voice and recognition. Moreover, the consequences are that the women's movement grows more hierarchical and ultimately exclusionary, and the challenges to the root inequalities of violence remain limited.

INTERLOCKING OPPRESSIONS AND FEMINIST RESPONSES

Most feminists have not offered comprehensive analytic and practical approaches to the entanglement of sexism, racism, classism, homophobia, antisemitism, among other oppressions, that shape the violence in women's lives. Mainstream feminist organizations address violence against women from within a generic, universal framework about women's status and oppression that is often based on the experiences of white middle-class women. From this framework, they add on "other" women. The result is that privileged white middle-class heterosexual Christian women continue to be the universalized center of public discourse on violence against women and they become the primary beneficiaries of the movement's research, support, advocacy, and activist activities. As a result, white middle-class heterosexual women who represent the leadership of mainstream organizations continue to create limited and sometimes dangerous programs and policies. These inevitably do not effectively serve most women because they do not challenge the multiple structural inequalities shaping women's experiences, and more importantly, in some cases they may make women's lives more difficult and dangerous. As such, racism, classism, and homophobia continue to divide and disempower organizations and projects despite the efforts of feminists of color and their allies to institute change.

In response to the critical challenges of feminists of color (including lesbians and bisexual women), and lesbians (including women of color), some organizations develop specific programs meant to address the needs of particular groups of women, defined by race, class, sexual orientation, national identity, and religion, among others. I have found that the differences between women often are discussed as cultural and religious, rather than social and structural. In some other cases, specific groups of African-American, Latina, Asian-American, Jewish, and lesbian women have organized ethno-specific or lesbian and bisexual specific projects. In the mainstream organizations oriented to "all women," the issues of structural inequality that create the differentiating impact of violence on women's lives are often reduced to cultural differences between women or to a set of "special issues" to consider in dealing with "other women." While it has been important to explore cultural differences among and between women and to integrate this understanding into service provision, it is an inadequate response to the structural inequalities shaping women's lives. A cultural approach does not address the structural forces of racism, classism, ethnocentrism, homophobia, and anti-semitism that shape social and institutional responses to violence against particular groups of women. The "cultural diversity" approach, in fact, in some ways can further isolate women by "othering" through the objectification of "difference" because there is often no simultaneous interrogation of the specific cultural context of white heterosexual Christianity. Without challenging ethnocentrism in a way that disrupts the hegemony of white heterosexual middle-class Christianity, the inequalities only get reinforced. [45] For instance, I have been troubled in domestic violence work when I hear monolithic descriptions of "Latina survivors" that do not reflect the diversity and multiplicity of Latina identities in the U.S. These descriptions often lead service providers to make ethnocentric, often racist, generalizations about Latino cultures and male dominance. [46]

Another common response to the challenge of addressing multiple identities and interlocking oppressions is to argue that it is women's commonalities, rather than our differences, that will unite us as a movement. Some suggest that "we" lose focus if "we" try to deal with "everything." This idea must be deconstructed. The idea that "we" should focus on commonalities assumes that the differences are insignificant and unrelated to the experience and response to violence against women. This "we" often reflects white middle-class heterosexual and Christian privilege. This is clear when one considers that it has been the many women who are underrepresented in mainstream feminist ideas who continue to stress the importance of addressing social differentiations between women in the struggle to end violence. These differentiations explain why many women might not identify with a women's movement that focuses exclusively on gender oppression and that refuses to recognize, interrogate, and challenge white privilege. The commonalities between women when abstracted from their historical, social, political, and economic contexts may seem overwhelming, but only when privilege affords such abstraction. In response to the fear of losing focus, I would first suggest that such focus is only available to those who are privileged, who do not have multiple sources of oppression and sites of resistance. It is this privilege that needs to be deconstructed and challenged so that it no longer serves as a barrier to understanding the complexities of violence against women. With a recognition of difference and multiplicity among and between women as well as in the sources of violence, a more realistic vision of unity becomes possible—a vision based on political solidarity and a commitment to social and economic justice, rather than one based on an assumed definition of shared victimization.[47] Aurora Morales encourages feminists to consider another conceptualization of unity; she writes, "Rather than build unity through simplification, we must learn to embrace multiple rallying points and understand their inherent interdependence."[48]

What does this mean for feminist organizing against violence? For one, it means that feminists must refuse to reduce women to mono-particularistic identities based on one axis of identification. Instead, in our organizing, we must follow the lead of feminists of color who have created discourses based on interconnected realities, rather than common experiences, across different groups of women. A recognition and analysis of interlocking oppressions must be a part of all feminist antiviolence discourses; the goal would not be to isolate and define distinct identities, but to recognize that identities as well as contexts are multiple, changing, and connected. As a richly diverse group of women striving for socially just communities free of oppression, feminists must not allow organizations to simply accept a divided and unequal system where some lives are privileged over others. One step is simply to recognize and analyze our own positionalities and actions. As Castañeda asks, "Where do each of us stand on each of these interlocking elements? And what will each of us do with this historical legacy? I would ask each of us to interrogate ourselves, our organizations, our work places, our families—to examine our individual gender, sexual, racial, and class politics, and our power and privilege in each realm."[49]

From another related vantage point, Mari Matsuda, a critical race theorist, offers a strategic and directed method of uncovering the ways our lives are shaped through interlocking oppressions. She writes,

> The way I try to understand the interconnection of all forms of subordination is through a method I call "ask the other question." When I see something that looks racist, I ask, "Where is the patriarchy in this?" When I see something that looks sexist, I ask, "Where is the heterosexism in this?" When I see something that looks homophobic, I ask, "Where are the class interests in this?" Working in coalition forces us to look for both the obvious and the nonobvious relationships of domination, and, as we have done this, we have come to see that no form of subordination ever stands alone.[50]

This methodology encourages an active recognition of the ways that privilege and oppression operate in women's lives and in the experiences, social responses, and resistance to mistreatment, discrimination, harassment, and violence.

Feminists must seek to build upon the knowledge and experience of interlocking systems of oppression and privilege in all of our analyses and strategies. As bell hooks, among others, has argued for years, feminists must move from an identity and shared victimization politics to one grounded in political solidarity. Leslie Roman describes this as a shift from "'identity politics' to the *politics of coalition* across different groups of women (and men) for the purpose of challenging racism, imperialism, sexism, and homophobia in their interrelated and contradictory forms."[51] The shift in feminism must be away from a concept of unity based on commonality and sameness, to a concept of unity grounded in difference and radical diversity. As Barbara Smith writes, "What *I* really feel is radical is trying to make coalitions with people who are different from you. I feel it is radical to be dealing with race and sex and class and sexual identity all at one time. I think *that* is really radical because it has never been done before."[52]

DENIAL AND THE DISTANCE BETWEEN US (AND THEM)

In my efforts to address the violence in women's lives, I am constantly confronted with the question of why there is not more outrage in response to endemic violence against women. On days when I feel my own paralysis, when I just can't take in another horror story of a life, a heart, a soul stolen in one form or another, I include myself in the audience for this question. While more public attention has been focused on violence against women over the past thirty years, the response to women's outcry has not been consistent or substantive across communities (including, I might add, the feminist, lesbian, and gay activist communities of which I am a part). Women (and increasingly men) who speak out against violence continue to risk denial, dismissal, blame, and resentment from families, friends, social networks, communities, police, media, and criminal justice systems. I wonder why it continues to be so hard even for progressive feminists, leftists, queer activists, even sometimes for other survivors, to believe survivors of abuse, to offer support, to find ways to hold perpetrators accountable, and to commit themselves to a social justice movement to end violence against women. Despite increased knowledge of endemic interpersonal, familial, and institutional violence against women, organizations that seek to address this violence—through counseling, shelter, advocacy, education, and prevention—continue to be met with little social support and major cuts in funding.

It seems that part of the apathetic and distanced response stems from pervasive denial and minimization of the mistreatment, abuse, and violence in women's lives. If we deny the prevalence of abuse and violence within and outside of social institutions, then we don't have to face the painful realities of mistreatment, abuse, and violence in our own lives. As Cherríe Moraga writes, "Without an emotional, heartfelt grappling with the source of our own oppression, without naming the enemy within ourselves and outside of us, no authentic, non-hierarchical connection among oppressed groups can take place."[53] She writes further, "to remember [what it feels like to be a victim] may mean giving up whatever privileges we have managed to squeeze out of this society by virtue of our gender, race, class, or sexuality."[54] If we minimize the impact of abuse and violence, we are not compelled to take them seriously enough to act against them. More importantly, denial makes it possible for us to differentiate ourselves from both victims and perpetrators, as if our lives are not affected by the prevalence of personal, social, and institutionalized inequalities in this society.

Contemporary discourse provides many examples of cultural denial—for example, the lack of sustained discussion in the media of violence against women, the focus on individual acts separate from larger contexts of endemic violence, and the production of sensationalized narratives that separate "us" from "them," the victims from the perpetrators from the onlookers. Moreover, when there is denial, minimization and trivialization of systemic discrimination and violence, we—as members of human communities—do not have to question our own complicity in relationships of power and control. We do not have to interrogate how the institutions where we live, work, and participate are structured along the lines of hierarchy and power and how social inequalities structure the conditions of our lives. If we are in denial about endemic discrimination and violence, we do not have to take responsibility for our own connection to the misery of others through our active silence or complicity.

Within the academic and public discourse about violence, writers often distance themselves from the realities of discrimination, abuse, and violence through the use of disembodied language. Some write and speak about violence from an impersonal and objectified perspective where they are the experts on "others"— both victims and perpetrators. Abstract and disembodied analyses separate survivors of violence from the onlookers, from the social contexts, as well as from the perpetrators. Such separations disconnect those seeking to address violence from the emotions (anger, rage, and grief) that are necessary to successfully confront the complex realities of violence in its multitude of forms within broader social systems of oppression—including misogyny, racism, classism, antisemitism, ablebodism, ageism, and homophobia—in which we are all involved.

I myself have struggled with the "us/them" dichotomy, despite many years of feminist antiviolence advocacy and activism. For me, it has been a constant struggle between the feminist who speaks out against violence from a sociopolitical framework, and the raging and sad woman who has been violated over and over again, who has witnessed violence against the many women and children in her life, and who, through teaching and activism, has heard thousands of stories of mistreatment, harassment, rape, battery, and murder. For me, the statistics are the women I've known and heard about throughout my life—and each one matters. Dworkin describes aptly my experience of this when she writes, "As a feminist, I carry the rape of all the women I've talked to over the past ten years personally with me. As a woman, I carry my own rape with me. . . . Piles and piles and piles of bodies that have whole lives and human names and human faces."[55]

The more I've named and analyzed my own experiences of abuse and violence, the more I've been able to move out of the "us/them" mentality that runs through feminist academic, political, and social discourses of violence, and that has sometimes operated in my own activist speaking, writing, and teaching. When I first gave speeches against rape, I did not integrate my own stories into my analysis. Some of the experiences, particularly the sexual and physical abuse I experienced as a child by my father and a neighbor, I tended to contain in the phrase "my crazy family." Even the experiences of sexual assault from men outside of the family, I tended to minimize and blame on myself. I often felt that what had happened to me was different (read: "my fault," or "not really that bad") and so I had trouble validating my personal experience within my own political analysis. At times, the separation between my analysis and my own life made it harder to sustain my energy and motivation in the antiviolence movement and even harder to connect with the anger, grief, rage, and compassion needed to participate fully. In retrospect, I can see that I still blamed myself for the violence and I minimized its ongoing effects on my life.

Institutionalized projects against violence often reproduce "us/them" dynamics which make it difficult for survivors to be public, outspoken and self-respecting in feminist organizing and to be able to speak both to our victimization and to our strength and power. It is deeply troubling to me when I hear researchers as well as service providers refer to women who are survivors of violence as "victims." The feminist movement's initial use of the term "survivor" rather than "victim" has been lost on many researchers. Increasingly I've heard that shelter workers use the term "victim" to refer disdainfully to women who are not responding "properly" to the social services provided them. Instead of drawing upon survivor strengths of endurance and resistance, some of the "experts" only see pain, victimization, and pathology. These responses marginalize and disempower women by locating the problem within the individual rather than with the broader social structures. Survivors as well as allies can use our pain and anger as the sources of our knowledge, strength, and resistance, and in this process encourage those who have been directly harmed to reclaim our bodies, minds, and souls and to become leaders in the movement for change. It is essential for survivors to be in the forefront of research, services, and political activism, and the initiatives developed must be accountable to survivors, not to the social systems that created the conditions of our lives.

Public discussions of sexual violence—speak outs, conferences, talk shows—often differentiate the experts who provide the analysis from the survivors who tell the personal and painful stories (and I've been on both sides of this). Survivor stories are not necessarily containable, controllable, clean, neat, straightforward, precise, nor consistent. Contradictory, mean, confusing, and messy stories do not make for easy media copy, for easy social psychological answers, nor for calm, reasoned responses. This makes people who see themselves as expert professionals uncomfortable. Some professionals are unwilling to honor the expertise that comes from direct experience and to recognize that survivor knowledge might be different from the knowledge of the "expert" who has not directly confronted her own experiences of violence as a survivor or witness. No one seems to question the claim of many "experts" that they have "not experienced violence." This claim seems dubious. I do not think any of us can separate ourselves from systems that perpetuate mistreatment, discrimination, abuse, and violence. The discomfort with survivors who are directly addressing the violence in our lives translates into further distance between the service providers and researchers and the survivors. It also serves to reinforce the victimization of survivors by maintaining their "victim" status.

Us/them differentiations increased in the contemporary feminist movement in part because of the way the movement became institutionalized and the ways that the issues became increasingly compartmentalized. In other words, because so many projects focus exclusively on rape or domestic violence or sexual harassment or discrimination, many are unable within these projects to conceptualize the inter-connectedness of the experiences, the sources of violence, and their social contexts.

The distance and emotional withdrawal that seem evident in some service provisions seem more in alignment with the perpetuation of inequality, rather than the opposite. In fact, dynamics of power and control plague feminist efforts against discrimination and violence; it might be a more effective move toward so-cial change if we included a systematic way of addressing the dynamics of power and control within our organizations. Why not look at practices of inequality not simply in relation to women as survivors of violence, but in relation to the struc-tures of our own organizations as well as to broader systems of oppression, power, and control in which we are all involved and responsible.

Cherríe Moraga asks some important questions in relation to the connections and divisions among women in the contexts of feminist organizing. She writes, "Within the women's movement, the connections among women of different backgrounds and sexual orientations have been fragile, at best. I think this phe-nomenon is indicative of our failure to seriously address ourselves to some very frightening questions: How have I internalized my own oppression? How have I oppressed?"[56] In speaking of women involved in the women's movement, Moraga writes, "for each of us in some way has been both oppressed and oppressor. We are afraid to look at how we have failed each other. We are afraid to see how we have taken the values of our oppressor into our hearts and turned them against ourselves and one another. We are afraid to admit how deeply 'the man's' words have been ingrained in us."[57] I believe these questions and concerns must be raised as feminists continue to chart their course in this coming century. They are especially relevant given the institutionalization of many of the organizations and initiatives feminists created to address and to end violence against women.

Ultimately, feminists struggling to create a socially just world must challenge and refuse the us/them mentality operative in so much of the work on violence. It only serves social divisions and hierarchies, and leads to limited and exclusionary strategies and visions. Us/them dichotomies are falsely constructed; they do not account for the many forms and levels of injustice, mistreatment, violence, and the responsibility of all of us for their perpetuation.

RECLAIMING IDENTITIES AND RESISTANCES

In ending, I want to challenge the current labeling of the movement against vio-lence against women as "victim feminism." The broad goals of our movement are to document the atrocities, to analyze their roots, and to struggle for social change and transformation. For many, this documentation is heartwrenching, painful, and has sometimes led to despair. It's impossible to build a movement on despair. This means that the language feminists use, the stories we tell, and the visions we create must speak to hopeful possibilities in terms of our identities and the social structures that shape and inform them.

In the last thirty years, the feminist struggle to end violence against women has sought to create language to describe, to protest, and to transform the conditions of our lives. Feminists created and redefined terms such as "battered woman," "wife battering," and "sexual harassment," among others, to clarify the social and political ramifications of interpersonal/institutional violence against women. Yet this language often gets incorporated into a social landscape that pathologizes women rather than critically analyzes the social underpinnings of the violence. As bell hooks says of the term "battered woman":[58] it is "used as though it constitutes a separate and unique category of womanness, as though it is an identity, a mark that sets one apart rather than being simply a descriptive term. It is as though the experience of being repeatedly violently hit is the sole defining characteristic of a woman's identity and all other aspects of who she is and what her experience has been are submerged."[59] She suggests that many women do not take on the label because it "appears to strip us of dignity, to deny that there has been any integrity in the relationships that we are in."[60] Rather than a term of empowerment, bell hooks suggests that "battered woman" is seen by many as a "stigmatizing label" which reinforces the notion that "the hurt woman . . . [is] a social pariah, set apart, marked forever by this experience."[61] While hooks recognizes that "we are indeed often scarred, often damaged in ways that do set us apart from those who have not experienced a similar wounding," she suggests that part of healing is removing the scar. She writes, "This is an empowering process that should not be diminished by labels that imply this wounding experience is the most significant aspect of identity."[62]

The danger of solely conceptualizing ourselves in terms of victimization, hurt, and damage is that it reinforces how social and cultural institutions have constructed us. Dorothy Allison in *Two or Three Things I Know for Sure* offers perspective on the importance of telling her own stories, rather than the story that others, including feminists, might impose upon her. She writes:

> What is the story I will not tell? The story I do not tell is the only one that is a lie. It is the story of the life I do not lead, without complication, mystery, courage, or the transfiguration of the flesh. Yes, somewhere inside me there is a child always eleven years old, a girlchild who holds the world responsible for all the things that terrify and call to me. But inside

me too is the teenager who armed herself and fought back, the dyke who did what she had to, the woman who learned to love without giving in to fear. The stories other people would tell about my life, my mother's life, my sisters', uncles', cousins', and lost girlfriends'—those are the stories that could destroy me, erase me, mock and deny me. I tell my stories louder all the time: mean and ugly stories; funny, almost bitter stories; passionate, desperate stories—all of them have to be told in order not to tell the one the world wants, the story of us broken, the story of us never laughing out loud, never learning to enjoy sex, never being able to love or trust again, the story in which all that survives is the flesh. That is not my story. I tell all the others so as not to have to tell that one.[63]

Feminists must not ignore the victimization, the isolation, the lack of support, the pain of betrayal, or the despair of battery and rape in women's lives. Women continue to live in communities where intimate, intragroup abuse and violence are not recognized and it's necessary to describe their painful realities. If we are in denial of the ways in which we have been victimized, then personal change and social transformation are impossible. Speaking out about the harm done and labeling the experiences as battering, rape, incestuous assault, and/or attempted murder are essential components of healing, recovery, self-determination and social change. However, identifying women who've experienced abuse as *only* or predominantly victims and survivors of abuse, violence, battering, and rape eventually reinforces our status as victims by reducing us to what someone else did to us.

When we only describe the individual damage to each other and when we solely seek validation and support for the individual pain endured, it can lead to depression and despair. This strategy within the broader feminist movement against violence contributes to its inability to sustain a broad spectrum of support and active engagement.[64] Over the years, many lesbians I know have moved away from activism against violence because they felt it was too depressing, negative, and painful. bell hooks provides some insight into this phenomenon when she writes:

Naming the pain or uncovering the pain in a context where it is not linked to strategies for resistance and transformation created for many women the conditions for even greater estrangement, alienation, isolation, and at times grave despair. Rather than aiding the process for self-recovery, many women felt a sense of disintegration as though their lives were becoming all the more fragmented and broken. . . . Longing for self-recovery, not simply the description of one's woundedness, one's victimization, or repeated discussion of the problems, many women simply became disillusioned and disinterested in feminism. . . . [65]

Women's lives are not simplistic nor are they stagnant. Women who struggle, who resist the violence, who work with others to change the conditions of our lives have tremendous courage, power, endurance, and strength. Reclaiming our rights to control our own minds and bodies is a liberating experience, to say the least. When we move from an exclusive focus on victimization to one that celebrates and encourages collective resistance and self-determination as well as social responsibility, we expand our vision of a socially just society free of pervasive violence against women.

Feminists must be careful when we talk about abuse and violence; we must not, in the process of documenting the problem, further pathologize women. Feminists must publicize the positive benefits that accrue when we resist, challenge, and change attitudes, behaviors, and institutions which inhibit and sometimes destroy us. To do this, we must communicate a faith that communities and institutions do have the capacity to stop violence and that we will benefit positively from doing so. I believe feminist efforts will be able to sustain themselves in a politically progressive way when we emphasize the ways in which our work encourages women to gain better control over our lives and our relationships, and to improve our communities. One way to do this is to draw upon the strengths of women who have experienced, survived, resisted, and challenged violence. We all, in different ways and at different times, actively seek to change our lives. Why not label ourselves resisters, instead of survivors, emphasizing that women can and have changed, escaped, fought back, resisted, critically analyzed, created change, and thrived in their lives. Dorothy Allison's essay, "Survival Is the Least of My Desires," is inspiring in this regard. She writes, "I'm interested in a lot more than mere survival . . . we must aim much higher than just staying alive if we are to begin to approach our true potential."[66]

As activists and educators, we need to publicize success stories of women who resist and challenge injustices, including abuse and violence, who work to create and nurture just relationships and institutions, and who embrace a hopeful vision of a socially just society. Imagine what it might be like to go to a speak out on violence, and to hear women tell the stories of violence in conjunction with their stories of resistance—stories of women who fight all forms of oppression; women who left batterers, who stood up to harassers or bullies, women who defended themselves against rapists; women who refuse to accept a racist and homophobic system; women who support women who kill in self-defense; women who support other women; women who are healing from sexual abuse; women who are fighting the sexist and racist criminal justice system, women who organize community efforts against harassers and rapists, women who are taking back control over their lives, women who are challenging and changing institutionalized racism and homophobia in the women's movement, and women who are working together to end violence against women and the social inequalities that support it. When we think about writing our testimonies, creating placards for demonstrations, and designing pamphlets, why not celebrate women's resistance to violence, rather than solely the violence that women face.

In addition to the stories of abuse and violence, why not also talk about what enabled many of us to recognize the abuse, to leave relationships, to fight back, to challenged institutionalized indifference, to seek solidarity with others, and to collectively organize for social change? Why not focus on what enables us to survive, or on what has made it possible for women to reclaim our lives, our bodies, our minds? As Dorothy Allison (1994) writes, "to make any contribution to other lives, I know that I must first begin in the carefully examined specifics of my own. I must acknowledge who has helped me survive and how my own hopes have been shaped. I must acknowledge the miracles in my life."[67] Locating women's strengths, courage, and resistance, and recognizing what makes them possible, are essential to sustaining involvement in a movement for social justice.

When feminists offer hope for change and visions of strong, beautiful, and positive communities and relationships, we invite involvement. Creating change in ourselves, in relationships, in institutions, in communities is possible, and each change increases the potential for all of us to come together as stronger communities in the face of increasingly hostile forces in this country. We need to build a movement that enables all of us to make the changes we need to make in order to challenge, refuse, and fight back against victimization and mistreatment in all of its many forms.

2

LESBIANS, PROSTITUTES, AND MURDER:
Deconstructing Media Distortions[1]

What is the value of a woman's life? This question haunts me daily. In the United States social, historical, and cultural context, the question has no simple answer. It depends on race, class, sexual identity, and marital status, as well as on the politics of the situation, the interests being served by the valuation, the life being protected or incriminated. In this chapter, I explore the social construction of violence, murder, and power in the news media when victims or perpetrators are identified as either lesbians or women working in prostitution.[2] I am interested in how media constructions inform and shape social value hierarchies that reinforce gender, racial, sexual, and class inequalities in this society.

Violence against lesbians and women working in prostitution in this country—police brutality, psychiatric stigma and consequent punishment, and daily harassment—has a history of being socially legitimized and condoned. Both lesbians and women working in prostitution have been labeled and treated as criminals and "deviants" for not living within or representing a normatively defined femininity; prostitution in this country is illegal, and while lesbianism is more accepted in some urban areas of the country, both lesbians and prostitutes continue to be the targets of assault, battery, and murder. Joan Nestle's essay "Lesbians and Prostitutes: An Historical Sisterhood" makes the connection between the two group identities historical and material. She writes, "Whores, like queers, are a society's dirty joke."[3] Nestle links the lives of lesbians and prostitutes concretely when she describes how in the "bars of the late fifties and early sixties where I learned my Lesbian ways, whores were part of our world. We sat on barstools next to each other, we partied together, and we made love together. The vice squad . . . controlled our world, and we knew clearly that whore and queer made little difference when a raid was on."[4]

Given heightened awareness of violence against women in this society, many scholars, activists, and concerned citizens criticize the mass media for glorifying, sensationalizing, and/or eroticizing violence against women as entertainment.

They argue that the media encourages and incites individual men to do violence against women; in other words, media violence produces criminals who are increasingly uncontrollable in their attacks on women. Others, however, argue that the problem is not simply the capacity for such media to incite individuals to violence, but rather the way in which the media reinforces social power hierarchies and control through its construction of violence. From this perspective, one must consider which kinds of violence are socially constructed as legitimate and which are considered illegitimate, which violence is condoned and which is punished. As George Gerbner argues, "The power to define violence and project its lessons, including stigmatization, demonization and the selective labeling of terror and terrorists, is the chief cultural requirement for social control. . . . Media violence is a political scenario[;] . . . it is a demonstration of power: of who has it, who uses it, and who loses it."[5] The main social function of media is to "maintain, reinforce, and exploit rather than to undermine or alter conventional conceptions, beliefs, and behaviors."[6]

In this chapter, I argue that the media marginalizes most lesbians and women working in prostitution through neglect and indifference with regard to the violence they experience, especially when they are poor, working-class, and/or women of color. A privileged race and/or class identity seems to increase the value the media accords a woman's life. This constructs a context of social apathy in response to endemic violence against some women, as opposed to compassion and concern for socially privileged women. It reinforces the idea that lesbians and/or women working in prostitution, particularly those who are poor and/or women of color, are less valued and thus expendable. By defining lesbians and women working in prostitution as social outcasts, the media constructs them as legitimate targets of violence, which in turn reinforces social hierarchies.

Simultaneously, the media reinforces the social power of white men by legitimating their violence against women in general, and most particularly against "deviant" women, like lesbians and women working in prostitution. Race and class clearly figure into this construction of "deviance": Not only are poor women of color often portrayed as women in prostitution, but they are also portrayed as expendable.[7] While the news media portrays the mostly white men who serially murder women as individually deviant, they also lend a sympathetic eye to the killers' motives and background, particularly in terms of how women in their lives have mistreated them.[8] It is significant to note that violence against women perpetrated by men who do not have race and/or class privilege are not given the same social legitimacy, most particularly if that violence is directed against white middle-class women.[9] Mostly the media neglects or registers indifference with regard to intraracial violence against women within communities of color, although when such violence is reported, racial, class, and/or cultural stereotypes and bias become the explanatory frameworks; the men and women are not given the benefit of individualist explanations for the violence. In significant contrast, media reports consistently sensationalize interracial violence perpetrated by men of color against white women. Witness the media response to the killing of Carol Stuart when her husband, the actual murderer, initially implicated an African-American male, or how the media racially constructed the young men involved in the Central Park Jogger rape, or the media's sensationalism in the O.J. Simpson case.[10] In these cases, the media constructs interracial violence against white, especially middle-class, women as brutal atrocities. The violence is attributed to the racial and/or class backgrounds of the perpetrators, and the media calls for swift and urgent action. These responses are in sharp contrast to how the media constructs the violence perpetrated by white middle-class men. The perpetrators here are constructed as individuals with individual histories and identities; their violence is often made "understandable" in media constructions. Witness the media's response to the St. John's University rapists who sexually assaulted a black West Indian woman. The media constructed the white middle-class athletes as up and coming young men and tended to interpret the incident from within a "boys will be boys" framework, which is mostly reserved for white middle-class men.[11] Thus, it is important to recognize that the media does not construct violence against women in a generic or universal way. In fact, the media is fairly predictable in its differential construction of both victims and perpetrators, and legitimate and illegitimate violence, in terms of its reinforcement of existing race, gender, sexual, and class hierarchies.

When lesbians and/or women working in prostitution cross the lines of power and control by using violence against men, their deviance is confirmed, they are sensationalized and vilified in the media, and the need for social control is reestablished. The media's sensational treatment of Aileen Wuornos—a lesbian and prostitute convicted for the murder of six white middle-aged men—initially compelled me to consider the similarities in how the media socially constructs violence when the perpetrators are identified as lesbians and/or women working in prostitution. News stories used Wuornos's lifelong history of abuse and her involvement in prostitution to frame her story as one of "revenge" against men, and they used her lesbian identification to say she was a "man-hater" out to kill men. Labeled as lesbian and as prostitute, Wuornos became, for "the establishment," a symbol of fear and terror. I was curious as to how these two "deviant" identities were constructed as explanatory frameworks for Wuornos's "unwomanly" actions. The media sensationalism in response to Wuornos stands in stark contrast to the mediated social apathy regarding the large numbers of women who have disappeared and are murdered across the country, an apathy perpetuated by way of labeling the women involved as "prostitutes."

TO BE VALUED, ONE MUST FIRST BE VISIBLE AS A HUMAN BEING

"I think it's very plausible that Aileen Wuornos was fighting her own disappearance."

—Leslie Ernst,
"Forum I: Women Who Kill," *Critical Condition* (1993)

"I put prostitutes and gays at about the same level, and I'd
be hard put to give somebody life for killing a prostitute."

—Jack Hampton,
a Texas state district court judge, in 1988[12]

Lesbians and women working in prostitution are often invisible in the media.
While the 1990s were deemed primarily a media success for some lesbians—k.d.
lang on the cover of *Vanity Fair*, a *Newsweek* cover story about lesbian life and
culture, high-profile coverage of the Ellen DeGeneres and Anne Heche love
story, among others[13]—this visibility was very limited in its selection of lesbian life
and it has not been fully sustained nor expanded. The stories highlight "successful," professional, and mostly white middle-class women who are not portrayed as
challenging the norms of white middle-class femininity by their existence. Media
stories about women working in prostitution in the United States tend to fluctuate
between constructions of the "happy hooker with a heart of gold" who loves her
work and is loved by her customers and constructions of prostitution as a "social
problem" that threatens the so-called moral fabric of society. Interestingly, I found
most of the articles featuring individual "successful" women who work as "call
girls" in *Cosmopolitan,* a magazine with a primarily female readership, while in
mainstream news media, the focus is on street prostitutes, whose existence is said
to constitute a "social problem."

Gregory Herek argues, "Through cultural heterosexism, homosexuality is
largely hidden in American society and, when publicly recognized, is usually condemned or stigmatized."[14] Consequently, reports of harassment, assault, and murder of lesbians are mostly absent from mainstream news. I had great difficulty, for
instance, obtaining news stories about the murder of lesbians, let alone harassment or assault of lesbians. In the early 1990s when I initially researched this
topic, the *New York Times Index* did not even have a category specific to lesbians;
it said, "See Homosexuality," and under "homosexuality and homicide," almost all
of the articles are about violence against gay men. Part of the reason for this is that
when women are harassed, assaulted, or murdered, news stories may not discuss
the fact that the victims are lesbians, or the lesbianism is muted, despite its potential relevance to the incidents. For instance, the initial news reports about Debra

Reid, a battered lesbian who killed her lesbian lover in self-defense, fluctuated between defining their relationship as being one between roommates, friends, or lovers. Some articles which referred to the women as lovers had headlines using the word "friends." It was not until several years later when she sought commutation of her prison sentence on the grounds of being a battered lesbian that the case became a *lesbian* case. Once her case became defined as a *lesbian* case, Reid became a "lesbian slayer" in at least one news report.

In the 1988 case of two white middle-class lesbians who were murdered while on vacation on a Caribbean island, the first three *Boston Globe* articles constructed the women as professional and well-known psychotherapists in the Boston area, who "shared their lives as a couple."[15] Their identities as professional white American tourists in the Caribbean were what gave their deaths importance. The implications for tourism and the issue of anti-American or antiwhite motivation in the killing were central to the stories. The word "lesbian" was not highlighted until the fourth article, which focused on the mourning and fear the deaths had generated in the lesbian community, which was defined as "a Boston subculture largely obscure to straight society."[16] It is in this article that the possibility of homophobia as a motive in the murders is raised and then quickly dismissed with quotes from island authorities. While the article dismisses homophobia as a motive, it implies that lesbian visibility may be a cause. It reads, "Many lesbians, unlike the two whose stabbed and bludgeoned bodies were found last week[;] . . . tend to mask their sexual orientation, [and] embrace private, quiet, home-centered lifestyles."[17] Nevertheless, neither the issue of homophobia nor that of sexism is ever given serious consideration as causes for the murders. Thus, the issue of antilesbian violence is never central to the story or to later reports on violence against women or lesbians and gay men.

In many of the serial murder cases I researched, I suspect that some of the women murdered were lesbians, but such information remains obscure in the accounts. The women are mostly defined as prostitutes. In the "true crime" book *The Search for the Green River Killer*, the possibility of lesbian existence is mentioned. Here the writers, who were journalists for the case, mention off-handedly the lesbian relationships of women who knew the murdered women, but they never discuss this aspect of the women's identities and its potential connection to their murders.[18] In sum, information about antilesbian violence is difficult to find.

The gay and lesbian movement has put antigay violence on the social and political map of this society. "Sexual orientation" is included as an official category in the 1990 version of the Hate Crimes Statistics Act.[19] In media reports about antigay hate crimes and violence, however, specific focus on lesbians is rare. The term "gay bashing" continues to call up images of mostly white middle-class men being bashed by young heterosexual men, as in the case of the brutal killing of

Matthew Sheperd. While the word "lesbian" is included in the general statements made about the increasing level of violence against the gay and lesbian communities, the examples and the analysis are predominantly based on violence against white middle-class gay men. For instance, the *Boston Globe* carried an article about a national study on gay victims of murder in 1994.[20] While the article mentions that the study focuses on "lesbians and gay men," its content presumes that men are the primary victims of antigay killings. They report that in 95 percent of the cases, the victims are male. This statistic, however, may be due to the way that crimes are reported and classified; activists and reporters alike assume that antigay violence is mostly perpetrated against men, not women, and that violence against lesbians has more to do with sexism than homophobia. Victoria Brownworth, in an article on the invisibility of antilesbian violence that appears in an issue of *The Advocate* devoted to antigay violence, reports on several antilesbian assaults which were not classified as homophobic despite the fact that the "assailants allegedly cited the women's sexual orientation as the reason for the assault."[21] The other articles in the issue, however, barely mention violence against lesbians. The invisibility and marginality of lesbians reinforce the idea that violence targeting lesbians is less pervasive than that against gay men. Racial exclusion underlies the social construction of antigay violence as well. While large-scale studies of antigay violence reveal that lesbians and gay men of color are more vulnerable to violence, most of the national reports on violence are based on sample populations consisting of predominantly white, mostly middle- to upper-middle-class gay men.[22] But this limitation is never mentioned in the media reports, thus reinforcing the construction of the problem as one exclusively affecting one group within very diverse gay and lesbian communities.

The harassment, rape, and murder of women working in prostitution are also either socially invisible or conceptualized as "just life." Pimps, johns, and the police often harass, assault, rape, and batter women working in prostitution, but those few media stories discussing this violence seem to assume it is "consensual" because the woman involved *is presumed to be* a prostitute. For instance, with regard to a woman's report of rape by a Boston police officer, the first news story in the *Boston Globe* used the word "rape" at the beginning of the article.[23] The remainder of the article, however, used the term "sex" or "sex acts" to describe encounters in which police coerced women into sex with threats of arrest if they did not comply. Thus, the claim of rape—the alleged focus of the story—is essentially erased by the end of the article. Moreover, the incident would never have made it into the media had the woman not been approached by two journalists from the *Boston Herald* immediately after she exited the police car. Violence is a daily reality facing women involved in street prostitution. A group in Minneapolis, Minnesota called Women Hurt In Systems of Prostitution Engaged in Revolt

(WHISPER) has an ongoing oral history project focused on women's lives in prostitution; they have found that 76 percent of the women report being beaten by their pimps; 50 percent report being kidnapped by pimps; 79 percent report being beaten by a customer; and 50 percent report being raped by customers.[24]

When women working in prostitution are murdered, it is often because they are targeted as prostitutes.[25] As Margaret Baldwin writes, "To be a 'prostitute' is to be rapable, beatable, killable, and *why* women are (righteously to non-controversially) raped, beaten and killed."[26] Men who rape and murder women working in prostitution often justify their violence by saying they are punishing the women, that the women ask for it or consent to it by the fact that they are engaged in prostitution. Moreover, it is very difficult to estimate the number of women murdered, especially those involved in prostitution, not only because the FBI does not have a category that would indicate this information but also because of the 'disappeared' status of women and girls involved in the practice."[27] "Disappeared" refers to the many women who are reported missing every year; the police often assume that the women are involved in prostitution or drugs and have therefore "disappeared" by "choice," so they do not follow up on the reported disappearances. As Phyllis Chesler suggests, "Serial killers may be responsible for the daily, and permanent, disappearance of thousands of prostituted and non-prostituted women, each and every year, all across the United States. . . . [And they] are rarely ever found or convicted."[28] Baldwin gives us a listing of just some of the numbers: "Up to thirty-one women murdered in Miami over a three year period, most of them prostitutes; fourteen in Denver; twenty-nine in Los Angeles; seven in Oakland. Forty-three in San Diego; fourteen in Rochester; eight in Arlington, Virginia; nine in New Bedford, Massachusetts; seventeen in Alaska; ten in Tampa," and so on.[29] According to Jane Caputi, "police officials [in mid-1980s] say that there are somewhere around four thousand serial murders annually in this country, most of them murders of women, although exact sex ratios are not given."[30]

The media response to the disappearance and murder of women involved, or assumed to be involved, in prostitution is overwhelmingly one of indifference. As the Combahee River Collective points out about the murders of twelve black women in Boston in 1979: "At first there was hardly any attention paid to the deaths. . . . When articles and television coverage began to appear more frequently, the victims were universally described as runaways, prostitutes, or drug addicts who 'deserved' to die because of how they had lived."[31] This was clear in the media treatment of the serial killings being discovered in New Bedford, Massachusetts, in 1988. When the bodies were first discovered but not yet identified, the women were always referred to as women who frequented an area of New Bedford "known for prostitution and illegal drug activity." As the identities of the women became known, their lives were consistently constructed by way of reference to this presumed location and presumed set of activities, even when family members or others were quoted as telling a different story about the women. In San Diego, California, the police attached the label "NHI" to their so-called investigation into the murders of forty-five women that took place between 1985 and 1992. "NHI" is evidently a police term that translates to "No Humans Involved." This phrase is frightening for its overt banality and hatred. According to one officer, "These were misdemeanor murders, biker women and hookers." Another police officer, responding to a feminist oppositional art exhibit called *More Women Involved*, offered that "he had been trained to disregard the humanity of victims from the 'darker side' of life."[32] In the Green River murders, many of the women eventually found and identified had been reported missing for months. The police routinely ignored these missing person reports, despite pressure from friends and family, who were met with anger and resentment for taking up valuable police time.[33]

What we learn from the police is that they often have the same attitudes toward the women as the killers do, attitudes that the media legitimates and the general public comes to accept; as Caputi writes, "we learn [from official statements about such murders] that it is normal to hate prostitutes. The killer is even assured of solidarity in this emotion . . . . The logical inference is that the prostitutes are already guilty and thus deserving of the punishments meted out to them by self-appointed avengers, or 'streetcleaners' as the convicted murderer Peter Sutcliffe later referred to himself."[34] In the media reports that focused on the individual women murdered in the New Bedford, Massachusetts area, the stories were constructed to show how the women's life choices *led* them to their deaths; there was little discussion about the social conditions that would *lead* a man or group of men to serially kill women, whether the women work in prostitution or not.

And yet, before this picture begins to be too simplistically organized by gender, it is important to recognize that the murder of women is not *always* tolerated and excused. Some serial-murder victims are given the status of "innocent victims" and their deaths are deemed significantly tragic. Not surprisingly, in a racist and classist society this "innocence" is inevitably connected to women accorded social privilege in a white supremacist, hetrosexist, capitalist society; women of color and working-class or poor women are not afforded the same value as white and middle-class women. A woman's involvement in prostitution, drugs, lesbianism, and other so-called deviant activities seemingly diminishes her value. For instance, Elizabeth Sisco contrasts the media response to the murders of women who the San Diego police identified as involved in prostitution with the response to a male intruder who entered "bedrooms in a quiet, middle-class neighborhood" and brutally sexually assaulted and murdered five women. The response to the latter case? "The largest manhunt in San Diego Police Force history stopped him. Police held daily press briefings from a special command post set up in the neighborhood and a city councilman went door-to-door warning residents to take extra precaution." The murdered women in this case represented the "good-woman victim"; one, for instance, was "a college student who worked at a sporting goods store." In constructing a valued victim, the police and media "de-emphasized the fact that [this same college student] also worked part-time as a nude dancer. Nude dancing was not an occupation that fit this particular victim profile."[35]

In contrast, in the Green River murders, as in the serial murders of women identified as "prostitutes" around the country, the media response is apathetic at best, unless activist groups press for action. Again the differential treatment can be found in the words of a police investigator of the Green River murders who offers, "There was public attention in the Ted [Bundy] case . . . because the victims resembled everyone's daughter. . . . But not everyone relates to prostitution on the Pacific Highway."[36] Here the women in prostitution are not even accorded human status as individuals; instead they are collectively referred to as "prostitution." And the normative assumptions in the term "everyone's daughters" erase the daughters of working-class or poor families and/or families of color. By routinely referring to the serial murders of women as "prostitute murders," Elizabeth Sisco aptly says, the police and media encourage "us" "to believe that violence and death are known occupational hazards for sex workers, [so] we respond to their demise with apathy or a resigned willingness to blame the victim, to accept the murder of a prostitute as one of life's harsh realities. At the same time, we are relieved that such brutality could never be visited upon those of us who comply with societal mores."[37]

In many of these murder cases, the police claim the need to control information released to the media in order to more efficiently investigate the case. They justify holding back information on the grounds that more attention might provoke copycat murders and/or give the murderer the opportunity to hide evidence and leave town. However, the level of media involvement is often connected to the race and class status of the victims. For instance, the Boston news media handled two murder cases very differently. In one case, a young African-American woman was brutally gang-raped and murdered by a group of young men in her neighborhood. A brief article mentioned the murder in early November 1990, but nothing else was reported until the twentieth of November, when several young men were arrested.[38] At this point, community activists demanded that the media and the police explain why the neighborhood and the larger community had not been alerted.[39] While the media was forced to address the incident in more detail after community protests, the articles tended to focus on the difficulties in the young woman's life that led up to her brutal death, as if she herself set up the scenario.[40] In stark contrast, when an upper-middle-class law school professor was murdered in April 1991, less than a year later, the Boston newspapers carried major news articles immediately following the incident.[41] The neighborhood was alerted, and special networks for women's safety were put into place.[42] In this case, the news reports focused on the woman's important and established career, and on the tragedy involved in losing such a valued member of the community to murder.[43]

The Wuornos case provides another illustration of the strongly contrasting way the media and police respond to different murders. As Munster, one of the investigators in the Wuornos case, reports: "We don't normally go to the press, but we felt we had a responsibility to warn the public of the danger in picking up female hitchhikers or females posing as women in distress. . . . If we hadn't gone to the media when we did, there would have been a good possibility of additional victims, and I don't believe [the alleged murderer] would be in custody today."[44] In grave contrast, a *New York Times* journalist, asked to attend a press conference concerning the murder of the black women in Boston in 1979, responded: "Twelve Black Women murdered. That's not news. I could call any city in this country and get that statistic."[45] In another serial murder case in South Central Los Angeles, a predominantly black community where at least seventeen women were killed over a three-year period, the police didn't even notify the media until after the tenth woman was found.[46]

The label of "prostitute" or "lesbian," or the association of a woman with a negative stereotype of an entire neighborhood (usually attached to racial or class stereotypes), can be a way to diminish the value of a woman's life and, therefore, the necessity for an urgent social response to the violence against her. I find this diminishment even among students in the courses I teach on violence against women; in discussing media and/or police indifference to violence against poor women who are identified as or assumed to be involved in prostitution, at least one student will inevitably excuse this response on the grounds that "people don't care" about "these" women. In this construction, the women who are killed and their communities of family, friends, and acquaintances are erased from the category of "people." It is very difficult to challenge this construction, so "naturalized" in mainstream media. But it is imperative that those of us who are educators, writers, or activists do so.

"RESPECTABILITY" AND THE POLITICS OF VISIBILITY

"As I was being raped, I was called a dyke and a cunt. The rapist used those terms as if they were interchangeable. And as I talk to other women who have been raped—straight and gay—I hear similar stories. Was my attack antilesbian? Or was it antiwoman? I think the facts are simple. I was raped because as a woman I'm considered

rapeable and, as a lesbian I'm considered a threat. How
can you separate those two things?"

—Victoria Brownworth,
quoted in "An Unreported Crisis"[47]

"[L]esbian invisibility compounds anti-lesbian violence."

—Suzanne Pharr, quoted in
Victoria Brownworth, "An Unreported Crisis"[48]

Since the 1960s, the feminist and gay and lesbian movements have drawn attention to gender or sexually motivated harassment, assault, rape, and murder. Many
activists recognize that in order to stop the endemic violence, people must recognize and value the humanity of all people—regardless of gender, race, class, or
sexual identification. One way to do this is to make the violence a public issue in
the media, to demand that the media cover crimes against all women in a way that
frames the violence in the larger context of a white supremacist, male-dominant,
heterosexist, and capitalist society. However, in so doing, these movements, especially as they have become more institutionalized in this society, often reinforce
value distinctions between groups of women and men grounded in differences of
class, race, and sexual orientation. This has resulted in the invisibility or diminishment of lesbians and women working in prostitution in the feminist movement,
whose lives and identities do not fit a narrow and normatively defined white middle-class heterosexual femininity.

The feminist construction of the issue—violence against women—has often
erased and distorted the differences and divisions among women. For instance,
the impulse of the predominantly white middle-class women's movement against
violence is to explicitly downplay, deny, ignore, or resist socially constructed
differences and divisions among women. While claiming that the movement is for
all women, they implicitly construct valued "innocent" victims—those supposedly
most harmed by harassment, assault, and murder. Given the predominantly white
middle-class heterosexual orientation of the movement, the valued victims are inevitably white, middle-class, and/or heterosexual women. This value hierarchy is
apparent when some feminists, in an effort to socially legitimate the concern
about violence against women, insist that the violence is "not just" a problem for
poor women or women of color, but that it affects middle- and upper-middle-class
white women *as well* and therefore is socially significant. Thus, the importance attached to the issue becomes dependent on whether it affects those socially constructed as the "valued victims."[49]

Since mainstream media historically has undermined feminist challenges to
the status quo by associating feminism with "lesbian man-haters," feminists (het-

erosexual and lesbian) have not consistently insisted on *lesbian visibility* in public representations of the movement.[50] Many movement organizations disassociate themselves from lesbians in order to gain legitimacy, credibility, and respectability in the "larger" society. As Suzanne Pharr writes, "The word *lesbian* is instilled with the power to halt our work and control our lives. And we give it its power with our fear."[51] Despite the leadership of lesbian feminists in the creation of crisis lines, shelters, safe-homes, and speak outs on gender violence, many of these organizations erase this participation in their public representation. Given homophobia within and outside of the movement, and the fear it instills, feminists have tended to define, analyze, and respond to violence as strictly a gender issue, one that affects women similarly across all lines of division among women—race, sexual orientation, class, and ethnicity. Violence *against lesbians as lesbians*, or violence against Latina-, African-, Asian-, and Native-American women *as women of color*, or violence *against women working in prostitution* remains mostly invisible, undocumented, and unknown. The centrality of race, class, and/or sexual orientation differences in determining the social constructions, interpretations, and responses to specific incidents of violence is minimized or ignored.[52] The overriding assumption, unspoken but present, is that the women under discussion, the "valued victims," are for the most part *not* lesbians, *not* women of color, *not* poor women, *not* women working in prostitution. Reports in the media are not different from the mainstream white middle-class definition of the issue, thus perpetuating a social hierarchy of value and worth accorded to different groups of women.

The specific mandate to keep lesbians and women working in prostitution invisible and to keep poor or working-class women and women of color on the margins constructs a context where the public does not visualize women of color, lesbians, women working in prostitution, working-class women, and poor women as valued victims and survivors of violence and therefore as those needing or deserving services and those in the forefront of women's resistance to violence and oppression. In most cases, when victims/survivors of violence are identified in the media as lesbians or as women working in prostitution, especially when they are poor women and/or women of color, the social importance of the crimes involved is diminished. The violence is not recorded as an aberration or reason for outrage but, rather, as routine daily life. The feminist movement against violence participates in this construction by not demanding public recognition and response to violence specifically directed against women as lesbians, as members of racial and ethnic minorities, or prostitutes and raising public awareness about their heightened vulnerability to violence as well as the heightened indifference to their plight by social institutions.

In the past twenty years, feminists have sought to put men's violence against women on the public agenda as a social rather than a personal issue. The media has slowly begun to acknowledge the social aspects of the crimes against women occurring in the context of intimate relationships. However, the construction of the problem tends to retain an exclusive assumption of heterosexuality. Feminist activists and service providers themselves presume that violence against women is done by men, not other women. Lesbian battering by lesbians, or violence against lesbians by heterosexual women, remains mostly unthinkable. It is uncommon to see materials, programs, support groups, newsletters, or shelters that address violence against lesbians, lesbian battering, or lesbian survival (although this is changing). In part, this is due to the desire to construct women as "innocent" and passive victims of male aggression in order to enlist empathy for "good" women. As a result, for media events, the focus remains on men's violence against women in intimate, monogamous, noncontractual heterosexual relationships. Lesbians and women working in prostitution remain invisible or, at best, on the margins of this public discourse.

Over the years, lesbian-specific organizations like the Boston-based Network for Battered Lesbians have diligently and persistently fought the invisibility. It has been mostly battered lesbians in the battered women's movement who have brought these issues out into the open. But feminist activists against violence and service providers in battered women's shelters remain reluctant to insist on lesbian visibility in media coverage both as victims and perpetrators of violence. In 1989, Debra Reid, a lesbian in prison for the killing of her female lover, joined forces with her legal team and the Network for Battered Lesbians in seeking to gain public and legal recognition of lesbian battering.[53] Debra Reid was the only *lesbian* in the group of incarcerated women seeking commutation of their prison sentences. She faced consistent denial and resistance to her identification as a battered woman, from the group of incarcerated women to the media accounts of "the Framingham Eight," to the Advisory Board of Pardons, who eventually decided not to commute her sentence.

The resistance to her story had to do with a refusal to recognize the specific victimization of lesbian battery and to recognize how homophobia and racism contributed to that victimization (in the battery as well as in the original trial). Some media reports quote David LaFontaine from the Coalition for Lesbian and Gay Civil Rights, who dismissed the significance of Reid's case, stating, "Obviously, there are going to be individual cases of abuse, but my experience of gay people is I think as a whole they're a very nonviolent group of people." The gay and lesbian community's fear of increasing homophobic bigotry underlies the persistent refusal to recognize battering as a serious social issue. While this fear may be a legitimate one, the realities of intimate violence continue to disempower our communities when not addressed.[54] The existence of lesbian battering also contradicts the feminist rhetoric which has tended to maintain that men are always the perpetrators of violence and women are always the victims of violence. The denial about women's use and abuse of violence contributes to the construction of the valued and "innocent" victim, who passively endures violence and certainly never uses violence. In Reid's case, having to recognize the realities of violence involving women as both perpetrators and victims, and the inability to construct victims and perpetrators solely along the lines of gender or sexual orientation, were seen as potential liabilities to the accepted and exclusive frameworks of sexist or homophobic violence. The resolution ultimately of the Advisory Board of Pardons, and subsequently the media, was to construct a story of "mutual abuse," where both Reid and her partner were equally responsible for the violence in their relationship. Reid's claim of self-defense in response to being attacked by her lover was thus erased. The construction of violence among lesbians becomes one of mutuality—lesbians beat each other up, and it is hard to distinguish one from the other. The need for social concern and response to lesbian battering are diminished, and at best, lesbians are once again relegated to the margins of the discourse on battering.

As I noted earlier, most of the public media attention to antigay violence focuses on gay male victims of violence, mostly white gay males. One of the myths perpetrated in the movement is that lesbians are not vulnerable to attack *as lesbians* but, rather, simply as women. For instance, Beatrice von Schulthess, in the only essay on antilesbian violence in the anthology *Hate Crimes: Violence Against Lesbians and Gay Men,* opts for misogyny as *the* primary explanation for antilesbian violence.[55] She writes, "I no longer frame the issue of violence against lesbians only in terms of sexual orientation. Instead, I conceptualize lesbianism as an extension of gender and conceptualize antilesbian violence as an extension of misogynistic violence." Based on her survey, the harassment and violence lesbians experience fall "along a continuum ranging from exclusively antiwoman at one end to exclusively antilesbian at the other."[56] But she notes that most of the violence begins as antiwoman and escalates to antilesbian. Those surveyed also report that most of the harassment was verbal, rather than physical. However, on closer inspection, we find that the lesbians of color surveyed reported more physical violence, but since they are not adequately represented in the sample, their experience does not inform the conclusions. It may be that the lesbians in her sample are also primarily middle-class. Thus her analysis is based on the experience of a very limited group of women. It would be important to know, for instance, whether the women interviewed are able to pass on the street as heterosexual. If so, this might explain their experience of being targeted first as women and only later as lesbians. Ultimately, von Schulthess contributes to the nonrecognition of explicitly antilesbian violence experienced by lesbians who do not pass as heterosexual. The stories of lesbians documented in Nestle's edited anthology, *A Persistent Desire,* and in Leslie Feinberg's semiautobiographical novel, *Stone*

Butch Blues, stand out in stark contrast to the conclusions offered in von Schulthess's study.[57] In the stories illuminated in these books, lesbians were targeted for abuse and violence because they were identified *as lesbians* by the police and by men on the street. It was the identification of them as "gender outlaws," rather than simply as women, that made them more vulnerable to the violence. When I first began to think about antilesbian violence, I too saw it as primarily antiwoman, but that was grounded in my own experience as a white middle-class lesbian who is often assumed to be heterosexual. Upon reflection, the stories of my lesbian friends who do *not* pass as heterosexual and who have been harassed and assaulted *as lesbians* came to the surface. As activists, we must begin to recognize and publicize the specificity of this violence and its victims. Otherwise, lesbian, gay, and feminist activists participate by exclusion in accepting the violence against some lesbians as "just life."

Similarly, feminist media campaigns in general do not highlight the abuse and violence perpetrated against women working in prostitution. Those few feminists who focus on violence against women working in prostitution have met with virulent criticism and hostility on the grounds that this focus somehow erases women's agency in choosing prostitution as an arena for work. The U.S. feminist debate over prostitution rages on, and meanwhile, a significant number of women working in prostitution continue to disappear. The life realities of women working in prostitution often are not on the antirape and battered women's movement agenda. Emanating from the tendency to construct "innocent victims" for the purposes of gaining public support and establishing social legitimacy, in combination with class, race, and sexual prejudices, activists and service providers may distance themselves from women who do not fulfill the requirements of the "innocent victim." This results in the systematic invisibility of women working in prostitution, who are relegated to the margins of discourse and practice. As with lesbians, feminists tend toward the "It's not me" response with prostitutes. As Baldwin writes, "The fate of a woman's claims on justice, we all seem to know somewhere, crucially depends on her success in proving that she is not, and never has been, a prostitute."[58] She goes on to quote Dworkin, who says, "The woman's effort to stay innocent, her efforts to prove innocence, her effort to prove that she was used against her will is always and unequivocally an effort to prove she is not a whore." Baldwin argues that much feminist legal work has sought to distinguish "with great delicacy and equal urgency between 'prostitutes' and 'other women.' The political rescue of 'real womanhood' from conditions of prostitution, within the spheres of life believed occupied by 'normal women' has been the mainstream feminist tactic advanced within many of our campaigns."[59]

This disassociation can only be labeled appalling in the face of evidence which suggests that women working in prostitution and lesbians, who are poor and women of color, may be the most vulnerable to violence and murder. The way to change the socially constructed value hierarchy among women who are victims of assault and murder is for activists to recognize the humanity of all women, to challenge the socially constructed differences between women, and to make visible and central to our campaigns against violence the women who are most vulnerable to violence and who currently are on the margins of media discourse. In other words, activists must refuse to participate in the construction of a value hierarchy in an effort to establish social legitimacy and concern about violence. The media will not change without public pressure and activism; the responsibility for forcing the issue is ours. Otherwise, our rhetoric should be more honest and specific about what violence and victims we are talking about.

LESBIANS, PROSTITUTES, AND MAN-HATERS

> "A woman, by definition, is not violent, and if violent, a female is not a woman."
>
> —Jeffner Allen, quoted in
> Lynda Hart, *Fatal Women*[60]

While lesbian existence is mostly absent from, or at best marginal in, mainstream social constructions of violence, the hegemonic culture associates lesbians with the perpetuation of violence and hatred; lesbians and man-hating seem to be intricately intertwined in the popular imagination. In some ways the threat of lesbianism seems to have more to do with lesbian autonomy from men—translated simultaneously into lesbian hatred of men, or overidentification with men—than with lesbian sexual activities (images of which are consumed in mainstream heterosexual pornography). The angry and indignant response to lesbians seems connected to those lesbians who are perceived as assuming and/or usurping the rights to male behaviors and actions, including violence. In turn, lesbians are said to have an intense animosity toward men, presumably because lesbians challenge men's exclusive claim to a "masculinized" authority or power. There seems to be a fear that because we are assumed to be autonomous from men's control, lesbians might not experience as much constraint in using violence as a weapon, one historically reserved for men (at least in public discourse). The discourse of deviance about lesbians, however, applies mostly to those perceived to be crossing gender boundaries. The threat to the social order, it seems, is the "butch" lesbian, not the "femme," and the working-class lesbian, not the middle-class one. For instance, in the working-class bars of the 1940s and 1950s, the police singled out and assaulted lesbians who dressed and looked "like men" more frequently than those perceived as "real" women.[61]

Since women are, by definition, not supposed to be violent, then women who are violent must be labeled as not real women—unfeminine, malelike. Lynda Hart insightfully argues that lesbian identity has served as "a site where women's aggression has been displaced. . . . [T]he female invert's *aggressiveness* was what marked her as deviant and therefore dangerous, *not* her object choice."[62] Hart shows how the construction of the "female offender" in criminology and the "invert" in sexology at the turn of the century were one and the same discourse. In summarizing the early criminologist Lombroso's construction of the "female offender," Hart draws out the linkages:

> Her propensity is to approximate the dress, behavior, appearance, and eroticism of the male. She is marked by an absence of maternal affection, indicating further that she is more like a man, even a normal man, than she is like a normal woman. She retains the sex of a female but acquires the gender attributes of masculinity. She is tyrannical, selfish; she wants only to satisfy her own passions. Love is replaced in her by an "insatiable egotism." She is incapable of resignation and sacrifice, and her desire results in acts of tyranny. . . . She is, in fact, remarkably like Ellis's congenital invert. . . . The congenital invert and the born female offender marked the limits of cultural femininity. And they did so as a couple, not separately, but together.[63]

This construction of lesbians as "not women" and as aggressive and man-hating can be seen operating in the explanations offered for Aileen Wuornos's behavior in killing. After Wuornos was arrested, descriptions such as the following inundated the media reports: "America's first female serial killer is a man-hating lesbian who posed as a prostitute to lure at least seven men into her web of death."[64]

Despite Wuornos's claims to self-defense, *the* major question in the media was whether Wuornos could be classified a "female serial killer." Robert Ressler, a former FBI agent and expert on serial killers, was quoted widely. He distinguishes Wuornos from both male serial murderers and women who murder more than one person. He defines a "true serial killer" as "a predator, one who for his own motives is hunting down people with murder in mind." Sexual issues are central, according to Ressler: "Serial murders stem from a man's inability to deal with women on a sexual basis, or from unresolved sexual problems and inadequacies." He says that Wuornos is "an enigma."

Historically, women who kill more than one person have not been classified as "serial killers"; murder by women is interpreted as categorically different. According to the traditional framework for murder by women, the assumption is that women kill people with whom they are in close association—children, husbands, patients under their care in hospitals, for example. Skrapec suggests that women who kill more than one person are considered *aberrant women* but still within the confines of femininity—individual, isolated, and needing of explanation; they are "[t]ypically presented as case studies and summarily typecast as 'black widows' (women who kill a series of husbands, their children, and other relatives), 'angels of death' or 'mercy killers' (women who kill patients in their care), and the like."[65] Thus, Wuornos is supposedly different. Dr. Kathy Morall, a forensic psychiatrist, labels Wuornos an *aberrant* female killer, rather than a representative one; she says, "Because of the confusion in sexual identity—you have a person making an effort to put herself in the place of a male, physically and mentally." She says, "There's nothing to prevent Miss Prissy in a prom dress from going around and shooting forty people, but historically we haven't seen it."[66] Ressler offers, "If Wuornos is seen to be a serial killer, we have to rewrite the rules. With women the base may be hatred, mental disorder, even monetary reasons—there could be a number of possibilities."[67] James Alan Fox, another expert on murder, also distinguishes between Wuornos and other female serial killers; he says that women "generally kill people they know. They kill for particular reasons, such as jealousy or revenge. My guess is that the motive in this case was actually control, power, dominance. It could be that these men were trying to take control, and submission, perhaps, is not something she was into. This may have been some attempt to get back at men."[68] In fact, Wuornos's difference seems to be her unwillingness to accept women's subordination and powerlessness in response to men's violence.

The media mapped this difference onto Wuornos's lesbian identity, which was used to explain her aggressiveness, hatred, and indifference to men, and therefore her motivation to kill. Despite the fact that Wuornos has only been in two lesbian relationships in her life and does not seem to identify as a lesbian, the media persistently defines her as both a lesbian and a man-hater.[69] Ressler says, for instance, "There may be an intrinsic hatred of males here, as well as an identification with male violence which helped push her across the line into what has been considered a 'male' crime."[70] The comments of one of Wuornos's childhood friends were enlisted to construct the connection further; she is quoted as saying, "I know she hated men. . . . She had no dates, no major crushes. If she was with a boy, it was always for the money. She had no close friends. And not a single adult ever helped her, absolutely not one."[71] A worker at a convenience store Wuornos frequented says, "She struck me as a very aggressive person. . . . The way she carried herself, the way she flexed her muscles. Whenever a nice-looking male customer would come in—I mean, I looked, Ty[ria Moore, Wuornos lover at the time of the killings] looked, but Lee [Aileen] didn't look. Or if she did, she snarled."[72] Wuornos's motives are most often ascribed to hatred and revenge arising from her sexual identification and her abusive past, not from the immediate circumstances of the crimes.

Neither sexist attitudes nor misogyny are called upon to explain the serial killings of women by men, despite the fact that most perpetrators of serial murder are male and most victims female. Instead, the murders are conceptualized as arising from the perpetrator's individual pathology, not his masculinity nor his gender identification. For instance, the journalists who wrote the "true crime" book on the Green River killer, in line with the experts' profile of the killer, write that the killer "does not [have], nor has he ever [had,] an aversion toward women." This is in stark contrast to Wuornos, whose violence the media consistently links to man-hating. The Green River killer's motives are nonetheless connected to gender, but they are not labeled as such. Rather, the motives seem only "natural" within the social reality of contemporary gender relations. The experts say that the killer must be someone who "has felt that he has been 'burned' or 'lied to' and 'fooled by women one too many times.' In his way of thinking, women are no good and cannot be trusted and he feels women will prostitute themselves for whatever reason and when he sees women openly prostituting themselves, this makes his blood boil."[73] Wuornos, on the other hand, despite the recognition that she experienced years of sexual and physical abuse as well as poverty and prostitution, is characterized as a deviant "man-hater" who kills without cause. There is no "natural" explanation. In the language of the prosecution, she is "a remorseless, diabolical killer" who was a "candidate for the electric chair if ever there was one."[74] According to Phyllis Chesler, the prosecutor portrayed Wuornos as a "predatory prostitute" whose "appetite for lust and control had taken a lethal turn;' and 'had been exercising control for years over men' and who 'killed for power, for full and ultimate control.'" She points out that the prosecutor was the same man—a born-again Christian—who, as Ted Bundy's "minister" on death row, "tried to delay Bundy's execution."[75]

Yet, in a strange way, media stories characterized Wuornos's actual lesbian relationship in terms of love and friendship. They portray Tyria Moore, Wuornos's lover at the time of the killings, as an innocent and feminine lover, "the wife" of Wuornos, who, according to most of the stories, Wuornos loved. No stories suggest that Wuornos was violent toward Moore, though they report that Moore was increasingly afraid of Wuornos given her suspicions about the killings.[76] Again, the crime of lesbianism in the stories is not about the relationship between the women but about Wuornos's autonomy, anger, and seeming rejection of men. The problematic "sexual identity" that makes her unfeminine and hateful toward men is then linked to her inherent propensity to murder. At the same time, the sexual aspect of their relationship is downplayed. In one made-for-TV movie, for instance, Wuornos and Moore are portrayed as friends, not lovers.[77]

Both the media and the police, primary sources of information, seem to fluctuate in their identification of Wuornos as a prostitute. Sometimes they minimize her work in prostitution; instead, they paint Wuornos as someone who targeted men for murder in the tradition of male serial killers. They minimize the context of prostitution in making sense of the relationship between Wuornos and the men she killed. The men are, for the most part, constructed as completely innocent victims. A *New York Times* article describes the victims as middle-aged men who "traveled in their jobs and were frequently on the roads."[78] In this story, Wuornos lured the men to remote areas in order to kill them. Major Henry, one of the investigators, is quoted as if he was asking an open-ended question: "What was it that led him and others to let their guard down? We think there may have been some offer of sex involved." Another account reads, "They said they believed that some of the men were killed after picking up, or stopping to help, their assailant on the highway." In one article an investigator named Munster claimed that Wuornos was not working as a prostitute at the time of the murders and that she was killing in order to rob the victims of money. In this report she is characterized as having "sought out expensive cars, sometimes stopping them by throwing herself in their path so the driver was forced to brake." He also claimed that after "the first killing she began ordering the victims to take off their clothes. Why? It's physical evidence."[79] Evidence for these claims is never offered, and they contradict other statements of Sergeant Munster and other investigators. The stories attribute complete innocence to the men and premeditation and lethal intent on the part of Wuornos, despite her claims of rape, attempted rape, and physical assault.

Some stories did raise the possibility of self-defense in response to the violence or the threat of violence that Wuornos may have encountered, but the stories retain contradictions that undermine Wuornos's claim. For instance, Munster says that "[Wuornos] was often described to us as obnoxious, aggressive, not sexy. . . . Most men put her out without any money at all. So that may have been part of it. . . . But really she was just a female predator who needed money."[80] The refusal of "most men" to pay for sexual services is passed over without comment. Horpeza, another investigator for the case, said that "Wuornos tried to turn eight or ten tricks a night." According to him, Wuornos said, "All I wanted was to get my money for sex. If I could do it clean, no problem. When somebody gave me a problem, that's when the incident happened."[81] The mistreatment and economic exploitation of women in prostitution are never addressed as a problem *for the women involved in prostitution*, and as such, as a possible motive for Wuornos's behavior. The allusions to the men's violence in the articles are never addressed as cause; it serves as background, but not one that might explain the killings. When raised, it is often countered with a discussion of Wuornos's desire for power and control over men in general, which is defined as unnatural, illegitimate, and arising from unjustified hatred.

Neither the media nor Wuornos's defense team sought out information about the men who were murdered. Phyllis Chesler points out that Richard Mallory, the first man killed by Wuornos, had a history of violence, according to his former girlfriend. This woman told one of the investigators that Mallory "had served ten years in prison for burglary, suffered from severe mood swings, drank too much, was violent to women, enjoyed the strip bars, was 'into' pornography, and had undergone therapy for some kind of sexual dysfunction."[82] Chesler's own investigation found that Mallory had "done many years in Patuxent Prison, in Maryland, as a sex offender. In [his] criminal record he was described as an 'impulsive and explosive' individual who will get into serious difficulty, most likely of a sexual nature. . . . Because of his emotional disturbance and his poor control of his sexual impulses, he could present a potential danger to his environment in the future."[83] This information would have helped support Wuornos's claim of self-defense, but her own defense team never followed up these leads. Moreover, the Judge would not allow information about Mallory's past behavior into the trial. Wuornos's defense teams also did not draw on experts who could speak to the high level of violence and threat of violence that many street prostitutes face on a daily basis, testimony which could have bolstered Wuornos's claim of self-defense.[84] Instead, her defense team tended to characterize her as "a terribly deprived victim," "a damaged, primitive child," who warranted mercy rather than hatred.[85] None of the mainstream media articles developed the self-defense claims. Instead, they relied on the police investigators' speculations. The mainstream media articles did not address the endemic violence women working in prostitution experience at the hands of pimps, johns, and/or the police; nor did they seek out experts on rape or abuse trauma, or feminist legal experts familiar with women's self-defense cases.

The story of Wuornos—a woman who worked in prostitution for many years, who faced the possibility of daily abuse and violence as part of her job—is severely minimized in the reports. Wuornos's claims of self-defense were mostly absent from the media stories. As described by Candace Skrapec, Wuornos "asserted that Mallory [the first male killed] had raped, tortured, and threatened to kill her, and that she had used the handgun in her purse, which she carried for protection, to save her life. . . ."[86] Wuornos claimed that she killed the other men under similar circumstances.

THE FRAMING OF WOMEN WHO MURDER

> "Passion and/or pathology have been the key historical constructs for explaining, and containing, women's aggression. Women like Aileen Wuornos are not supposed to exist."
> —Lynda Hart, *Fatal Women*[87]

"As long as we insist on maintaining our innocence, we lock ourselves into helplessness. In this way we become complicit with our oppression."
—Melanie Kaye/Kantrowitz, *The Issue is Power*[88]

"When 'violence' appears against 'oppression,' it is a negation of institutionalized violence. Such acts are acts of bravery. . . . It is a betrayal of humanity, and of hope, to represent such acts as shameful, or regrettable."
—Ti Grace Atkinson,[89] quoted in
Melanie Kaye/Kantrowitz, *The Issue is Power*

It seems very rare in this social landscape for the claim of self-defense against rapists, batterers, abusers, and potential killers to get a hearing in the media. Mainstream media stories that seem sympathetic instead obscure the claims to self-defense by highlighting the psychology of victimized and abused women. Those empathetic to women who kill sidestep the issue of self-defense by focusing on past histories of abuse and trauma, presumably to gain public sympathy for the woman as a victim. The psychology of the victim is used then to explain why she resorted to violence; violence is assumed to be behavior uncharacteristic, unnatural, and unreasonable for women. Phyllis Murphy, co-chair of Florida's chapter of the Gay and Lesbian Alliance against Defamation, criticized the media treatment of Wuornos for the way they "sensationalized her lesbianism rather than her abusive childhood. There are a lot of abused children who grow up to do violence, both homosexual and heterosexual. The prosecutors are playing up her hatred of men."[90] Donald Suggs offered abuse as the explanatory narrative, in contrast to the homophobic explanations of "criminal experts": "Ressler [former FBI agent] sees in Wuornos's lesbianism an 'intrinsic hatred of males,' which he apparently considers to be more of a motivating factor in her anger and in the killings she has been accused of committing than her history of violence and sexual abuse."[91] Absent from both discussions is Wuornos's own explanation of self-defense against violent men.

Caught between competing explanations and defenses of Wuornos, Suggs concludes, "While it would be difficult not to feel queasy about Wuornos's actions, the bigoted assumptions underlying the media coverage of the case are also a sordid proposition. Whether or not Wuornos is ultimately found to be a serial killer [,] . . . lesbians and gays must neither apologize for the way many women are forced to defend themselves nor allow the actions of one troubled lesbian to become a pretext for attacking an entire community."[92] Suggs seems caught in the dilemma of whether to recognize that Wuornos may have legitimately killed the men in self-defense or to define her actions as those of a "troubled individual." The past history of abuse and trauma are used to explain Wuornos in psychological terms as a victim-turned-perpetrator, rather than to recognize abuse and violence as legitimate causes for Wuornos to fight in defense of her life. The anger attributed to Wuornos is defined as unreasonable or unusual.[93] Wuornos is constructed as a woman whose victimization has made her judgment and behavior aberrant and pathological. This construction of pathology undermines and dismisses, without further investigation, Wuornos's own argument of self-defense. It shifts the focus from the violence and threat of violence that Wuornos faced on a daily basis and in these particular circumstances to her personality and perception of reality.

Using past history of abuse as explanatory framework in cases of self-defense deflects attention away from the circumstances surrounding the killings, and it pathologizes the women fighting to defend their lives. As Lynda Hart says, "The appeal [to past trauma] will rest on the very pathology that reproduces the social conditions in which Aileen Wuornos performed her desperate actions."[94] Hart points out that Wuornos herself refuses this narrative:

Aileen Wuornos is "guilty" under the law; but she refuses to enact the "guilt" that secures the fiction of law's justice. She confesses to the acts but is still unrepentant. And although we might find her incredible when she insists that her "past" has nothing to do with the crimes she has committed, there is something fascinating, and unnerving, in her implacable self-defense, her disregard for a linear narrative of a life's trajectory that begins with victimization and ends in retaliation. . . . By refusing to accede to the narrative of her "traumatic past," Aileen Wuornos repudiates not just a personal history but also the story of "vengeance," with its ever-threatening promise of repetition.[95]

Nonetheless, Hart, like Chesler, recognizes that constructing such a story of abuse and trauma might have been Wuornos's only chance of not being given the death sentence, which she inevitably received.[96] But in so doing, it dismantles Wuornos claim of self-defense—it "even more powerfully asserts that Wuornos's perception of a 'clear and present danger' was not *real*."[97]

Wuornos claimed in interviews with the media that she committed each of the six killings in self-defense. She argued that as someone who worked in prostitution, she was in contact with many men every day whom she did not kill. She claimed, then, that she killed *these particular* men because they raped her, attempted to rape her, or in some way threatened her life. Wuornos testified that she killed the first victim, Richard Mallory, in self-defense after he raped and sexually abused her. Her story is as follows:

So we go into the woods. He's huggin' and kissin' on me. He starts pushin' me down. And I said, wait a minute, you know, get cool. You don't have to get rough, you know. Let's have fun. . . . I said I would not [have sex with him]. He said, yes, you are, bitch. You're going to do everything I tell you. If you don't I'm going to kill you and [have sex with you] after you're dead, just like the other sluts. It doesn't matter, your body will still be warm. He tied my wrists to the steering wheel, and screwed me in the ass. Afterwards, he got a Visine bottle filled with rubbing alcohol out of the trunk. He said the Visine bottle was one of my surprises. He emptied it into my rectum. It really hurt bad because he tore me up a lot. He got dressed, got a radio, sat on the hood for what seemed like an hour. . . . Eventually he untied me, put a stereo wire around my neck and tried to rape me again. . . . Then I thought, well, this dirty bastard deserves to die because of what he was tryin' to do to me. We struggled. I reached for my gun. I shot him. I scrambled to cover the shooting because I didn't think the police would believe I killed him in self-defense. . . . I have to say it. I killed them all because they got violent with me and I decided to defend myself.[98]

As Hart describes, media commentators continually questioned Wuornos on her version of reality.[99] They would suggest to Wuornos that the public does not believe that prostitutes can be raped because they agree to sexual relations for money. Wuornos unapologetically insists that women working in prostitution know the difference between sex and rape, that they *can* be raped and that *she* was raped. She often offered graphic details of the rapes she experienced. When an interviewer suggests that the killings were evidence that she was out of control, Wuornos responds: "Those men are out of control. I'm sick and tired of those men out there thinking they can control us and do whatever they damn well please with our bodies and think they can get away with it."[100] Wuornos herself refuses the story of the completely victimized and insane woman turned killer. Instead, she forthrightly presents herself as someone who was trying to save her own life. Although neither the media nor her defense team took the threat to her life seriously, Wuornos had no choice. In her narrative, Wuornos refers to Mallory's reference to the destiny of other women's refusal—"You're going to do everything I tell you. If you don't, I'm going to kill you and [have sex with you] after you're dead, just like the other sluts." Given prostitutes' high rate of vulnerability to serial murder, as delineated earlier in this chapter, and the specific cases in the state of Florida, Wuornos had every reason to believe she was in serious danger of being killed. But in this society, which tends to demonize lesbians, pathologize women, and stigmatize women working in prostitution, Wuornos is unnatural, her narrative unbelievable, and her claim of self-defense socially illegitimate.

The tendency to resort to individual psychology as an explanation of women's use of violence in self-defense seeps into feminist analyses as well. For instance, in the spring of 1994, a local group of feminists offered to create an exhibit on Debra Reid's case for their art show on feminist activism. On the night of the opening, I was shocked to find an exhibit which characterized Reid as a "battered woman" with sole reference to the childhood abuse she experienced in her family. Absent from the exhibit was the story of how Reid's lover had systematically battered her—physically, emotionally, sexually, verbally, and economically—for most of their five-year relationship. Despite the fact that her commutation petition was grounded in a self-defense claim, the events which led up to the killing were not described. It was as if her history of child abuse explained the killing, rather than the actual events of the night in question and the history of the couple's relationship.

The challenge for activists is to be able to make the claim of self-defense for women without pathologizing them. Rather than solely emphasizing a woman's psychological state as an explanation for her actions, arguments must be made for a woman's right to self-defense in response to real violence and threats to her life. As Susan Madden writes, "For a woman to fight back means that she values her self enough to fight for it. And for society to support her in that fight would mean a recognition of her innate human value, her right to live unmolested and without fear, and her freedom from intimate captivity" (1981, 146). This is a very different argument from one that talks about the psychological state that induces a woman to resort to violence.

In *Fight Back! Feminist Resistance to Male Violence,* Melanie Kaye/Kantrowitz challenges us to think about the possibilities: "imagine: every day in the paper, instead of a story about a woman who was attacked, raped, beaten, tortured and/or murdered—information which certainly has its effects on us—there were a story about a rapist or batterer who was beaten, shot, stabbed—even public humiliation would be better than nothing."[101]

In a very provocative article, "Imagined Violence/Queer Violence," Judith Halberstam suggests "imagined violence" as a strategy for disrupting the power-and- violence equation that the media socially constructs.[102] Halberstam defines "imagined violence" as "the fantasy of unsanctioned eruptions of aggression" emanating from those who June Jordan describes as the socially constructed *legitimate* victims of violence—"the wrong people, of the wrong skin, the wrong sexuality, the wrong gender." Rather than shying away from exploring the capacity for violence among the oppressed, Halberstam argues that "our violence needs to be imaginable because the power of fantasy is not to represent but to destabilize the real. . . . Imagined violence does not advocate lesbian or female aggression but it might complicate an assumed relationship between women and passivity or feminism and pacifism."[103]

Similarly, rather than seeking to disassociate from women who fight back against violence to defend their own lives or the lives of others, and rather than pathologizing women's life histories to neutralize their actions, the real challenge to the social value hierarchy would be to recognize, support, and socially validate such women's actions and behaviors. To disassociate from and/or pathologize "deviant" women who are fighting for their/our lives is not a strategy toward fundamental change in the social order. It might help a few women out, but in the meantime it accepts and perpetuates the dehumanization and marginalization of many women. In "Poem About My Rights," June Jordan eloquently refuses the construction of legitimate violence. She writes: "*I am not wrong: Wrong is not my name* / My name is my own my own my own."[104]

The argument that I have been making in this chapter is that mainstream media indifferently accepts violence against women who are identified as lesbians and/or women working in prostitution. This makes the violence "legitimate" and "understandable" in the current social reality. Moreover, the media demonizes and pathologizes lesbians and/or women working in prostitution when they become "a problem" or "threat" to the status quo, which creates a context where violence against them becomes socially legitimate and acceptable. A major strategy for disrupting this construction of social power is to persistently challenge the terms on which it is lodged. At the very least this means that as writers, educators, and activists, we must insist that we ourselves, as well as the media, make visible and socially significant the violence against all lesbians and all women working in prostitution, especially violence against poor, working-class women of color who are the most vulnerable to violence. We must persistently refuse the construction of "deserving victims" whose disappearances and deaths are unworthy of social urgency and outrage. And we must publicly defend the right of women, all women, to defend our lives, not as pathological responses of "troubled" women but as reasonable responses to vicious, brutal, and life-threatening attacks.

3

LESBIAN AND BISEXUAL WOMEN'S BATTERING:
Homophobia, Heterosexism, and Violence

Lesbian and bisexual women's stories of woman-to-woman mistreatment, harassment, rape, and battery continually challenge me to politicize our experiences. This politicization does not come easy. At a workshop on lesbian battering in the late 1980s given by the Network for Battered Lesbians in Boston, Massachusetts, I finally began to get it. As I listened to lesbian stories of physical, sexual, verbal, and emotional abuse and recognized their interconnections, I felt thrown into a whirlwind of emotion and confusion, as well as clarity. The truth-telling of this session profoundly changed my work as a teacher and activist in the women's movement against violence. The collective voices no longer allowed me to simply personalize the dynamics of power and control operating in many of our personal and social relationships. It was no longer viable for me to remain in denial about the realities of women's use and abuse of power, to minimize the impact of woman-to-woman violence in women's lives, nor to rationalize the violence as stemming from the sexism and misogyny women experience from men. I began to recognize women's patterns of power and control over other women, including violence, and to work with others to find ways to hold women accountable for their actions.

My process of recognizing lesbian and bisexual women's interpersonal abuse and battering has been one of rethinking my own life and the lives of women I've known as friends, sister activists, colleagues, and students. Until this session in the late 1980s, I had found it hard to name abuse in lesbian relationships as a *political issue with structural roots*. For one, I desperately wanted lesbians to be different from the men I had known in my life. To label abusive the patterns and behaviors in lesbian relationships that I both experienced and witnessed seemed, on the surface, to threaten my hopes for a different life. Yet through my own experiences, I knew that my hopes for a different life could not be based on denial of the realities of destructive human relationships.

I remember being at a Take Back the Night march in the early 1980s. As I listened to the stories of rape and battery, tears streamed down my face as I thought of my friend who canceled out on me that day. She was in an abusive relationship with another woman. I found myself silently disagreeing when a speaker claimed that "women don't rape or batter," but I didn't have a language or a context to challenge these "truths." Over the years, I have had many lesbian and bisexual friends, acquaintances, and students who were being harassed, abused, and battered by their girlfriends. Since 1987, I have taught at least one course a year on Violence Against Women, and each year, lesbian and bisexual women students tell me stories of rape and battery by women, including lovers, friends, co-workers, teachers, professors, doctors, sisters, and mothers. I too have struggled in lesbian relationships characterized by abusive power and control tactics, and yet for years I viewed the abusive patterns of my lovers as my own fault. The self-blame instilled from a history of violence since childhood stood strong in the face of the abusive behavior being directed at me.

Despite the difficulties most feminist activists have had politicizing this knowledge, lesbians and bisexual women have continued to speak out about the realities of woman-to-woman mistreatment, harassment, rape, battering, and murder; many seek support and justice through the feminist antirape and battered women's movements and/or the gay, lesbian, bisexual, and transgender-based movements. In each arena, woman-to-woman interpersonal violence is often denied and/or ignored, and yet lesbians, bisexuals, gay men, and transgender individuals continue to push organizations to address the urgent needs of those harmed by rape and battery. A number of studies document the incidence and experience of woman-to-woman physical battery to be in anywhere from 22 percent to 46 percent of lesbian relationships.[1] Pam Elliott points out that these studies primarily document physical violence; studies documenting a broader range of abuse indicate that approximately three-fourths of relationships involve dynamics of emotional, verbal, sexual, and/or psychological abuse.[2]

In many cases, lesbians and bisexual women who are being battered by their lovers have few resources and thus may find themselves increasingly in life or death situations. It is often difficult, if not dangerous, to rely on the police who continue to build on their history of brutality and/or indifference toward gay, lesbian, bisexual, and transgender folks.[3] The criminal justice system continues to be inaccessible and sometimes hostile to those who seek protection through restraining orders or who seek justice in civil or criminal courts.[4] Social services are not routinely open and accessible to lesbians and bisexual women.[5] Only recently have lesbians and bisexual women involved with women been welcome in some battered women's shelters (most shelters do not accept lesbians, and most support services for battered women are not accessible to lesbians and bisexual women involved in same-sex relationships).[6] Steve Friess notes that "None of the nation's 1,500 battered women's shelters are devoted to lesbians, although some have caseworkers who focus on lesbian clients. And most crisis hot-line operators answer the phone expecting traditional battered women situations."[7] Moreover, as Elliott points out, "Even as lesbian victims have become somewhat welcome in many traditional heterosexual programs, the attempt was made to force these lesbians into the heterosexual models for service and accountability."[8] Gay men and transgender folks have even fewer resources, although slowly this is changing.[9] While queer-based community social services in metropolitan cities increasingly address domestic violence, they tend to serve white, middle-class, English-speaking, and male members of the lesbigay and transgender communities.[10] With little to no community accountability, those who are being battered are that much more isolated, alone, and vulnerable to escalating abuse.[11]

DENIAL AND MINIMIZATION

Neither the women's antiviolence movement nor the gay, lesbian, and bisexual movement against violence adequately addresses same-sex interpersonal violence. The reasons for this may not be all that difficult to surmise. They are shared by many who struggle against institutionalized sexism, racism and classism, police brutality, hate crimes, and poverty, in addition to homophobia. Feminist and lesbian and gay movements are, in many ways, grounded in an identity politics formed to address one primary axis of oppression and to focus on external sources of oppression, i.e., sexism or homophobia. This unidimensional form of identity politics limits both the range of people served and issues included. Moreover, as Kimberlé Crenshaw points out, when antidiscrimination scholars and activists define the issues solely along one axis of identity, most base their analysis and policy on the more privileged members of broadly construed group identities.[12] For example, the feminist movement's analysis of sex discrimination often assumes that the experiences of white middle-class heterosexual Christian women are normative for women because gender is the primary axis of their oppression. The multiple sources of most women's oppression—racism, classism, heterosexism and homophobia, antisemitism, xenophobia, and colonialism, among others—are often invisible and unanalyzed. Moreover, the impact of social privilege and power is also invisible. The result is a limited, narrow, and incomplete analysis of the conditions of women's lives.

The denial of woman-to-woman rape and battering in feminist movements against violence hinges on a number of organizing assumptions related to the narrowness of a gender-exclusive agenda. One is the assumption that women are mostly the victims of violence, not the perpetrators. In the case of battering, for instance, feminists argue that social institutions organize themselves along the lines of gender inequality where

> men as a class wield power over women. As the dominant class, men have differential access to important material and symbolic resources, while women are devalued as secondary and inferior. . . . Even if individual men refrain from employing physical force against their partners, men as a class benefit from how women's lives are restricted and limited because of their fear of violence by husbands and lovers as well as by strangers. Wife abuse or battering reinforces women's passivity and dependence as men exert their rights to authority and control. The reality of domination at the social level is the most crucial factor contributing to and maintaining wife abuse at the personal level.[13]

With a focus on male violence as indicative of men's power over women, feminist analysis often ignores or minimizes both social inequalities between women and women's use of violence to establish power and control over other women and children.

Related to the minimization of women's abuse of power, many feminists (including heterosexual, lesbian, and bisexual women) assume that women's intimate relationships with women are based on equality and mutual respect because there is no apparent gender hierarchy within the relationship. By labeling the source of violence against women as (heterosexual) male dominance and patriarchy, many feminists (lesbian and heterosexual) assume that lesbian relationships are free of oppressive mistreatment, harassment, coercion, assault, and violence because men are less intimately connected to our lives. They assume that because no men are present, then power is not an issue; and, since it is assumed that women are not socialized toward power, control, and aggression (physical and sexual), then we wouldn't wield it.

When feminists acknowledge women's abuse of power, the tendency is to rationalize its use as a response to gender oppression. In my own experience, one of the major stumbling blocks I faced in addressing women's abuse was my tendency to rationalize and excuse the abusive patterns and behaviors of other women by focusing on their victimization as girl children and lesbian and bisexual adults. As a survivor of discrimination, abuse, and violence myself, I have tended to empathize with women along the lines of victimization and oppression. This tendency often prevents me from identifying and naming women's unequal power, abusiveness, and violence. It inhibits me from holding women accountable for their abusive and violent behavior. Also, I have not always recognized my own privilege and position of power as a middle-class white lesbian and its impact on women with whom I work in the university, in social and political organizations, among other contexts. I have rationalized women's abuse of other women. I have used concepts like "horizontal hostility" to describe women's oppressiveness toward each other. I have explained women's abusiveness in terms of their personal histories of abuse, and I placed the blame on their abusers and the system of male dominance that perpetrated such abuse. These strategies do not challenge unequal power and they do not stop abuse from happening. They do not encourage women to be responsible for their actions. In fact, they perpetuate inequality and violence through an active inaction and passivity.

The focus on women's victimization along with the nonrecognition of multiple sources of women's oppression and privilege has meant that feminists mostly do not politicize women's violence as a serious social issue worthy of attention. The unwillingness to address women's violence is consistent with the tendency to minimize unequal power relations between women. Despite the efforts of many to document and challenge the racism, classism, homophobia, heterosexism, antisemitism, and ableism among other forms of oppression between women, many mainstream white middle-class heterosexual Christian-based feminists have not radically taken on the realities of women's power and privilege. Since most feminist frameworks have located the source of women's oppression in male dominance, and since these conceptualize women mostly as victims/survivors of sexism, many do not analyze the interlocking systems of oppression and privilege in which women differentially experience and use power and privilege in this society. Thus, few feminist antiviolence theorists analyze women's abusiveness in relationship to women's differential involvement in systemic racism, classism, and homophobia within and outside of feminist organizations or to histories of women's complicity and involvement in violence. The result is that women's experiences of abuse and violence by other women simply accumulate without challenge.

Another roadblock in feminist work against intralesbian/bisexual women's rape and battering is homophobia and heterosexism. Herek defines heterosexism as "an ideological system that denies, denigrates, and stigmatizes any nonheterosexual form of behavior, identity, relationship, or community. [It] is manifested both in societal customs and institutions, such as religion and the legal system, and in individual attitudes and behaviors."[14] Heterosexism limits and obscures feminist analysis of men's violence against women as well as the work on lesbian and bisexual women's battering. A heterosexist feminism presumes that women survivors of men's violence are heterosexual, that homophobia is not a source of violence against women, and that heterosexual, lesbian, and bisexual women are not each impacted by heterosexism and homophobia.[15] In most surveys, studies, and analyses of (heterosexual) men's violence, violence against lesbians is invisible and homophobia is not cited as a source of women's oppression. Historical analyses of rape, for instance, rarely include the sexual abuse and rape of working-class lesbians in the 1950s by the police[16] or sexual abuse in psychiatric institutions.[17] This is due in part to the heterosexism of feminist analysis that assumes women are targeted exclusively on the basis of gender, as well as the U.S. feminist tendency in mainstream antiviolence work to focus on interpersonal rather than institutional sources of violence. The result is that violence against lesbians and bisexual women is invisible in the literature and in activist initiatives to end violence against women. Moreover, analyses of the forces of racism, classism, antisemitism and xenophobia is also missing from the theories of the incidence of violence, as well as the institutionalized ways that the society responds to violence. Similarly, domestic violence research, support, and advocacy presumes heterosexuality to be the norm and gender to be the analytic framework. When antirape and battered women's programs do include lesbian and bisexual women's relationships, they discuss them under the category of "special issues" and the information is provided as an addition to an otherwise unchanged framework.

Within lesbian, gay, bisexual, and transgender organizations, the antiviolence projects primarily have been directed toward hate crimes. The analytic framework here has been homophobia and heterosexism.[18] Lesbigay-based activists and advocates argue that homophobic bigotry and heterosexist institutions are the main issues and barriers to be addressed. In this work, lesbians and bisexual women are often invisible, and in studies of lesbians and bisexual women, often women of color, immigrant women, and poor women remain mariginalized, if not invisible, in the reports. The mainstream efforts addressing hate crimes based on sexual orientation focus on white gay men; gender-based crimes like rape are not typically included in hate crime statistics, and lesbians are not typically visible in rape statistics. This invisibility in hate crime literature is often attributed to the false notion that lesbians are not targeted to the same degree as gay men.[19] Victoria Brownworth points out the dire implications of such an assumption; she writes, "With attacks on women soaring, lesbians face an assault rate higher even than that faced by gay men, but neither women's nor gay service agencies for victims are providing adequate support. And when assaults involve rape, lesbians simply have nowhere to turn."[20] A report from the Community United Against Violence (CUAV) in San Francisco suggests that violence against "lesbians was occurring at twice the level of violence against gay men in the city."[21] Another study from the Philadelphia Lesbian and Gay Task Force (PLGTF) notes that the "incidence of homophobic violence was ten times higher than the incidence of violence against the general population and that the rate of anti-lesbian violence was 17 percent higher than violence against gay men." Moreover, the studies that do include lesbians often do not address the specifics for bisexual women.

One of the barriers to addressing violence in the lives of lesbians and bisexual women, according to Suzanne Pharr, is that "There is an assumption that women take care of themselves, that women's organizations, feminist organizations, will take care of these women. But I think feminists of all sexual orientations also often presume that lesbigay communities will address the issues and concerns of lesbian and bisexual women. As a result, lesbian and bisexual women's invisibility compounds anti-lesbian violence."[22] This includes lesbian and bisexual women's relationship violence. Without public acknowledgment, without visible public resources, and without institutional supports, lesbian and bisexual women who are being abused by their partners remain isolated.

In addition, lesbigay and transgender activists are reluctant to take on rape and battering within lesbian, gay, bisexual, and transgender relationships. Many fear that public discussions of same-sex domestic violence will contribute to public homophobic, heterosexist, transphobic, and/or biphobic attitudes and mistreatment. Given the recent controversies over social policies such as the military "don't ask don't tell," the failure of the federal legislation to outlaw discrimination on the basis of sexual orientation, the increased number of states passing heterosexual-only marriage statutes, and the debate over legal recognition of same-sex partner relationships, many feel such discussion will foster further justifications for discrimination.[23]

Some lesbian, gay, bisexual, and transgender activists believe that addressing these issues divides already disempowered communities. Not surprisingly this fear arises whenever issues of power and inequality are raised. As a white antiracist activist, I hear it often from white middle-class lesbians and feminists. Many argue that the only way to "protect" a community is to be uncritical and supportive, and yet the question is: supportive to whom? And for what purpose? It is always easier to talk about accountability and personal responsibility when the perpetrator is not one of "our" own. It's easier to point the finger at gay bashers and Christian fundamentalists for their homophobia than to address the very same practices of exclusion, mistreatment, and violence when perpetrated by women and men in our self-defined social groups. Similarly, it has been easier for lesbians to decry heterosexual men for their violence against women, but much more difficult to challenge women engaged in similar behavior either against their children or their women partners. Yet, oppression and violence, not our efforts to address and change them, divide us. Unity and solidarity are not possible when we allow existing systems of oppression and privilege, including abuse and violence, to go unchallenged.

WHAT IS WOMAN-TO-WOMAN BATTERING?

In *Naming the Violence*, Barbara Hart carefully and concretely defines lesbian battering as that pattern of violent and coercive behaviors whereby a lesbian seeks to control the thoughts, beliefs, or conduct of her intimate partner or to punish the intimate for resisting the perpetrator's control over her. . . . Lesbian battering is the pattern of intimidation, coercion, terrorism or violence, the sum of all past acts of violence and the promises of future violence, that achieves enhanced power and control for the perpetrator over her partner.[24]

Charlene Allen and Beth Leventhal point out, "We need to understand that anyone with the desire to control his or her partner and the willingness to do whatever it takes to achieve, consolidate, and maintain that control can batter."[25] Moreover, as Hart points out, "The same elements of hierarchy of power, ownership, entitlement, and control exist in lesbian family relationships. Largely this is true because lesbians have also learned that violence works in achieving partner compliance."[26]

The strategies to gain power and control are similar across the sexual orientation spectrum. Munia offers a vividly concrete listing of some of these strategies; she writes:

Domestic violence is getting beaten up by someone we love. It can involve pushing, hitting, kicking, biting, pulling hair, throwing objects, stomping, grabbing, punching, choking, blocking an exit, or using a weapon. Domestic violence is getting forced or coerced into unwanted sex or sexual acts by someone we are in a relationship with. Domestic violence is being isolated—prevented from going out, getting a job, going to school, or seeing family or friends—by our partner. Domestic violence is being threatened (of violence, of being outed) by our lover. Domestic violence is getting yelled at by our girlfriend or boyfriend. Domestic violence is having our money controlled by our partner. Domestic violence is put downs, name calling ("stupid," "ugly," "crazy") or humiliation by our soulmate. Domestic violence is having our feelings or beliefs devalued by the one we love. Domestic violence is not being allowed to make decisions for ourselves without consulting our lover.[27]

Woman-to-woman abuse, rape, and battering are *just as* serious as heterosexual men's abuse, rape, and battering—just as violent, just as hurtful, just as life threatening, just as manipulative, just as damaging.[28] Feminist efforts to address lesbian and bisexual women's battering must challenge the minimization, trivialization, and/or denial of women's use and abuse of power as well as disrupt the ideology of women's passivity and nonviolence.[29]

The differences between the strategies of batterers in same-sex relationships and those in heterosexual relationships are the ways abusers use social homophobia, biphobia, and heterosexism to further control and threaten those being victimized. If you are closeted to your family, to your employer, to your school, the batterer can threaten to out you if you leave or if you try to seek assistance. If you have children, she can threaten your custody rights. She can tell you that no one will believe you, that the police will not intervene, that the health care system will not respond. If you are bisexual and the batterer is a lesbian, she can use your bisexuality against you in the lesbian community to decrease your chances of support. The batterer can isolate you from family, co-workers, and acquaintances by emphasizing that they are homophobic, biphobic, and/or heterosexist and thus unreliable in terms of support. Social homophobia, biphobia, and heterosexism create a specific backdrop to the perpetuation of same-sex battery and rape. Heterosexual male batterers use heterosexism and homophobia to their benefit as well; heterosexual male batterers, for instance, rely on homophobia when they accuse the women they are battering of lesbianism as a way of maintaining control over them.

Generally, any batterer has a vast array of social resources from which to draw to establish power and control. And they do. Batterers use the social realities of racism, xenophobia, ableism, classism, and many other forms of oppression to increase their own power and control. They are able to do this because of the multiple sources of oppression operating in this society. Thus, battering does not rely on any one system of sexism or heterosexism exclusively. The purpose of rape and battering is power and control and perpetrators will use any oppressive system that can be orchestrated for this purpose. They do not tend to be exclusive about their choice of strategies.

Lesbians and bisexual women often feel confused about the application of the term battering to their relationships. Among the lesbians and bisexual women I know, many claim that the "real battering" or "real rape" happens only in isolated instances. Some have suggested to me that what's being called "battering" is really only generalized mistreatment common to intimate relationships. Battered lesbians and bisexual women often face similar comments and assumptions that their experiences don't constitute abuse, that their batterers have hard lives and so can't be expected to be perfect, and that the abuse isn't that bad because it's between "socially equal" individuals. One difficulty of naming abuse is that the definition of battering is so grounded in heterosexualized gender constructions. The social images of domestic violence continue to conjure up systematic physical battering and/or direct threats of physical violence. We are not used to labeling emotional, verbal, and economic abuse as abuse. For instance, Munia suggests that what is often referred to as "dyke drama" may be abuse in that it often includes patterns of behavior whereby one partner secures power and control in a relationship. She

suggests that abusive strategies may include "purposefully triggering jealousy, pro-
voking feelings of hurt and rejection, and pushing buttons that are known to trig-
ger negative emotional responses."[30] While emotional abuse may be harder to
label, it can be just as destructive. As Christie Chung puts it, "[When someone
says] 's/he strangled me,' people get it right away. . . . But if they say, 's/he's calling
me names, s/he doesn't like the way I dress, s/he always wants to use my car,' it's
harder to call it abusive, and yet it serves the same purpose of power and control."[31]

I am consistently made aware of the importance of this definitional issue in
my teaching as in my own life. In my educational efforts, women who are currently in abusive relationships may have difficulty identifying their experience as
domestic violence. I must consistently emphasize the systemic patterns of power
and control strategies over and above particular acts of physical or sexual violence.
I underline the relationship dynamics and the patterns of isolation, possessiveness
and jealousy, verbal and emotional abuse, victim-blaming, in addition to physical
violence, in my teaching, activism, and friendship networks. Tonja Santos talks
about the impact this definitional confusion had on her own life; she writes, "Had
I been able to associate 'battering' with the way she made me feel and the control
she exercised over me, rather than with the rigid definition that is generally accepted, I may have felt that the word 'battered' applied to me as well as analyzed
my situation differently."[32] If one defines battery as strictly physical violence, then
the powerful forms of psychological, verbal, and economic strategies of power and
control are not defined as problematic and abusive; these very strategies are those
that produce and maintain the abusive power and control of one partner over another and they often are simultaneous with physical violence.

It seems to me that there are differences between mistreatment, abusive behavior, battering, sexual assault, torture, attempted murder, and murder; all
abuses are not the same, even though they may be connected in people's experience. Moreover, the sources of the problem and ultimately the solution are going
to vary depending on the relational context. This is not to judge the significance of
the hurt or pain caused by "lesser" or "greater" forms of mistreatment and/or
abuse, with varying levels of systemic control and force, emotional and physical
violence. But they are qualitatively different experiences that require different responses. Educators can include all of them in prevention efforts, but indiscrimi-
nantly lumping them under one label—battery—may discourage, rather than
encourage, a discussion of what options are available to address the range of mistreatment, abuse, and battery women are experiencing. A variety of terms would
allow lesbians and bisexual women to recognize, name, and challenge abusive
power and control behaviors in relationships, even if they do not fit into common
conceptions of domestic violence. For instance, lesbians who are being mis-

treated, but do not see it as battery, might more readily label the treatment as un-acceptable and worthy of change despite the feeling that it is not battering. Les-bians who are being abused might be able to define the behaviors as more than mistreatment, more systematic, and realize that, if not addressed, they could be-come lethal. This process would allow lesbians and bisexual women to find them-selves along a continuum, to recognize that naming the problem is the first step to changing it, and to move us toward self-determination.

EXPLANATIONS OF WOMEN'S VIOLENCE AGAINST WOMEN

Since the analysis of interpersonal relationship violence has been primarily in terms of (heterosexual) male domination, many scholars, advocates, and activists are unsure of how to explain same-sex domestic violence. On the one hand, many argue that abuse is abuse, and that domestic violence cuts across all groups de-spite race, ethnicity, class, sexual orientation, religion, or any other socially con-structed difference. Some reject feminist analysis on the grounds that since women are known to be violent and men can be victims of violence, then sexism cannot be the explanatory framework. For instance, David Island and Patrick Letelier reject feminist analysis; they offer a psychological approach that defines individual personality traits and relationship dysfunctions as the sources of inti-mate violence.[33] One of the challenges of feminist analysis is to account for same-sex violence from a framework that locates that violence in multiple structures of power and oppression. One way is to differentiate the sources of domestic vio-lence for heterosexuals and for lesbians and gay men. As Pam Elliott, for instance, argues, "Sexism creates the opportunity for heterosexual men to abuse their part-ners, and homophobia, a tool of sexism, creates the opportunity for gays and les-bians to abuse their partners."[34] Some also point out that heterosexist social institutions (police, courts, social services) perpetuate battering because they are inaccessible or hostile to lesbians.[35]

These approaches assume, however, that one can separate sexism from the lives of gay men, lesbians and bisexual women, or homophobia and heterosexism from the lives of heterosexual women. They tend not to address how sexism in-forms lesbian and bisexual women's battering, or how heterosexism and homopho-bia impact heterosexual battering (including its impact on women's fears about going to a women's shelter).[36] They also do not conceptualize how racism, clas-sism, ethnocentrism, and other forms of domination and privilege shape lesbian and bisexual women's experience of violence and the differential responses of so-cial institutions to that violence.

Instead of shifting the analysis of intrawoman abuse completely away from sexism to an analysis of heterosexism and homophobia, it seems more effective to develop an analysis suggested by Patricia Hill Collins and Kimberlé Crenshaw that explores the interlocking systems of oppression that perpetuate interpersonal as well as public institutional violence. [37] These systems of hierarchy and domination depend upon violence and the threat of violence to maintain themselves. Sexism, racism, homophobia/heterosexism, classism, among other systems of oppression and privilege create the endemic and yet differentiated violence in women's lives. They fuel the different and yet interconnected forms of violence, they impact the differential personal experiences of and resistance to violence, and they shape the differentiated social and institutional responses to violence. This systemic framework differs from the current method of handling "diversity" in the domestic violence and antirape movements in that it looks at the interlocking systems of oppression and privilege, and their differential and differentiating impact on all of us.[38]

In other words, the existence of same-sex battering does not mandate the rejection of a feminist structural analysis of sexism; it does alert us to the recognition that intimate violence is connected to multiple systems of interlocking oppressions and cannot simply be understood through one axis of domination. In the following section, I lay out some broad dimensions of interlocking systems of oppression and privilege that shape the experiences of and responses to intralesbian and bisexual women's violence.

OPPRESSIVE STRUCTURES AND CONTEXTS

In order to address interpersonal lesbian and bisexual women's violence, it is essential to understand the contexts that shape and perpetuate it, beyond individual cases of sexual assault, abuse, and/or battery. Here I offer a broad outline of some isues to consider in the general context of the United States, although particular communities and regions will render more specific, nuanced, and local dimensions. In efforts to stop intralesbian and bisexual women's violence, the local and specific contexts must be considered; and yet I hope this general portrait will help provide some direction to these efforts. Lesbians and bisexual women in the United States live in a white supremacist, male dominant, homophobic, heterocentric, and capitalist society whose mainstream institutions are at best contradictory in their interpretive and very real responses to our various identities and experiences. While a few prominent white middle- and upper-class lesbians have experienced some small measure of success as public figures (political figures, prime time TV actresses, musicians), most lesbians and bisexual women continue to be invisible and/or defined and treated as deviant, pathological, sick, man-hating, aggressive, and/or violent, among other things. Suzanne Pharr writes:

Many of the lesbians I meet have been deeply wounded by the ravages of homophobia. Some have told their families they were lesbian and were rejected; others were accepted but only conditionally so. Some have lost jobs, custody of children, acceptance in the church of their choice, friends; others have been incarcerated in prisons or mental institutions. Some have left their homes and families to live far away, only to learn that there is little acceptance of their sexual identity anywhere. Feeling so much alienation from the heterosexual world, many have put all their hopes and needs into their love relationships or their lesbian communities and have felt anger and despair when both showed human failings.[39]

Lesbians and bisexual women often experience a sense of isolation, social difference, ostracism and/or hostility from family, non-lesbigay friends, acquaintances, co-workers, colleagues, neighbors, as well as from social institutions such as schools, religious institutions, and social clubs, among others. As Steven Onken writes, "Persons who are gay, lesbian, intersexual, bisexual, or transgender have grown up in homes without parental or societal role models who share these orientations and identities. Their parents, families, friends, and communities often adopt the values and attitudes of the mainstream, becoming environments perpetuating patriarchal, heterosexist, genderist, and sexist myths and stereotypes."[40] Systems of racism, classism, ethnocentrism, and xenophobia also contribute to the isolation of many lesbians and bisexual women. This social isolation in combination with underlying hostility compounds intralesbian and bisexual women's abuse, rape, and battery. It means that lesbians and bisexual women may not seek out support, may not speak about what is happening to them, may not believe that they'll gain support from social institutions, nor sometimes from queer organizations. Batterers depend on this social isolation for their strategy to establish power and control over their partner through individual isolation. The individual isolation meshes well with the social isolation to entrap the one being battered.

Rhea Almeida et al. argue that the public discrimination and abuse of the racially and sexually different significantly impact the experience of relationship violence. They write, "By publicly identifying and labeling a group, the dominant culture establishes a foundation for the public abuse of those marked 'other.' The 'other's' status in terms of visibility and invisibility is then defined by the dominant class, as are the public and private issues central to oppression."[41] Lesbians, gay men, and bisexuals experience a multitude of forms of public abuse that shape their identities, experiences, and possibilities. For instance, hate crimes and the threat of hate violence significantly shape the life experiences of lesbians and bisexual women.[42] The sources of these crimes emanate from multiple systems of domination. Onken lays out a few; he writes:

Sexism, genderism, heterosexism, monosexism, and patriarchal hierarchy are social diseases of domination with enculturation so pervasive that no individual is immune. . . . Not complying with gender and sexuality norms and the moral and medical model modes of treatment (i.e., suppression, aversion and conversion therapy, and sex reassignment surgery) has resulted in past (and current) institutional violent practices of invisibility, isolation, hospitalization, imprisonment, marginalization, rejection, discrimination, harassment, assault and death. Being open about sexual identities has resulted in such individual acts of violence as name-calling, verbal harassment, physical harassment, physical beatings, and murder.[43]

The experiences of intimidation, threats, and acts of violence by institutions as well as individuals compound our experiences of interpersonal same-sex rape and battery. Again, the public violence works in tandem with the privatized violence. The impact of homophobic, racist, sexist, xenophobic discrimination and violence increases isolation, anxiety, fear, and hopelessness. Given broader experiences of social and institutional homophobia and heterosexism, the trust in social supports is often minimal.

Reports indicate that lesbians and gay men experience discriminatory treatment in most social institutions—sports, employment, government, military, prisons, and health care. The consequences of institutionalized invisibility, mistreatment, and inconsistent social supports are increased isolation, alienation, and fear of public identification. One major social arena of mistreatment is education. Lesbians and bisexual women are subject to attack on the grounds of gender identification, gender transgressions, and/or perceived sexual orientation. Nora S. Gustavsson and Ann E. MacEachron note that while "exact rates of incidence are unknown, as many as half of lesbian and gay students may be physically harassed at school with more than 90 percent subject to verbal abuse."[44] The AAUW reports that in 1993, "more than 80 percent of girls (ages eight through eleven) had experienced some form of sexual harassment."[45] Most studies of sexual harassment do not specify antilesbian and homophobic mistreatment, and yet such treatment can dramatically impact the abilities of young lesbian, bisexual, and questioning women to address mistreatment and violence within their relationships. Sexual harassment policies often do not address same-sex and homophobic harassment. Young lesbians and bisexual women end up unprotected by school policies and practices. The ways that the mistreatment, discrimination, harassment, and abuse evidence themselves in lesbian and bisexual women's lives can shape the experience, response, and available options for those being battered and raped.

The feelings of fear, isolation, and lack of safety are compounded by institutional indifference as well as hostility in response to reports of public and private violence. These realities are brought home to me in the story of Michael Scarce, a survivor of rape and of rampant homophobia as a college student. The homophobia on his college campus created a situation in which he did not feel he could call out for help when he was being raped in his dorm room. In recognizing the collusion of a homophobic environment with an individual rapist, he writes, "I now blame those thirty floormates for my rape as much as I blame the man who assaulted me. They created and shaped a space, both actively and through negligence, in which I was gagged, effectively silenced, and unable to resist. Their intimidation weakened my spirit, lowered my self-worth, and forced me to appropriate a victim mentality that impeded me from regaining control of my life."[46] Many queer students on college campuses face homophobia and heterosexism, in a multitude of forms, often in addition to racism and classism, and as a result, many do not seek out the support of school support services and administrations.[47]

Media invisibility and distortion of queer identities further impact the self-identity and experience of lesbians and bisexual women generally and these compound same-sex harassment, rape, and battery as well. As Almeida et al. write, the lives of lesbians, bisexuals, and gay men are "not publicly acknowledged; rather they are devalued."[48] The limited range of images, stories, and perspectives about multiple and varied lesbian and bisexual women's identities and experiences contributes to social isolation that in turn contributes to the isolation of women who are being battered. With little public visibility, many do not have access to information, resources, or discourses to make sense of their experiences of relationships, including abuse and violence. I am reminded of the significance of these absences in many of my discussions with young lesbians. Their sense of what is possible is often limited; the isolated fear of public exposure in tandem with few images and stories of lesbian lives create a context of seemingly limited options. Lesbians who are being battered may fear that this relationship is the best they can do, some may feel that lesbian relationships are just more difficult in general because of the external pressures of homophobia, and some may not have a broader context from which to evaluate their relationships. This is particularly true for women who are in a lesbian relationship for the first time. Controlling and possessive lovers, introducing their girlfriends to lesbian life for the first time, often rely on their girlfriend's ignorance of lesbian life and culture to set the terms of the relationship (see Battered Lesbian Fights for Recognition, this volume). Media and cultural invisibility and distortion contribute to intralesbian and bisexual women's battering and rape. Few places exist where lesbian and bisexual relationships are openly represented and discussed. While a growing number of magazines, films, short stories, novels, and nonfiction books exist, their accessibility is often limited and even there, few address serious relationship issues such as rape and battery.

The discriminatory substance and practice of the legal system further reinforce violence against and between lesbians and bisexual women. Discrimination against lesbians and bisexual women is legal in many states—partnerships are not recognized; sodomy laws remain on the books; domestic violence statutes do not necessarily apply to same-sex relationships; and discriminatory practices in education and employment are not considered unlawful.[49] Moreover, as noted earlier, lesbians, bisexuals, and gay men have a history of being harassed and brutalized by the police. In this context, queer folks may not even entertain the idea of looking to the police or criminal justice system to protect and/or support them. Moreover, when they do, they often experience indifference and sometimes hostility on the part of the police, judges, and other officials of the criminal justice system. The sources of the indifference and hostility are institutionalized and socially endemic homophobia, sexism, racism, classism, and/or antiimmigrant attitudes. Indifference to same-sex domestic violence exists not because the police support the right of one lesbian to beat up her lover or that they uphold a right to familial privacy (often factors in their nonintervention in heterosexual partnerships). Instead, the police and judges may be indifferent because they do not perceive lesbians as worth protecting, or they assume that lesbians are generally violent and can handle themselves, or they don't take it seriously because the violence is between two women.

The experiences of lesbians and bisexual women in the legal system are shaped by multiple systems of oppression, not simply heterosexism and homophobia. For example, sexism, as well as racism and classism, are operating when judges decide that the violence in a white middle-class lesbian relationship is nothing more than a "catfight." These systems are operating when a white middle-class lesbian professional's violence is made invisible through a protected privacy afforded the middle-class and through the common, though false, assumption within the gay and straight communities that middle-class professionals are not violent. When judges decide that a lesbian is a batterer because she "looks and acts like a man," sexism is operating sometimes in collaboration with race and class oppression. The assumption that an African-American woman must be the batterer in an interracial relationship demonstrates the interconnectedness of sexism, racism, and homophobia. As Angela West explains with regard to a specific case of lesbian battering involving two African-American lesbians, "Black females have traditionally been viewed as much more hostile and aggressive than women of other races. . . . The stereotype that Black women are 'angry' and 'domineering' often results in their criminal convictions . . . "[50] Similarly, the civil system's resistance to recognizing gay men's violence is due in part to the ideas that men are not supposed to be victims and that they should be able to defend themselves. Both of these ideas stem from sexism in addition to heterosexism.[51] Thus the needs of lesbians and bisexual women are multiple and cannot be reduced to a homogeneous conception of lesbian and bisexual identity, and the systemic changes necessary to make the police and courts more accessible must not be limited to a monolithic critique of heterosexism and homophobia.

Feminist and queer-based social service and healthcare institutions exist in major cities, but are sparse in more rural areas. Moreover, they are not always hospitable, welcoming, and open to all lesbian, gay, and bisexual people. The same social systems of oppression of the broader society operate within these institutions. They tend to reproduce the power and hierarchical relations along the lines of gender, race, class, ability, religion, and nation, among others.[52] Racial polarization structures lesbian and bisexual women's communities as it does the broader society, thus many lesbian and gay social networks and organizations often reflect social power differences, not simply group-based cultural preferences.[53] This means that, for instance, not all lesbians, bisexuals, and gay men have equal access to queer-based organizations. Working-class and poor lesbians and bisexual women, for instance, who are in violent relationships, may not know about queer-based community and health organizations that serve a predominantly middle- and upper-middle-class community; they may not feel welcome and/or they may experience discriminatory and prejudicial treatment when they attempt to use these services.

The accessibility of feminist and queer-based organizations addressing violence must not be assumed. Our organizations must be mindful of institutionalized exclusionary and prejudicial practices based in a range of systems of oppression. Vazquez suggests that the problem of exclusionary organizations comes from "the single lens focus on oppression based on sexual orientation and the misguided notion that we can address racism and sexism within our movement through consciousness raising without a political agenda that specifically addresses racism, sexism, and economic injustice . . ."[54] This means that organizations must go beyond "outreach" and educational trainings about "others," and focus more directly on how organizations institutionalize and perpetuate social divisions and hierarchies in services, advocacy, and policies.

In sum, the experience of intimate violence takes place in broader social contexts that shape the experience of violence and often perpetuate it. When public institutions continue to render lesbigay identity and life invisible, marginalized, and distorted, they collude in isolating and marginalizing lesbians, bisexuals, and gay men. The social realities of public discrimination and violence contribute to the experiences of private intimate violence. Each compounds social marginality and individual isolation and devastation. In order to effectively address and eventually prevent interpersonal and public violence, we must dismantle broader structures of inequality.

IDENTITY-BASED SERVICES AND ADVOCACY

Increasingly, services, organizations, and networks are forming to address intralesbian/bisexual women's rape and battering. The approach and strategies of these groups are being negotiated and developed. Given the multiple, interlocking, and conflicting systems of oppression, feminists of color, and lesbians, and immigrant women, among others, argue that the generic universal approach to abuse and battering is not only ineffective but can be dangerous. Due in part to the homophobia and heterosexism of battered women's service organizations and the sexism of gay organizations, some lesbian and bisexual women activists have created specific organizations to address the abuse and battering in women's intimate relationships with women.[55] Such organizations assume that lesbians and bisexual women who are battered and formerly battered have a distinct set of needs and concerns. Yet, this distinctness must not be seen as homogeneous either. As Beth Leventhal and Sandra Lundy point out, "when the issue of queer domestic violence has been addressed at all, it has generally been in 'one size fits all' terms that ignore and disrespect our diversity."[56] In contrast, strategies within lesbigay transcommunities must be multiple and varied. The identities and life experiences of lesbian and bisexual women vary considerably across contexts. Cultural, historical, linguistic, political, economic, and social factors shape the contexts of our lives and must shape the support and advocacy services and the resources developed to prevent and eliminate violence in intimate relationships.

A typical response within mainstream battered women's movement organizations has been to simply marginalize same-sex domestic violence as a "special case" with special needs within an otherwise generic program. For instance, some battered women's organizations add a section to their trainings on lesbigay rape and battering; typically, volunteers are introduced to a discussion of sexual orientation, the system of heterosexism and homophobia, and the particular issues related to same-sex domestic violence. The inclusion of same-sex rape and battering has been a step forward, and yet it has limitations. It has been important to acknowledge that same-sex violence exists, to critically challenge homophobia and heterosexism, and to discuss the differences between lesbian and bisexual women's rape and battering and heterosexual men's violence. The inclusion directly addresses the heterosexism and homophobia of volunteers, counselors, educators, and advocates; and it shows how these systems impact the personal experience of rape and battering and the social response to this violence by the courts, agencies, and schools, among other public institutions.

In general, however, the service providers, volunteers, and activists continue to operate from a generic feminist analysis (implicitly based on white heterosexual Christian middle-class women), with an added section on "other" women. In trainings about same-sex domestic violence, we/they discuss this group of "other" women in terms of particular issues that lesbians and bisexual women might face. The feminist framework of sexist oppression and power is often muted. The particulars of lesbigay lives are associated, usually, with cultural specificities and sometimes social and political status. Typically, the trainings assume that lesbians and bisexual women fit into one identity category, that our experiences can be generalized, and that the main issue we face is heterosexism and homophobia. The multiple identities of women—gender identity, race, class, ethnicity, religion, nationality—are homogenized into a lesbian/bisexual/gay identity; our issues are considered separate from the generic group of women. The result, as Martha Lucía García aptly points out, is that "The women we serve are not seen as whole individuals with unique realities. Instead, for the sake of 'manageability,' they are fragmented into components that are simpler for us to handle."[57] One strategy to counteract such compartmentalization would be to address the complex contextual realities of women's lives—including racism, classism, homophobia, xenophobia, and ethnocentrism—in ways that don't reduce the wholeness of women's identities into fragmented factors. Our understanding would come from an analysis of context, rather than from descriptive characteristics attributed to group-based monolithic identities.

Service providers, advocates, and activists would do well to recognize the fullness of women's lives—including systems of oppression and privilege, cultural and social context, and women's negotiation and response to violence. Sexism, heterosexism, and homophobia, as well as systems of class, race, and nation, all impact women's experiences and potential responses to violence. The particulars of these systems depend on the multiple identities of women involved and their developed modes of coping, resisting, and surviving. For instance, for immigrant lesbians and bisexual women, García writes, "Just as we cannot separate U.S. women who are experiencing abuse from the society they live in, we must also look at how immigrant lesbians are affected by globalization of the economy, war and political strife, and the widening gap between rich and poor that forces many to leave their home countries in search of work and a better economic life in the United States."[58] In addressing the needs of women, the multidimensionality of their contexts must be considered as well as their own unique location and experience within these contexts. One organization that is building such a program is Asian Women's Services in San Francisco. They are making their battered women's programs and services accessible to lesbian and bisexual women. They have policies to challenge homophobia and heterosexism of the staff as well as women they serve, and they are doing further research into the particular needs of the lesbian and bisexual women's communities to determine particular programming and services.[59]

My approach to violence in lesbian and bisexual women's communities has grown out of my experiences as a self-identified lesbian, whose context is in urban, mostly, but not exclusively, middle-class and white politically active communities. My perspectives about naming the violence, about the needs of lesbian and bisexual women, and about how available and accessible resources are, have often been based on the configurations of my own particular identity and context. I must identify and address the limitations of this in my teaching and activism. For instance, my involvement in Debra Reid's case in the early 1990s made me humbly aware of these limitatons. I met Debra Reid, a formerly battered African-American lesbian who accidentally killed her lover in self-defense, in the early 1990s, when I was approached to write an essay to publicize her clemency petition.[60] Over the course of many conversations with her, the differences between us became very apparent—differences in our relationship to lesbian identity and life experience, as well as in our access to information and resources. During the time she was being battered by her lesbian lover, she was living in a small town in western Massachusetts. She was new to the area (originally from Virginia), she was working-class poor, she had never been in a relationship with a woman, and she did not identify with the term "lesbian." She had no knowledge of support systems and resources that would address the needs of poor African-American women in relationships with women. Even had she lived in Boston, she may not have known of the existing lesbian and gay social, legal, and health services as they seem to serve predominantly white middle-class politically-aware communities. I, on the other hand, was living in Boston as a middle-class white lesbian feminist activist who had been involved with feminist, gay, lesbian, and bisexual movements for the previous fifteen years. Many of the established organizations in Boston were geared to me, not to Debra Reid. How could outreach, services, and resources be changed to meet the needs of a much broader range of lesbians and bisexual women? This is the question that must be asked and answered as we move forward.

Any efforts to create services for lesbian and bisexual women must be grounded in the experiences and perspectives of the different and varied groups of women who live in the particular and local contexts. The importance of this continues to be brought home to me. Sulis, for instance, encourages me to consider the biphobia that exists in lesbian and gay organizations and social groups, including those in which I participate, and its impact on domestic violence. As she suggests, a bisexual woman who is being battered by a woman may experience further isolation and control because of the alienation she feels from established organizations.[61] Moreover, her batterer can use biphobia to maintain her control over the resources she perceives to be available. Services, advocacy, and activism must address the different and overlapping identities and contexts of lesbians and bisexual women in order to address the fullness of our individual and social lives.

BATTERING AS A COMMUNITY ISSUE

The endemic nature of violence in this society demonstrates the need to move be-yond an analysis based in social psychology. Interpersonal violence in this society is integrally linked to gender, racial, class, and state-orchestrated hierarchies, power, and violence. Making connections with broader systems of oppression and privi-lege help us to refocus our attention from individual pathology to social relations of power and inequality. Such a shift encourages the development of strategies that are grounded in broad-based conceptions of individual and social change.

Violence against lesbians and bisexual women, both intragroup and inter-group, is a community-based issue that is connected with many other forms of mistreatment, abuse, and violence. If educators and activists understand that abuse and violence are endemic to particular social, political, and cultural con-texts, then the focus of change efforts would not simply be on the individuals in-volved. When we approach intimate violence through an isolated focus on the individuals, couples, and/or families, when we focus solely on the particulars of the intimate violence, and when we abstract the individuals out of their commu-nity contexts, our strategies for stopping violence will ultimately be limited and in-effective. As Gustavsson and MacEachron write in relation to social services for gay and lesbian youth,

> Americans appear comfortable with misdirected responses to societal vi-olence and are willing to provide limited remedial services. Lesbian, gay, and bisexual youth can receive professional mental health services for de-pression and substance abuse. Social service agencies treat these issues as individual, personal problems with therapies designed to help the client cope. This inadvertantly maintains the status quo, as the victims of soci-etal violence are isolated and blamed for their own problems.[62]

Feminist educators and activists must support local and national efforts to change institutional policies and practices so that they address the multiple and intercon-nected sources of discrimination, stigmatization, harassment, and violence.

On a local level, individuals can make a difference in our self-defined com-munities. If we made our smaller social groups responsible to its members in terms of challenging interpersonal abuse and violence, a difference could be made. This strategy recognizes that all of us contribute to interpersonal abuse and violence as active perpetrators and bystanders. When we remain actively passive as onlookers to abusive relationships, we help perpetuate them. When we actively minimize or rationalize abusive behaviors, we contribute to them and to their impact on the recipient of the abuse. Instead, we might create strategies in our social groups that recognize, label, and challenge abusive attitudes and behaviors. At the very least, our small social groups might develop ways to support lesbians and bisexual women seeking to leave relationships, to confront abusive girlfriends and partners, and to access support services. This approach challenges the privacy of relationships which often serves to protect and perpetuate abuse. It encourages discussion and critical reflection about our relationship dynamics and behaviors. It also supports lesbians in violent abusive relationships who are seeking to change and/or leave these relationships, and it encourages self-determination. I have experienced a lot of resistance to this approach. Some argue that it would interfere in private relationships and that it might lead to false accusations. They remind me often that there are always "two sides" to every story. I agree that we run these risks, and yet, I also know that mistreatment, abuse, and violence are perpetuated in part because of the shields of privacy and its ensuing isolation. One solution to this is to facilitate ongoing discussions in our social groups about intimate relationship dynamics. When relationship dynamics are subject to public and collective discussion, interpersonal manipulation and abuse are less likely to germinate. I believe that if we openly and freely discussed the dynamics of mistreatment, abuse, rape, and battery among lesbians and bisexual women—without shame—then perpetrators would feel less comfortable abusing their partners. In such a context, if we felt uncomfortable with destructive relationship dynamics, we would have more information from which to make judgments and decisions about our relationships.

We might also find ways to hold women accountable for their abusive actions and behaviors, not for the rest of their lives, but until they stop behaving in negative, hostile, and violent ways. When the issue of accountability is raised, some argue that lesbians who batter are in need of our support *as lesbians*. Melanie Kaye/Kantrowitz criticizes what she perceives as a strategy of ostracizing or excluding batterers from events, forums, or general communities.[63] This is a common and recurrent worry that arises whenever the issue of accountability is raised. In response to potential exclusion, Kaye/Kantrowitz asks: "Why is this? So our communities remain pure? Do we think we can shove wrongdoers 'out there,' like garbage, for someone else to clean up? Where are they supposed to go? Who will deal with our abusers, our shadow, our difficult and dangerous ones, if we don't?"[64] Kaye/Kantrowitz's questions sidestep the issue of accountability and erase the life of the lesbian being battered who in many cases is being treated like "garbage" by this "difficult and dangerous" one. The question cannot be whether to ban or not to ban batterers, or to identify or not with the abuser or the abused. Rather, the question has to be how can we prevent, stop, and change the endemic abusiveness in many of our relationships. We need to experiment with and explore various strategies that lesbians and bisexual women activists have tried.

In order to answer the question of how to prevent violence, we must explore approaches that allow us to address the sources for lesbian abuse and battering within the broader society's hierarchical relations of power and control. At the same time, we must hold lesbians accountable for their actions. Accountability means that the lesbian or bisexual woman agrees to stop being abusive and to take responsibility for her actions and for the consequences of those actions. Accountability would also mean that a lesbian or bisexual woman is willing to change her behavior without blaming the one she abused and battered. The refusal to confront mistreatment, abuse, and battering allows the violations to continue unquestioned and presumably accepted. Meanwhile, the lesbian who is being battered remains isolated and on her own.

In the immediacy of violent and threatening circumstances, banning someone from participating in our social groups may be necessary and essential for the safety of a woman being battered. On the other hand, in the absence of threat, banning someone from a public gathering who has been known to batter in the past seems problematic. At a session on lesbian battering at the national lesbian conference in Atlanta in 1992, a lesbian participant mentioned that in one of her relationships, she felt that she was both the batterer and the battered. Rather than explore her claim, the facilitators asked her to leave the group. She left in tears. I disagreed with this decision. If the session had been organized exclusively for lesbians who had only ever been recipients of battering, and who had never participated in battering as an active batterer, then I can understand the decision to ask this woman to leave. But the session was not labeled as such and no one in the workshop knew her or identified her as a threat. As a solution, banning an individual self-identified as someone who has battered in the past, who is not battering or threatening to someone at the event, and at an event not exclusively oriented toward those who have only directly experienced battering, assumes that everyone else that remains *is safe*. As Liz Kelly asks, "Does the view that we create 'safe' places for women who have been abused lead to a perception that the only problem is the few women who are thus excluded?"[65]

I do not believe that anyone can guarantee, without reservation, safety. What we can guarantee however, as individuals or as a group, is that if we perceive and/or are told about mistreatment, abuse, rape, and/or battery, that we will not be passive bystanders or minimizers and rationalizers. We can create a context that encourages collective responsibility for the mistreatment, abuse, and violence that exists. When this is done, then interpersonal mistreatment, abuse, and violence become public issues that are ripe for prevention and change. The possibilities for fundamental change, in other words, are located in the larger social context, rather than solely in the specific individual cases.

WHERE DO WE GO FROM HERE? A VISION OF SOCIAL JUSTICE

Interpersonal mistreatment, abuse, battery, and rape among lesbians and bisexual women are social justice issues, not simply personal ones. They emanate from broader contexts of social inequalities that feed into the specific forms of mistreatment and violence that in turn further shape these contexts. A social justice framework in relation to intralesbian/bisexual women's violence can improve feminist research, service, advocacy, and activism. Without it, our efforts become mere bandages to wounds fed from multiple sources and circumstances. A social justice framework encourages the development of intervention and prevention efforts that are aimed at community practices, not simply individual and relationship behaviors and dynamics. Education and outreach efforts might be oriented toward building responsive and responsible communities, rather than simply helping individuals to identify battery and rape for themselves. The question guiding the efforts would be: how can we educate and motivate social groups, institutions, and organizations to take responsibility for the interpersonal and institutionalized mistreatment, abuse, and violence that surround us? It is important to move beyond simply teaching people not to use violence or to leave violent relationships, and instead to work to build more just and equal relationships that respect the dignity of each individual.

As many before me have argued, the underlying hierarchies, relations of domination and subordination, and social inequalities must be addressed in order to stop and prevent interpersonal violence.[66] The mistreatment, abuse, and battering within lesbian relationships are integrally linked to the forces of social discrimination, abuse, and violence in employment, education, criminal justice, health institutions, and on the streets. They are connected as well to the harassment, rape, and battery orchestrated by the state, for instance, in the criminal justice system, in prisons, and in the military. Efforts are limited and counterproductive when they treat interpersonal privatized harassment and abuse as if they are separate and distinct from public forms. Organizing to connect the private and public forms of violence will help create a more comprehensive and holistic approach to creating more socially just communities.

PART II

PRODUCING AND CONSUMING SEXUALIZED INEQUALITY

4

PORNOGRAPHY'S STORIES:
Eroticizing Inequality, Hierarchy, and Historical Atrocity

Feminists who critically analyze and fight the mass industry of heterosexual pornography do so because it socially produces and institutionally practices sexual and racial exploitation, objectification, abuse, and violence against women. The mass industry of pornography, built from the structures and dynamics of social inequalities, promotes implicit and explicit ideologies of sexism and racism that justify and legitimate mistreatment, harassment, and sexual abuse. Moreover, the pornography industry often perpetuates mistreatment, exploitation, abuse, and violence through its production, use, and mass distribution.

In contrast to the moralistic perspective on pornography proffered by the right wing, the salient issue for feminists has not been the sexual explicitness of pornography nor its public availability. Rather, it is the industry's misogyny, racism, and bigotry, the structure and dynamics of eroticized inequality, and the sexual abuse and violence which occur through its production, consumption, and distribution.[1] Feminists are less focused on individual tastes or preferences, and more concerned with the social practices and actions endemic in an industry which produces social relations of inequality and violence that reproduce in turn structural systems of oppression and privilege in the world.

The profitability of the mass industry of pornography is dependent on gender, racial, economic, political, and social inequalities and bigotries at several levels. The structure of the industry's labor force reflects racial and economic inequalities. The industry mass produces and distributes sexual images and stories constructed in ways that create sexual entertainment from the dynamics of social inequality. The mass market appeal of pornography to men in particular is that it is created for male audiences who culturally identify at some level with this hegemonically constructed heterosexual white male masculinity. For feminists, as Andrea Dworkin suggests, "Social inequality is created in many different ways. In my view, the radical responsibility is to isolate the material means of creating the inequality so that material remedies can be found for it."[2]

Feminists critical of the industry analyze and deconstruct the ideological constructions of gender, race, and sexuality in terms of their participation in naturalizing, legitimating, and therefore perpetuating sexualized and racialized harassment, abuse, and violence. Many of us look to the pornography industry, as well as other mass media cultural industries, including fairy tales, music, literature, and other cultural forms in an effort to understand the acceptance of pervasive mistreatment of and violence against women.[3] The analysis of pornographic texts offered in this chapter is grounded in my belief that these constructions contribute to social contexts where pervasive mistreatment, abuse, and violence are denied, minimized, and trivialized. Pornography's cultural productions legitimate social inequalities as normative and consensual.

The products of the multibillion dollar heterosexual male-dominant pornography industry rely upon the dynamics of dominance and subordination for their sexual appeal; they do so by drawing upon historically constituted structures and institutionalized forms of inequality, discrimination, and violence.[4] I am less concerned here with the particular meaning and significance of isolated images, and more concerned with the ways that pornographic texts collectively reinforce inequality to produce social entertainment. As Tracey Gardner writes with regard to the racism of pornography, "I want you to understand that when a person of color is used in pornography, it's not the physical appearance of that person which makes it racist. Rather, it's how pornography capitalizes on the underlying history and myths surrounding and oppressing people of color in this country which makes it racist."[5] Sexism, racism, homophobia, classism, and xenophobia are central to the functioning of heterosexual men's pornography and its connection to mistreatment, abuse, and violence. By making social inequalities into social and cultural entertainment, pornographic cultural productions encourage apathy, indifference, and hostility toward those working to build a more socially just society. In this chapter, I offer an analysis of pornographic stories to illustrate how inequality is made into entertainment. Of course, this is only one aspect of the larger critique of the mass industry of pornography and is not meant to be comprehensive.

PORNOGRAPHY'S STORIES AND THE REPRODUCTION OF INEQUALITIES

The eroticization of male supremacy in pornography is enmeshed with racial, class, ethnic, and other inequalities in the society that are also institutionalized in law, medicine, education, and religion. Pornography tells stories about women's naturalized desires to be sexually subordinate, objectified, submissive, and powerless. These stories are cultural stories that have a significance beyond the immediate impact on individual consumers. The stories construct social meanings that are connected to many other cultural stories in the society produced by mass culture industries. These stories become the lens through which we interpret and understand actions, behaviors, and events. I am interested in the lens created by stories in pornography as an industry of mass culture and how this lens frames our understanding and evaluation of women's stories of mistreatment, harassment, abuse, and violence. My questions here concern the relationship between the stories in heterosexual male pornography and their relationship to social and political realities. I am interested in the ways that inequalities are reinvigorated, reinforced, perpetuated, legitimated, and justified through the stories in these pornographic texts.

The stories, told by the mass culture industry of pornography, about women's pleasure in submission and pain contribute to the fact that men who rape, convicted and nonconvicted, believe that women derive sexual pleasure from forceful, abusive, and violent treatment. The general public also believes these myths. Men and women assume that the women consented to the sex (assault) or in some way were responsible for the sexual experience (assault), especially in the cases of women of color, poor women, and/or prostitutes.[6] Due to the fictionalized entertainment medium, pornography's stories desensitize men and women to sexual abuse and violence. In the words of Dworkin, pornography "numbs the conscience, makes one increasingly callous to cruelty, to the infliction of pain, to violence against persons, to the humiliation or degradation of persons, to the abuse of women and children."[7] According to Catharine MacKinnon's review of much of the social science research on pornography, it illustrates that without much question

> Pornography destroys men's ability to *perceive* either the existence of sexual force and degradation, or the harm of it. The use of force and degradation becomes fused with their perceptions of what women are for and what men may legitimately do to us.[8]

Mass mediated pornography contributes to the cultural silencing and dismissal of women's objections and resistance to discrimination and violence. For instance, the mass production of pornography's representations of women's bodies silence the women represented on its pages by accompanying the photographic representations with first-person narratives giving the impression that the women themselves are writing about their own sexual identities, desires, and practices. Pornographic stories also can silence women (not in the photos) who are sexually assaulted because the stories say this is what women want and need. The mass cultural production of pornography also contributes to the silencing of women's resistance to forced sex by promoting pathologizing terms of prudery and frigidity to women uninterested in heterosexual men's sexuality. It silences women as well because the stories often discredit women's charges of sexual assault by couching abusive threatment as consensual and positive. Finally, it silences women's claims to human worth and dignity through processes of mass objectification and sexualization of women's bodies that are then bought and sold on the mass market.[9]

Pornography perpetuates sexual abuse and discrimination in the real world of social inequality by portraying sexual harassment and abuse as a source of sexual pleasure and entertainment. Sexual relations in this society are considered individual and private. By placing the inequality and bigotry in a sexual, and thus supposedly private arena, the pornography industry's producers and consumers are mostly uninterrogated in the broad public arena. For many it remains a taboo topic except in the most general terms. If we deprivatize the sexual entertainment arena, the links between the stories of sexualized inequality in the pornography and the harassment, abuse, and violence that women (and men) experience become more apparent.

This deprivatization is one of the accomplishments of the contemporary feminist antipornography movement; feminists have created an unprecedented public discussion of pornography's sexism and racism, and its connections to violence against women. Since the mid to late 1970s, groups across the country, like Women Against Violence Against Women (WAVAW), Women Against Violence in Pornography and Media (WAVPM), and MediaWatch, among others, have sought to publicize the substance and practices of the pornography industry. The actions have included protests, marches, group tours of pornography districts, pickets and boycotts of films which glorify sexual abuse and violence, public hearings on the impact of pornography, slide show discussions on the pornography industry's products, as well as direct action politics and civil disobedience against the industry.[10] These actions have each drawn attention to the industry's activities and its harms to women. Feminists have also sought to create legislation that would hold producers and consumers of pornography accountable for the direct harms of specific pornography's production, consumption, and mass distribution.[11] The slide shows and public hearings in particular document, through example, how pornography constructs and perpetuates sexualized and racialized bigotry, exploitation, harassment, and violence against women. They deconstruct the ideology of white, male, heterosexualized domination; they show how pornography presents sexual force as what women desire, and how it legitimates discrimination and abuse by making them sexually arousing and entertaining.[12] The slide shows and public hearings have helped to demystify the secrecy and taboo aspect of the pornography industry. This has been important, particularly for women who have not been directly involved in the industry, since pornography has historically been produced for the privatized sexual entertainment of men and because the women involved in pornography have often been stigmatized, criminalized, and at the very least excluded from mainstream recognition and respect.

The public discussion of pornography encourages women and men to recognize that the industry does not simply traffic in "sexual expression" but rather in misogynist and racist discourse and practices. Feminist activism has created a forum for public discussion about the personal and social implications of this mass industry. Contrary to most critiques of the feminist antipornography movement, the strategies have not been directed toward an absolute ban against sexually explicit material in general. The goals have been critical analysis and public protest to provoke discussion and industrial accountability for the harms created through pornography, each with the hope of change and transformation. It is in this spirit that I offer the following analysis of pornography's sexualization of inequality.

MAKING WHITE HETEROSEXUAL MALE SUPREMACY SEXY

Pornography is not creative or original in its exploitation of historical and social power dynamics. It takes already existing inequalities and makes them sexy and entertaining. Just as mainstream culture industries justify inequality and hatred on the basis of biological determinism—anatomy is destiny—so does pornography. Pornography reproduces inequality in part through repeated and cumulative constructions of racially gendered bodies that are differentiated and opposed in form and function.

Like mass media and popular culture, pornography treats women differently according to race and color. Mainstream heterosexual men's pornography geared to the white male population rarely includes women of color, and when they do, they present the women differently from white women. Luisah Teish points out that "While white women are pictured as pillow-soft pussy willows, the stereotype of the Black 'dominatrix' portrays the Black woman as ugly, sadistic, and animalistic, undeserving of human affection."[13] Mainstream heterosexual men's pornography portrays white women, particularly with blonde hair and blue-eyes, as prized sex objects. The mass pornography industry perpetuates white beauty standards that are set up as normative and universal in mainstream popular culture. Thus, they create a sexual-racial hierarchy between women based on skin color and ethnic features.[14] Dorchen Leidholdt illustrates this differential treatment in her description of *Playboy's* June 1982 issue where the "Playmate of the Year" is a "tall, slender, light-skinned blonde" who is characterized as a "very expensive possession"—she "reclines in white fur on the cover and naked beneath the gold net inside." The "Playmate of the Month," on the other hand, is an Asian-Latin woman who is photographed "frolicking with animals and licking a snow cone, she is depicted as a creature of nature, a happy, simple child."

Darker-skinned women, who appear in cartoons, are ridiculed and put down; in one, "a plump Mexican housekeeper who sits barebreasted on her elderly white employer's lap downs Tequila and a group of domestic workers [are] cleaning the Playboy Club after hours, their heavy middle-aged bodies encased in skimpy bunny costumes." MacKinnon provides some clues to the range of racism against Asian women when she reports: "The pornography of Asian women is almost entirely one of torture. The women are presented so passive they cannot be said to be alive, so bound they are not recognized as human, hanging from light fixtures and clothes pegs and trees."[15] These stereotypes and racist representations permeate this society, and are integral to the lack of response on the part of social institutions to violence against women of color. They are also directly related to the systematic exploitation of different groups of women historically.[16]

In part because of this differential treatment in the mainstream pornography, Tracey Gardner argues that Black women may approach the issue of mainstream heterosexual men's pornography differently from white women:

> Soft-core pornography is an extension of mass advertising and the beauty market; it is the Beauty Queen revealed. Until recently the Beauty Queen was by definition white: fair complexion, straight hair, keen features, and round eyes. Soft-core pornography was the objectification of white purity, white beauty, white innocence.[17]

For Black, Asian, and Latina women, the message of popular culture is that they could be "whores but not beauty queens."[18] Alice Walker's short story, "Coming Apart" eloquently addresses these issues. She shows how the racial and gender politics in pornography's representations cannot be separated from the history of racism and sexism in this country. In particular, she discusses pornography's connection to the history of slavery and how sexualized racism impacts Black women, in particular in relation to Black men as well as white women. She accomplishes this through the story of a heterosexual Black couple's struggle over the man's use of pornography and its impact on their intimate relationship. The woman in the story confronts her husband's use of first white mainstream pornography, and then mainstream Black pornography, in terms of how it participates in sexualized racism against Black women. She poignantly portrays the impact of white beauty standards and their relationship to the self-image of a Black woman as well as to how the pornography interferes with the growth possibilities of an intimate heterosexual relationship.[19]

Walker addresses how pornography depicts white women as objects, while depicting Black women as animals. Patricia Hill Collins elaborates: "As objects white women become creations of culture—in this case, the mind of white men—using the materials of nature—in this case, uncontrolled female sexuality. In contrast, as animals Black women receive no such redeeming dose of culture and remain open to the type of exploitation visited on nature overall. Race becomes the distinguishing feature in determining the type of objectification women will encounter. Whiteness as symbolic of both civilization and culture is used to separate objects from animals."[20]

Pornographers create specific magazines and books around various groups of women of color, including *Lusty Latin*, *Mulatto Splits and Tits*, *Oriental Fetishes*, *Sexy Señoritas*, *Slut from Shanghai*, *Brown Juicy Bitch*, *Asian Suck Mistress*, *Asian Anal Girls*, *Black Whore*, *Black Beaver Fever*. These magazines are mostly addressed to a white male gaze, although consumers range in identity. Some claim that by featuring women of color in the pornographic representations, the industry is attempting to equalize the race bias. Producers do not necessarily have equality in mind. William Margold, a video producer who specializes in interracial porn videos, for instance, openly reports: "When I put Blacks in my videos, I project my fantasies, not theirs." His video *Hot Chocolate* features "Black people calling one another 'niggers' and hitting one another with spareribs." He says, "I did these videos because they portray Black life like it really is. They have soul."[21] Paul Fishbein, publisher of *Adult Video News*, admits that the videos are racist and that the projected audience is white men, not Black.[22]

Pornography available under the broad rubric of the industry eroticizes and/or fetishizes other characteristics of women as well. As Gail Dines-Levy reports, "we also have pornography that you can't imagine. Pornography like amputee pornography, where people have sex with the amputated limbs of other people. We have pregnancy pornography, where women who are pregnant are shown squirting milk over other women. We have urination pornography, which specializes in people urinating on each other. . . . We also have child pornography and abortion pornography."[23] There is also pornography eroticizing fat women (*Fat Fuckers*), old women, "ugly" women (*Ugly Girls that Love to Fuck*), and large breasted women (e.g., *Big Breast Bondage*, *Black Tit and Body Torture*, *Black and Stacked*).

The bodies of women and men are constructed in terms of erotic relations. Much mainstream heterosexual pornography presents the penis and/or its many symbolic phallic substitutes and women's orifices, including the vagina, mouth, and anus, as the basis for male domination and supremacy. Here power inheres in the ability to penetrate, and powerlessness in the desire and willingness to be penetrated. Dworkin explains:

> The possession of a penis is the symbol of and entitlement to a host of psychological, moral and existential attributes—primarily strength, power, and humanity. In contrast, the vulva is viewed as a mark of shame, a stigma representing weakness, duplicity, powerlessness, and the status of an animal or a thing.[24]

The penis and its phallic substitutes (including swords, knives, scissors, guns, pistols, rifles, tanks, various instruments of torture, steel rods, and cattle prods,[25] as well as household items, broom handles, vacuum cleaners, telephone receivers) are used in pornography and in real life to control and possess women. In the pornography, they symbolize not only status, but weapons of domination. The vulva and other female orifices, on the other hand, symbolize in the pornography the desire to be taken, controlled, and violated.

As in other hegemonic culture industries in the United States, women of color are particular targets of sexual stigma given the historical production of controlling images of sexual promiscuity.[26] In *Pornography: Men Possessing Women*, Dworkin's analysis of particular pornographic texts illustrates how the color of Black women's skin is sexualized such that dark skin comes to symbolize the stigma of sexuality. She analyzes the magazine *Black Fashion Model*, which, she reports, uses the standard methods of sexual subordination and violation, including "rape, bondage, humiliation, pain, fucking, assfucking, fingerfucking, cocksucking, cuntsucking, kidnapping, hitting, the sexual cruelty of one woman toward another, pair sex, gang sex . . ." However, here the pornography's construction works by sexualizing Black women's skin. Dworkin writes:

> Her skin with its color is her sex with its nature. She is punished in sex by sex and she is punished as a consequence of sex: she loses her status. All this punishment is deserved, owing to her sex, which is her skin. The genital shame of any woman is transferred to the Black woman's skin. The shame of sex is the shame of her skin. The stigma of sex is the stigma of her skin. The use of her sex is the use of her skin. The violence against her sex is the violence against her skin. The excitement of torturing her sex is the excitement of torturing her skin. . . . [27]

Dworkin argues that Black women's skin becomes "the specific sexual value of the black women in pornography in the United States, a race-bound society fanatically committed to the sexual devaluing of black skin perceived as a sex organ and a sexual nature. . . ."[28] The eroticization of Black skin in pornography contributes to the racist history and stereotype that Black women exist for the sexual use of men, especially white men, and the myth that they are always sexually available.[29] This is further connected to the fact that historically in this country, the rape and sexual abuse of Black women was legal, and continues to this day to be minimized and ignored.[30]

The constructed images and the stories that surround women serve to set up a naturalized inequality where men naturally need and desire to sexually humiliate, degrade, and violate women, and that women naturally accept, love, and de-find pornographic stories of teacher and student sexual encounters and relationships like *A Schoolgirl's First Time*. In some cases, the gender hierarchy competes with the teacher/student hierarchy as in products with titles like *Teacher Loves Rape*, or *Two Horny, Hot Teachers* where the male student seduces his female teachers. Employment contexts are ripe for sexualized storytelling given the social hierarchy between employers and employees. Pornographic magazines and fiction books that delve into these relations include *Have You Tried the New Secretary?*, *Hard Boss*, *A Secretary Spreads*, *Chained Slave Secretary*. Babysitting is another favorite; one can purchase *Babysitter in Bed* and *Chained Up Babysitter*. In each of these, it is the social inequality—of gender, race, age, social status, occupation—that becomes the cornerstone of sexual desire and arousal. Without the inequality, the sex appeal diminishes. What interests me is the interrelationship between these stories and the stories women, and increasingly men, tell about sexual harassment, sexual abuse, and rape in the context of these same hierarchies.

Given the gendered values of this society in combination with the sexual dynamics of power and powerlessness, pornography capitalizes on age hierarchies as well. A vast array of pornographic products and services sexualize age hierarchies. Writers and producers construct young, prepubescent women to be the most sexually enticing and attractive erotic objects for adult men's consumption. The younger a woman is or appears, the more virginal, vulnerable, and powerless she is portrayed, and thus the sexier (read sexually enticing and available) she is believed to be. Accordingly, the younger the girl (or boy) or woman appears to be in the pornography, the stronger the sexual arousal for adult male consumers.[33]

The mass legal and illegal industries of pornography participate in the sexualization and pervasive sexual abuse of children in and out of pornography. Children are bought and sold for prostitution and pornography in this country and around the world.[34] Legal pornographic products and services, however, are just as involved in perpetuating the sexualization of children for adult sexual pleasure and entertainment. Incest and adult/child sexual relations are common themes of stories and cartoons in mainstream pornography. Fictional stories and cartoons are a way to use children to provide entertainment and sexual stimulation with the disclaimer that they are not using "real" children. For instance, there are pornographic paperback book series on incest and adult/child sexual relations, with titles like *Spread Daughter Spread*, or *Daughters Hot for Dogs*, or *Daddy's Naughty Daughters*. *Hustler* had a regularly featured cartoon for many years called "Chester the Molester." The main character, Chester, regularly "seduces" or is "seduced by" young girls. Of course, according to the pornographic narrative, the young girls control and orchestrate the sexual relations with the adult men for their own sexual pleasure.[35] The cartoons often have the little girls asking for sex, bragging about sex, and/or trivializing the sex (e.g., one cartoon has a young girl leaving an adult man's house saying, "you call that molestation?").

Defenders of the pornography industry argue that these are just cartoons, just entertainment, just fantasy. Such responses seem too simplistic. For example, even for the author/creator of "Chester the Molester," Dwaine Beverly Tinsley, the interconnections between fantasy and reality are troubling. In 1991, he was convicted of five counts of sexually abusing his teenage daughter. A court overturned this conviction on the grounds that the cartoons were "unjustly" used in the trial as evidence.[36] While his conviction was overturned, the connections cannot be simplistically dismissed. The mass production of cartoons and stories celebrating adult/child sexual relations cannot help but have an impact on adult male readers as well as the children they may be sexually abusing. A scholar and activist on pornography, Gail Dines, once asked a family therapist who works with sexual abusers if she ever considered the role of pornography in abuse. When Dines mentioned *Hustler*'s "Chester the Molester," the therapist responded: "God, they come into my office and they call themselves 'Chesters.'"[37] Judith Reisman, in a study of *Playboy, Hustler*, and *Penthouse*, found many references to the sexual use of children for adult male's sexual pleasure. On average, she found that "nine sexually-oriented photographs and cartoons involved children per issue. These included photos of children and teens displayed in various stages of nudity, pictures of simulated sex between minors and adults, and cartoons which make light of child molestation and statutory rape."[38]

Legal pornography also often infantilizes young adult women models to sell sexualized gendered age hierarchies. For instance, paperback books exist with titles such as *A Virgin's Shame, Chained Youth, Girls in Bondage, Teen in Terror*. Magazines, like *19 and Bound, Young Love* ("261 Sexy Young Things"), and *Eager Naked Daughter*, contain statements on their covers claiming that all of their models are 18 and over. The writers and producers of this pornography create narratives as if they were the perspectives of the women models. They are constructed to be in control of the sexual activity being portrayed and the agents of their own desire. The pornographic stories have the characters saying that they want to be sexually used, tied up, bound, raped, tortured, and mutilated. The consumers believe the pornography. We have reports from children, and from adults who had pornography forced on them as children, that their fathers, brothers, uncles, religious leaders, and neighbors told them that the girls and boys, and the women in the pornography, liked it and wanted it, that they too would learn to accept and like what was being done to them.[39]

One method of infantilizing the women is through shaving the pubic area. It's a way of making the women seem younger, more virginal, more powerless and less human. Magazines specializing in shaving include *Shaved Sluts, Black Shaved Pussy, Teen Shave*, and *Shave Me and Fuck Me*. Often all the hair on a woman's body is shaved. Shaving dehumanizes women and it can diminish possibilities for human empathy and compassion. As U.S. militarism teaches us, dehumanization is key to convincing the murderers of the worthlessness and lack of humanity of the "enemy." It was a classic strategy used in Nazi concentration camps. Shaving makes women inhuman and indistinguishable. As Dines argues, "when you shave women's heads, they all look the same. We all become one. What pornography does is destroy the distinguishing features between women, because that basically could be any woman's body."[40]

The supposed sexual power of young girls is alluded to in the information given about adult models; for instance, in *Playboy*, alongside written descriptions of the women featured as the centerfolds are snapshots from their lives. The captions read, for instance, "Age one: Playboy material already;" or "Age two: Boy-chasing already." The description, photos, and captions function to convince the reader that this women's sexual desires have always already been oriented toward men's sexual pleasure. Mainstream pornography also features "intellectual" articles which support adult/child sexual relations. For example, *Penthouse*'s article, "Incest The Last Taboo," discusses the parts of the Kinsey report on sexuality that were suppressed which claimed that incest is "prevalent and often positive."[41]

It seems naïve and irresponsible to argue that there is no connection between this material, the prevalence of child sexual abuse and rape in this society, and the apathetic indifference and victim-blaming responses to survivor stories of sexual violence. The estimates are currently that one out of three girls and one out of five boys will be sexually abused before the age of eighteen. Despite the prevalence of child sexual abuse, there is a deadening apathy on the part of social institutions to stop its epidemic proportions. Pornography is a mass industry that creates and promotes sexual arousal/pleasure to the sexualization of young girls (and boys). It legitimates child sexual abuse by making it accessible and available to adults as sexual entertainment and fun. Moreover pornography puts the responsibility for the sexual activity on the young girls (and boys), not the adults, and may account for why police, judges, doctors, and juries continue to entertain ideas about young girls "sexual provocativeness" in response to claims of sexual abuse.

MAKING HISTORIES OF BIGOTRY, ENSLAVEMENT, AND GENOCIDE SEXY

Pornography makes histories of racism, colonialism, and Nazism sexy and entertaining, thereby legitimating, nourishing, and reinforcing ongoing stereotypes, bigotry, and imperial relations. The racism of pornography is not simply an issue of equal representation of different groups, nor simply an issue of the physical appearance of women in pornography. Again, as Gardner argues, it is "how pornography capitalizes on the underlying history and myths surrounding and oppressing people of color in this country which makes it racism. . . ." Historically in this country, white male slaveholders routinely raped Black women and castrated Black men, often with little to no opposition from their white wives. Pornography capitalizes on this history with publications like *White Masters: Black Slave Girls* and *A Cocksucking Slave*. Collins points out:

> Contemporary portrayals of Black women in pornography represent the continuation of the historical treatment of their actual bodies. African-American women are usually depicted in a situation of bondage and slavery, typically in a submissive posture, and often with two white men. As Bell observes, "this setting reminds us of all the trappings of slavery: chains, whips, neck braces, wrist clasps." The image of Black women in pornography is almost consistently one featuring them breaking from chains.[42]

The pornography industry capitalizes on the racist mythology of Black men's sexuality as well. For instance, pornographers create magazines and videos that present Black men ravishing and raping white women on southern slave plantations.[43] Some titles with this theme include *Nigger for Hire, Plantation Stud*, and *Slave Stud*.[44] This thematic pornography with its narrative story lines capitalizes on the ever-present societal myth that it is predominantly Black men who rape or want to rape white women. This myth creates a devastating reality for many Black men who are unfairly targeted by a racist criminal justice system which one-sidedly and systematically convicts Black men (and other men of color) for the rape of white women.[45] The pornography industry consistently produces cultural products that represent Black men as oversexed or bestial in their sexuality. This representation is directly connected to the history of white racist lynching in this country. Gardner quotes James Earl Jones, who makes explicit the interconnections between sexuality, racism, and sexism:

> By their lynching, the white man was showing that he hated the Black man carnally, biologically; he hated his color, his features, his genitals. Thus he attacked the Black man's body, and like a lover gone mad, maimed his flesh, violated him in the most intimate, pornographic fashion. When a white man makes such a personal involvement and takes the time to strip off or cut off penises and torture, beat and lynch a Black man it has got to be sexual, it's the result of repressed sex. It's finding a way out.[46]

Pornography that uses Black men often reproduces racist notions of Black male bodies. There are pornographic books completely focused on Black men's sexual organs, like *Long Black Super Cock*, but there are also a multitude of cartoons and caricatured images of Black men in many mainstream pornographic magazines which caricature and exaggerate Black men's bodies.

The sexualized racism of pornography sets up a sexual/racial hierarchy between men. In *Pornography*, Dworkin illustrates the sexual dynamics of racism, misogyny, and imperialist relations in her analysis of a pornographic scenario of a Mexican prison. The pornography describes the three participants as a Mexican man who is the jailor, a white U.S. American man in jail, and a Mexican woman who is described as an oversexed and insatiable women who is the white man's lover. The pornography says the Mexican woman is "the hot-blooded señorita," which Dworkin argues is "the ethnic slur cast so as to be both specific (she is Mexican) and evocative (she is the hot-blooded Latin or Hispanic woman . . .). She is the woman sexed by the climate." The pornographic narrative sexualizes Mexico in general and Mexican women in particular in such a way as to uphold the white racist and nationalist stereotype that the "Latin or Hispanic woman is the woman who cannot do without it."[47] In the fictional story, the Mexican woman will do anything, including having sex with the Mexican jailor, to be available to the Anglo man from the United States; Dworkin writes, "She is used by the Mexican policeman but she belongs to the Anglo boyfriend. She prostitutes herself for him, not because he wants it, but because she wants it."[48]

The significant sexual tension, Dworkin argues, is not between the man and woman, but between the two men. The Mexican woman is simply used in the drama between the two men who are differentiated according to an ideology of sexualized racism. Dworkin continues:

> The Mexican male is the figure of overt force and brute sexuality. Every aspect of his stance expresses the brutality of the fuck and a corresponding incapacity to feel. . . . The Anglo does more than fuck the woman; he touches her, approaches her nipple, puts his hand on her thigh, sleeps peacefully while she—never having enough—masturbates. . . . This, indeed, is basic to racist sexual ideology: the white male is the civilized male, the bearer of a civilized sexuality.[49]

The depiction of the Mexican man, Dworkin argues, is "precisely what licenses violence against him in a racist value system. His sexuality is a savage masculinity, while the phallus of the white carries civilization to the dark places."[50] Again pornography's ideology and portrayal of Latino men, as with Black men, fuels the racist social system which targets men of color as the rapists, thieves, and murderers against "good white men and their women." Pornography's sexualization of gender and racial inequality and bigotry makes the hierarchies seem normal and legitimate. Some exemplary titles of pornographic books that feed into racialized constructions of men of color considered threats to U.S. security include *Japanese Sadist Dungeon*, *Raped by Arab Terrorists*, and *Soviet Sadist's Slave*.[51]

Antisemitism is another common staple of pornography. The contemporary sexualization of antisemitism for entertainment and profit cannot be disassociated from the historical use of pornography before and during the Nazi war years. At that time, pornography fueled antisemitism, and contributed to the torture and killing of Jews. Nazi pornography portrayed Jewish men as rapists of Aryan women, and Jewish women as sexually insatiable and openly accessible for Aryan men to use and abuse. This propaganda continues with the proliferation of a genre of pornography that depicts and celebrates the Nazis' sexual torture of Jewish women on the grounds that the women reveled in this torture—such as book series with titles like *Concentration Camp Tortures* or *Dachau Desire*.[52] In the United States as in Nazi Germany, pornography capitalizes on the histories of racism, bigotry, torture, and murder by making them sexually arousing and entertaining, and justifies these atrocities by defining racial and ethnic men and women in terms of biological/racial determinism. Dworkin illuminates the racist sexual ideology of Nazi Germany which portrayed the

> Jewish male as a rapist, despoiler of Aryan women. He painted the Jewish female as a harlot, wild, promiscuous, the sensuous antithesis of the Aryan female, who was blonde and pure. Both male and female Jews were characterized as bestial in their sexuality. The wild animal is dangerous and must be caged. Hitler's first and most basic anti-Semitic appeal was not economic, that is, the Jews control the money; it was sexual—and it was the sexuality of the Jews, as portrayed by Hitler, that provoked the German response. . . . This is the paradigm of racist sexual ideology— every racially despised group is invested with a bestial sexual nature. So the force is marshaled and the terror is executed."[53]

Similarly, pornography helped to fuel the Vietnam war by presenting Asian women in racist and misogynistic ways. The U.S. military and international capitalism continue to participate in the buying and selling of Asian women in prostitution around military bases such as those in the Phillippines. Moreover, an international slave traffic in Asian women exists through industries of prostitution and in the mailorder bride business.[54] Racism, sexism, and imperialism combine in this part of the pornography industry to feed on the fears and bigotries of U.S.

Americans against Asian women and men. Some titles of pornographic books exemplary of these sociopolitical relations include *Oriental Fetishes*, *Geisha Girls*, *Asian Suck Mistress*, *Slant-Eyed Savages*, and *Slut from Shanghai* focused on Asian women, and *Oriental Cock*, *Japanese Sadist Dungeon*, and *Jap Sadist's Virgin Captives* focused on Asian men. This propaganda helps lay the foundation for continued bigotry, discrimination, and violence against Asian Americans and Asian countries.[55] This kind of propaganda is especially functional when, for instance, fears of Japanese power are exploited in U.S. media as a scapegoat for U.S. economic problems.

FACING THE REALITIES OF IMAGES

In opposition to the critical analysis offered above, feminist defenders of the pornography industry often define pornography as individual images, fantasies, and speech, separate from historical and material conditions and from institutional practices and actions of a mass industry. They suggest that we must distinguish between images and realities.[56] In contrast to the focus on social inequalities, they foreground individual consumer's interpretation and private use of pornography. Social issues of gender and racial inequality, they argue, must not be confused with the sexual dynamics of pornography linked to images and fantasies, not realities. As Deirdre English argues: "Images and fictional text are not the same thing as subordinating conduct. . . . Although ideas have impact, images of discrimination are not the discrimination."[57] She further explains:

> The fact remains that no matter how disturbing violent fantasies are, as long as they stay within the world of pornography, they are still only fantasies. The man masturbating in a theater showing a snuff film is still only watching a movie, not actually raping or murdering. . . . There is something wrong with attacking people, not because of their actions, but because of their fantasies—or their particular commercial style of having them."[58]

Pornography for feminists who defend the industry is a "mere" representation belonging to the minds of the individual producers or consumers. They speak about pornography as if it did not have to be produced and as if its effects only existed by choice and in the realm of individual privacy and sexual fantasy. They define the conflict over pornography, then, as one of individual interpretation, not social discrimination.

By conceptually framing the issue as one of interpretation, they appeal to a liberal tolerance that mandates that each individual has a right to his or her personal tastes and pleasures. This makes it possible to deny and ignore the breadth of the industry and thus how its products and services are integrally related to the many other arenas of social and political life. Some of the feminist defenders of pornography also minimize pornography's racism and antisemitism, including the eroticization of historic atrocities like U.S. slavery and the Nazi extermination of Jews under Hitler's regime. Some maintain that in a private sexual context, "separate from reality," Nazi symbolism is justifiable as sexual game playing. Pat Califia, for instance, in writing about lesbian sadomasochism, claims that playing out these social hierarchies in private is completely separate from their social realities. She argues that individuals can sexually explore the dynamics of power and hierarchy, often based in social bigotry, and get sexual pleasure, without it having anything to do with the perpetuation of the social bigotry.[59]

Of course such emotional distance from the racism and sexism may be less easy for those who are systematically hurt by the particular power dynamics in the social world of inequality. In an essay on incest and child sexual relations, Jean, a Black lesbian, writes: "The question of legitimate/illegitimate attractions across taboo lines—like race—is problematic for me. It's problematic for me to defend sexual fetishes, attractions, and interests which reflect political differences, imbalances, and hierarchies in other realms. White people can defend those choices more fully than I can, because I also have to concern myself with issues of race and class. I have to. I have no choice in the matter. My survival depends on it."[60] The sexualization of inequality for entertainment and profit also cannot be separated from social inequality because pornography's production depends on the exploitation of specific human beings, many of whom are used precisely because of these inequalities. But also the pornography would not have the same erotic impact without the existing social inequalities. As Jackie Goldsby points out,

> Though eroticizing difference is a nose-thumbing gesture of sorts against racial ideologies of power—when a white man specifies he wants to 'service' Black cock, he is, in that moment, relinquishing the privileged status the culture ascribes to him as 'top'—that reversal depends on accepting racial hierarchies as legitimate truth. Difference must be enforced, not transformed, and the privilege accorded it reinscribed if the sex is to keep its charge.[61]

The absolute distinctions between fantasy and reality made by defenders of pornography deny the historic and social realities of inequality. The intellectualizations hide the pervasiveness of sexual violence against women, which much pornography depends upon for its substance and market. It is clear from the analysis of pornography that the structure and dynamics of so-called "private" sexual relations are intricately connected to "public" social relations, i.e., "the personal is political." The two arenas are interrelated and mutually influencing (and in some contexts indistinguishable), such that attitudes, behaviors, and values are not distinct. As Audre Lorde writes:

> Sadomasochism is an institutionalized celebration of dominant/subordinate relationships. And, it prepares us either to accept subordination or to enforce dominance. *Even in play*, to affirm that the exertion of power over powerlessness is erotic, is empowering, is to set the emotional and social stage for the continuation of that relationship, politically, socially, and economically.[62]

Similarly Dworkin maintains that it is impossible to change racism and sexism if at the same time they are being mass produced for sexual pleasure and entertainment. She writes:

> It's one thing to try to eradicate a form of hatred if people are experiencing it as hatred. It's another thing when they have an orgasm because of the kind of hatred that they're feeling toward another person.[63]

Pornography's message that women *want* sexual abuse is connected to society's denial—both public and private—of the harm to women both in and out of the pornography industry. The police, the courts, and the public, when confronted with women who are seeking justice because of incestuous assault, rape, and battery by men in their lives, often believe that the women are responsible for what is done to them. At some level they believe that women want it, or ask for it, or deserve it, especially women who are involved in the industries of pornography and prostitution. The pornography industries facilitate, condone, and perpetuate these beliefs. They convince men (and women) to not believe women's stories of abuse.

Immense denial, disbelief, and victim-blaming are the major obstacles women face in seeking redress for abuse and violence. In addressing the invisibility of the harm to women in and out of pornography through sexual torture and violence, Dworkin writes:

> The central question is not: what is force and what is freedom? That is a good question, but in the realm of human cruelty—the realm of history— it is utterly abstract. The central question is: why is force never acknowledged as such when used against the racially or sexually despised?[64]

5

LESBIAN PORN STORIES:
Rebellion and/or Resistance?[1]

Ann Russo and Lourdes Torres

Throughout the 1980s and 1990s, many lesbians active in queer politics seemed to take up the banner of sexual liberation. Lesbians began to produce pornography by and for lesbians and lesbian bars began to feature erotic dancers and strip shows. Sex toy stores began to spring up in San Francisco, Boston, Chicago, and New York, and lesbian sex conferences as well as parties became common. Sexual desire and dynamics became more visible—lesbian sadomasochists began to claim a public voice and space, and butch-femme sexual roles enjoyed a public renaissance.

This burgeoning lesbian sex industry providing more forums for lesbian sexual expression is the backdrop for many lesbians when engaged in the feminist debates over the politics of the pornography industry. Feminists who focus on the inequalities and violence produced through pornography's production, consumption, and distribution are often in direct conflict with those who advocate women's rights to sexual expression and freedom, including the right to express sexualized power dynamics and to have access to pornographic products and services. Lesbian and gay pornography is a pivotal point of contention in feminist debates. Many feel torn between a feminist analysis of white male power and domination evidenced in the mass industry of pornography and an individual rights approach to sexual expression and practice through pornographic commodities. Many lesbians are hesitant to publicly criticize sexual practices in pornography because of the continuing struggle to legitimize the sexual lives of lesbians in the larger heterosexist and homophobic society. Many lesbian sex radicals and anticensorship feminists do not believe there is a connection between the industries of pornography and social systems of inequality and sexual violence. Many consume pornographic images and stories produced by the sex industries. They perceive sexual expression and practice to be individual choices and preferences, rather than social constructions tied to broader systems of unequal social power. Moreover, given the stigma attached to lesbian, gay, and bisexual sexual identities, some argue that the sexual expression of gay, lesbian, and bisexual communities must be protected from social critique so as not to contribute to persecution. Finally, some believe that the feminist analysis of pornography inhibits women's exploration of sexual practices and is therefore antithetical to liberation and freedom.[2]

Pat Califia's essay entitled "Among Us, Against Us: The New Puritans," was key in the early 1980s in framing the perspective of lesbian sex radicals. She begins the essay with her personal history of being titillated since she was a kid by sexy images and stories that had sadomasochistic dynamics. Califia claims that eroticism is individual, natural, and inevitable, and therefore must be defended from critical analysis. She writes: "The inner voice of eros is arbitrary, bizarre, impeccably honest, bountiful and so powerful as to be cruel. It takes courage to hear its demands and follow them."[3] She argues that pornography has been essential to the development of her sexual desire because in the broader society this desire is stigmatized and punished. Since sexual expression is a matter of individual desire, she perceives the feminist critique of the sexual dynamics constructed in pornography as an attack on individual women's sexual identities, desires, and practices, rather than a critique of a commercial industry. Sex radicals, like Califia, connect antipornography feminist politics to ongoing sexual repression and persecution of sexual minority communities. Thus, sex radicals often link feminist critical analyses of the pornography industry with intolerant, antisexual, and puritanical attitudes and public policies.

Feminists and lesbians who defend the pornography industry often make the slippery slope argument that the critical analysis of pornography feeds into repressive and punitive attacks on gay and lesbian sexual expression. They fear that any critical attention to sexually explicit material will be used selectively against gay and lesbian peoples. This argument has had a lot of potency among lesbians, bisexuals, and gay men in general because it has been true. The right wing continues to have a moralistic and repressive focus on gay and lesbian sexual identities and practices. This bigoted focus creates a dilemma for those of us who are both critical of the mass industry of pornography and its practices of inequality and who are also supportive of the sexual rights of lesbian, gay, and bisexual communities. The stigma, hatred, and violence directed against the sexual identities and practices of gay men and lesbians are realities that cannot be ignored. Right wing politicians, like Jesse Helms, do target gay, lesbian, and bisexual materials, often ignoring the mass industry of white male heterosexual pornography. The repercussions are significant. As Califia warns, "People would have even less access to information about sex and erotic material than they do now."[4] The heterosexism and homophobia of right wing antipornography campaigns, we believe, must be confronted and denounced, not ignored. In fact, feminists challenging pornography industries must critically denounce the homophobia and bigotry associated with right wing campaigns, as well as their sexism and misogyny.

The sex radicals, however, do not simply defend pornography; they promote lesbian pornography as a radical impulse against public authority and repression. Lesbian sex radicals argue that for too long women have been defined by our sexuality and that it is time that we define it for ourselves. Pornography, they argue, offers a space to explore sexuality as a source of women's power as opposed to our victimization. Lesbian sex magazines proliferate in the 80s and 90s—*On Our Backs* and *Bad Attitude* are the most prominent. Lesbian pornographers seek to create a lesbian dialect that is bold, hot, and speaks to lesbian sexual desires and needs. Lesbian pornography differs from representations of "girl-girl" sex so prevalent in heterosexual men's pornography in that it speaks to lesbians not to white heterosexual men.[5] The publishers of *On Our Backs* claim that lesbians portraying their own sexuality for lesbians is a radical act. Lisa Henderson, for instance, argues that lesbian pornographic images not only "transgress anti-porn feminist orthodoxy and the heterosexual mainstream, they also expose, demystify and affirm precisely that part of lesbianism that is so threatening: we take our place among women through sexual and political desire, and in the process declare some resistance to heterosexist and patriarchal cultural scripts."[6] Lesbian pornography presents women as powerful, desiring subjects, according to Susie Bright, co-founder and one-time editor of *On Our Backs*. She declares that pornography has to be seized by those who are disenfranchised by it.

The women who produce lesbian pornography claim that it is radical and transformative because lesbians are visible as active sexual subjects. Jill Dolan, a theater theorist, argues that because lesbian sex is totally excluded from traditional contexts, the most transgressive act imaginable at this point is to represent lesbian sex, especially its excesses. She states, "The explicitness of pornography is a constructive choice for practicing cultural disruptions."[7] By making sex acts explicit, lesbian pornography disrupts the dominant discourse around sexuality and gender, and makes visible the sexually invisible lesbian. This moves the specifically *sexual* aspects of lesbian identities, including public expression of lesbian sexual desires and practices, to the forefront of public consciousness. This is more radical than merely presenting a neutral discourse of lesbianism as a sexual preference for a partner of the same sex.

Lesbian producers and consumers of pornography often argue that they are engaging in transgressive sexual practices given that they are lesbians, and not heterosexual men. In contrast, feminists critical of the pornography industry do not presume that women (heterosexual, lesbian, bisexual) will necessarily produce pornography that is transgressive in its construction of sexual desire and dynamics.

Rather, many of us argue that for pornography to be truly transgressive it must challenge existing power structures and dynamics of inequality and must significantly disrupt the sexist, heterosexist, and racist sexual representations of the broader mass culture. Representing women engaged in "taboo" and "deviant" sexual practices and playing out roles that were previously unavailable to women in heterosexual pornography may be transgressive, and yet not socially transformative. Lesbian pornography may simply reinforce dominant discourses of sexualized power and inequality, rather than deconstructing them. The question for feminists critical of pornography is whether lesbians producing lesbian pornography transform normative constructions of sexuality, rather than merely adopting the white male gaze for lesbian consumers.

Sex radicals justify the sexualization of power relations in lesbian pornography on the grounds that it produces sexual pleasure for women, as it does men, and thus must be protected as an individual right. Yet, the uncritical celebration of all lesbian, gay, and bisexual sexual expression simply on the grounds that it produces sexual pleasure seems problematic from a social justice perspective. As Jenny Kitzinger and Celia Kitzinger suggest, "Sexual excitement cannot be taken as inherently radical nor can our 'pleasure' be assumed to be an unproblematic criterion by which to assess images of lesbian sex. Lesbian pleasure is not constructed in a heteropatriarchy-free zone. . . . Taking pleasure in sex scenes which enact power struggles or which play with the symbols of fascism may reflect the measure of our complicity in our own and other people's oppression."[8] In a movement toward social justice, it seems problematic simply to exempt the cultural products and practices of lesbians, gay men, and bisexuals from social responsibility, especially when it comes to misogyny, racism, classism, and xenophobia, as well as sexual abuse and violence. Open discussion of lesbian and gay sexual representations and practices in terms of respect, equality, and consent can only contribute to the creation of a strong and more just community.

Lesbian, gay, and bisexual scholars, educators, and activists must critically consider the social and sexual implications of the growing international sex industry in gay, lesbian, and bisexual communities. If sexual desire is being constructed through dynamics of misogyny, racism, classism, and/or xenophobia and mass produced and sold, we must explore the social implications. A critical discussion of the sexual commodities and services being produced and sold by a growing queer pornography industry may feel difficult because of the realities of homophobia and the desire for sexual rights and freedom. The social climate has made many queer-identified women and men defensive of any critical discussion of these issues. While this defensiveness is understandable, activists must not retreat from the discussion. As educators and activists, we don't believe we should simply accept, minimize, and deny the production of inequalities in the queer sex industry just because they are connected to marginalized and demonized sexual identities. The analytic and strategic approach, however, must simultaneously address the forces of homophobia, sexual persecution, in addition to gender, race, and class inequalities, rather than ignore them.

The controversies surrounding the art of Robert Mapplethorpe exemplify the complexities of these debates. Many activists will point to the efforts to prohibit the exhibitions of Mapplethorpe's work as a prime example of state repression against lesbian and gay sexual expression. It is one of the cases used to warn feminists of the dangers of criticizing any sexual materials. The mainstream gay response to the attack on Mapplethorpe has been to defend him from critical analysis. While censoring efforts and the homophobia underlying them must be resisted, this must not also mean that the artistic sexual representations cannot be critically analyzed from a social justice perspective. For instance, some queer activists have interrogated Mapplethorpe's representations of Black men as they fit into a tradition of white racism that continues to produce racial inequalities in queer-based social groups and organizations. Essex Hemphill explores the racial implications of Mapplethorpe's art and its relationship to the failures of the white gay male community to engage equally and respectfully with Black gay men, personally, socially, and politically. He writes:

The white gay community of the 1980s was not seriously concerned with the plight of black men except as sexual objects. The black male was given very little representation except most often as a big, black dick. This aspect of white gay consciousness is best revealed by the photographs of the late Robert Mapplethorpe on the subject of black males. Though his images may be technically and aesthetically well-composed, what occurs in his work often enough to be of concern is his ability *artistically* to perpetuate racial stereotypes constructed around sexuality. In some of his images we are only shown parts of the anatomy—genitals, chests, buttocks—close-up and close-cropped to elicit desire. Mapplethorpe's eye pays special attention to the penis—at the expense of showing us the subject's face, and thus, a whole person. The penis becomes *the* identity of the black male which is the classic stereotype recreated and presented as *art*, as a *gay* vision. Mapplethorpe's "Man in a Polyester Suit," for example, presents a black man without a head, wearing a business suit, his trousers unzipped, and his fat, long penis dangling down, a penis that is not erect. It can be assumed that many viewers appreciative of Mapplethorpe's work, and those constructing sexual fantasies from it, probably wondered *first* how much larger would the penis become during erection, as opposed to wondering *who* is the man in the photo? Or *why* is his head missing? What is insulting and endangering to black men on one level is Mapplethorpe's *conscious* determination that the faces, heads, and by extension, the minds and experiences of some of his black subjects were not as important as close-up shots of their penises. It is virtually impossible to view Mapplethorpe's photos of black males and avoid confronting issues of exploitation and objectification.[9]

Most discussions of Mapplethorpe in white dominant lesbigay communities seemed to exclusively focus on the homophobia of the censorship efforts and their ties to the broader right wing antisex campaigns. The defense orchestrated for Mapplethorpe and other gay and lesbian artists contributes to a context where critical analysis is often squelched in the service of protecting lesbigay sexual representations from right wing attacks. While homophobia was and is at play in these censorship efforts, it is not the only issue at stake when considering the social implications of Mapplethorpe's sexual representations. As Jackie Goldsby points out, "For all the theorizing about censorship, the meaning of Mapplethorpe's racial aesthetic remained unarticulated in the analysis and protest."[10] The inattention to the reproduction of racialized sexual representations only furthers the racial divides within lesbigay communities.

Questions of unequal power, exploitation, and objectification are significant in movements for social justice, and must not be dismissed on the grounds that they might further societal homophobia. Critical discussion of gay and lesbian sexual representations and their connection to inequalities of race, class, and age within our communities creates the possibilities for equality and mutual respect between us. The purpose of such questions is not to deem sexual materials "good" or "bad," nor to argue for or against censorship. The purpose is to create a critical discussion about social relations within our communities in the efforts to create a socially just society. It is with such a conversation in mind that we offer the following analysis of lesbian sex stories from *On Our Backs* of the early 1990s. Our purpose is to contribute to critical discussions of lesbian-created sexual imagery in a social context of interlocking oppressions; our purpose is not to simply condemn or celebrate lesbian pornography. Our hope is to raise critical questions for lesbian and bisexual women's communities for discussion and dialogue, not to provide absolute answers.

ON OUR BACKS AND THE POLITICS OF LESBIAN PORNOGRAPHY

In the context of the feminist debates over lesbian pornography in the early 1990s, we did an analysis of the fictional stories in *On Our Backs*. We chose *On Our Backs*, a lesbian sex magazine produced in San Francisco, because it is a central contender in the debates over lesbian pornography. Published since 1984, at the height of the feminist sexuality debates, *On Our Backs* advertises itself as "entertainment for the adventurous lesbian" and contrasts itself with the radical feminist newspaper, *off our backs*. Its content described by Lisa Henderson includes mostly "women-only fiction, poetry, drawings, and photographs. It also features sexual advice columns, editorials on lesbian sexual culture and sexual politics, book, film and video reviews, display advertising for sexual and non-sexual services and supplies, letters to the editor, reports from lesbian events, occasional readership surveys, safer sex guidelines, and classified personal ads and announcements, among other attractions."[11] Henderson argues that representations of lesbian sex in magazines like *On Our Backs* are "a potentially transgressive and transformative site. What is socially marginal becomes symbolically central through a politicized appropriation of sexual taboo, a threat (in the service of lesbian desire) to the sexual codes of both straight society and anti-porn feminist orthodoxy."[12] For many, *On Our Backs* is a symbol of sexually transgressive lesbian politics and represents a progressive move toward sexual liberation.

In the following analysis, we ask whether or not the lesbian-produced pornography in *On Our Backs* constructs sexual desires, dynamics, and practices that challenge and/or transgress power dynamics structured along the lines of social inequalities. The analysis is based on a reading of the fictional stories published in sixteen issues in 1991 and 1992. We analyzed the stories in terms of their narrative story lines, constructed sexual dynamics, use of narrative voice, and descriptive language. In this analysis, we consider four key components of mass-marketed pornography involved in the subordination of women as outlined by Andrea Dworkin—hierarchy, objectification, submission, and violence.[13] While Dworkin mostly focuses on the sexualization of gender inequality, we use these components to define multiple forms of social inequality. We found that the stories in *On Our Backs*[14] offer a variety of discourse strategies ranging from objectified language to poetry and metaphor. The sexual dynamics in the stories are constructed mostly along the lines of power difference and hierarchy (e.g., age, social status, occupation). Most of the stories concern concrete, one-time sexual encounters between women, although one story features sex between a woman and two dolphins, and another portrays sex between two women and a statue that comes to life. Like the pornography produced for men from which lesbian pornography borrows heavily, the lesbian stories emphasize several motifs. Fifty percent of the stories deal with anonymous sex, that is, sex between strangers or persons who meet shortly before the sexual encounter. Sixty-eight percent of the stories represent sexual relations in public places, such as at the opera, a bar, a hallway, an office, a cemetery, or the woods. Fifty percent of the stories construct sexual dynamics characterized by dominance and submission and involve varying levels of violence, bondage, and humiliation.

LESBIAN STYLE OBJECTIFICATION

In about half of the stories, the authors use a range of objectifying language to de-scribe sexual desire, dynamics, and relations between the women. The story in our sample that used the harshest and most explicit form of sexual objectification was "Cum E–Z." The story is about a lesbian who purchases the sexual services of a woman working in prostitution. Presented as a first-person narrative, the story be-gins as follows, "You see that thing over there. You see that thing over there? She's $20.00. You got twenty dollars? Then you can fuck her."[15] As the protagonist searches for a woman who works in prostitution, the narrative voice explains, "Hunting for a female who meant nothing to her. A thing. Meat. A slut. A piece."[16] During the sexual transaction, the narrative voice again comments, "The idea that they didn't like being with a woman made it even better in a perverted kind of way, gave her a sense of power, increased her dominance."[17] Finally, at the end of the encounter, the narrator remarks, "A scene of degradation. Pain of the soul. But of freedom also. It's all about freedom and power and control."[18]

In this piece, the author eroticizes what we interpret as the annihilation of the humanity of the woman who works in prostitution for the purpose of the lesbian customer's sexual pleasure and power. The story strips the humanity of the woman in prostitution to her supposed essence—sex. She is referred to as an object, a thing, a piece of meat throughout the story. The dehumanized objectification of the woman as well as the sex is mirrored in the terse language of the story that is extremely simple and bare. The syntax is stripped to its core; throughout, most sentences consist only of a subject and verb, and often not even that. This story ex-ists against a backdrop of women who are prostituted, who are subject to rape, as-sault, and murder on a daily basis. We question the dehumanization of women in prostitution for the purposes of sexual entertainment. We ask: Whose pleasure? At whose expense?

Stories are also present in *On Our Backs* that rely less on objectification for desire and pleasure. These stories celebrate women and sex in a language that is poetic and more complexly nuanced. For example, in a short piece entitled "Lila," the narrator describes sexual encounters with another woman in ways that demon-strate human connection and intimacy. She states, "When I was the right temper-ature, when I could be wrapped in glory, when I could be trusted, and praising, and praised, she would start to sing. Her mouth would arrive between my legs, her tongue a palm leaf, burning, fanning, her teeth sticking my clit, two fingers in-side me moving like a small question."[19] This is the only story in our sample that developed intimate relations completely without objectification and that did not use social distance between the characters to construct the sexual dynamics.

LESBIAN SADOMASOCHISM—HIERARCHY AND RELATIONS
OF DOMINANCE/SUBMISSION

The lesbian sadomasochist community and their allies continue to be significant voices in setting the terms and questions of the feminist sexuality debates. Their identities and interests are central to the arguments in defense of the pornography industry and the rights of "sexual minorities." As an individual sexual identity and practice, sexual liberals and radicals both defend sadomasochism. As in other parts of the debate, sexual practices are individual and private choices and thus worthy of protection from social analysis.

Lesbians who defend sexual sadomasochism argue that antipornography feminists avoid and/or condemn sadomasochism out of fear, rather than knowledge. In the introduction to Samois's edited collection *Coming to Power* (1981), Katherine Davis writes, *"What we fear we try to keep contained."* By repressing, condemning, and/or ostracizing lesbians who identify with sexual sadomasochism, she argues, antipornography feminists deny the complex truths about women's sexual desires and pleasures. She writes:

> We must reexamine our politics of sex and power. The challenge of talking personally and explicitly about the ways we are sexual, and about how our sexuality differs, is not so much destructive as it is corrective, and necessary. The logical place to begin is to talk about our sexuality *as it is.* . . . We will find many differences among and between us, but it is better to do this work than to continually hide from our fears and insecurities. We must put the rhetorical weaponry aside and willingly engage each other, without simply jumping ahead into a new sexual conformity.[20]

Davis describes the book *Coming to Power,* for instance, as a "statement, a confrontation, and a challenge. It calls for a re-evaluation of existing lesbian-feminist ethics, saying, "You must own your 'illegitimate' children."[21] Lesbian advocates of sexual sadomasochism make analogies between the resistance and fear of sadomasochism and the homophobia of the late '60s and early '70s in the women's movement. They define sexual sadomasochism as a sexual identity, like queer identity, that has been unfairly stigmatized. Just as queer identities are defined as radical alternatives to compulsory heterosexuality, they label sexual sadomasochism as a deviantly radical sexual identity and practice. According to sex radicals, sadomasochism challenges a sexual orthodoxy that only sanctions "vanilla" heterosexual sex based in intimate relational dynamics that are free of power and control.

Feminists critical of sexual sadomasochism disagree. Linden, for instance, argues that s/m is "firmly rooted in patriarchal sexual ideology, with its emphasis on the fragmentation of desire from the rest of our lives and the single-minded pursuit of gratification, sexual and otherwise. . . . Sadomasochism is as much an irreducible condition of society as it is an individual 'sexual preference' or lifestyle: indeed, sadomasochism reflects the power asymmetries embedded in most of our social relationships.[22] Pornography produced by the mainstream white male-dominant heterosexual industry is grounded in sadomasochistic dynamics built on social inequalities. Sexual sadomasochism, from this perspective, explicitly eroticizes bipolar oppositions that resemble social power differences. In terms of gender dynamics, pornography's normal heterosexuality is sadomasochistic with men's sexual aggression constructed in relation to women's sexual submission. As Dworkin writes, "So-called normal sex occurs when the normal sexual aggressiveness of the male meets the normal masochism of the female *not* in an alley."[23]

As we noted earlier, many of the stories in *On Our Backs* reflect the sexual dynamics of sadomasochism. We determined this by assuming the definition of sadomasochism (s/m) offered by the lesbians who are its advocates and practitioners.[24] Pat Califia defines sadomasochism as "an erotic ritual that involves acting out fantasies in which one partner is sexually dominant and the other partner is sexually submissive. This ritual is preceded by a negotiation process that enables participants to select their roles, state their limits, and specify some of the activities which will take place."[25] The basic dynamic is an "eroticized, consensual exchange of power—not violence." The main components, according to Califia, are communication, roles, bondage, physical pleasure or pain, and humiliation. Given the context of "consensual" sexual relations, the dynamics of power, dominance, and humiliation are individual, private forms of sexual pleasure, and not abusive nor violent. In our analysis of the stories in *On Our Backs*, we found that one-half of the stories contain sadomasochistic sexual practices and dynamics as defined by Califia. Three of the sixteen are markedly sadomasochistic; the others use some bondage or dominant/submissive roles but are not constructed around fully developed s/m scenarios. In each of the stories, authors give the participants prescribed sexual roles of "top" and "bottom." They construct the roles along the lines of dominance and submission, and the sexual dynamics associate pain with pleasure.

According to Califia, the sexual roles in sadomasochist practices fulfill different desires for each of the participants. She suggests that the "bottom's pleasure comes from being dominated, from experiencing intense physical sensations and forbidden emotions, and from having her sacrifices witnessed by the top. The top's reward is the affirmation of her power and the sexual service she receives from the bottom. She participates vicariously in the delight and distress of her submissive."[26] In the sadomasochistic stories, the perspective that the reader is most often privy to is that of the bottom. According to the stories in *On Our Backs*, the character occupying the role of bottom openly desires this position and its accompanying scenario. She is free to stop the role-playing at any point during the sexual scene. The construction of the narratives from the bottom's perspective allows readers/consumers to set aside concerns about abusiveness and inequality, in order to gain sexual pleasure from the stories.

The scenarios themselves are built from existing inequalities, hierarchies, and sexual "taboos." For instance, one story, "Daddy's Little Girl," is of a sexual scenario of father-daughter incestuous sex. The characters in the story include an authoritarian, strict, incestuous "daddy" and a "little-girl" who wants to be humiliated, punished, and fucked. The "little girl" is played by an adult woman who travels 150 miles to act out this incest scenario with another woman. The woman visited will play "Daddy" to her "little girl." In the narrative, the woman who plays the "little girl" consents to the scenario and proceeds to construct it—"I wrote line after line for her, 100 lines, 200 lines. I beat myself for her, for me, for our father, just another variation on our theme. But it was never enough. I never felt cleansed, or redeemed, or free. Finally she ordered me to come to her."[27] The story is written from the perspective of the woman who plays the "little girl"—the story claims to be about her desire, her need. This narrative strategy, which is typical of heterosexual pornography, neutralizes the interpretation of particular sexual practices by locating the origin of the sexual practices in the desire and consent of the less powerful bottom, in this case, the adult who takes the role of the "little girl." The consumer reader is told that the scenario is constructed for the benefit and liberation of the bottom; it is about her "salvation." According to the story, the sexual encounter will help the bottom rid herself of guilt through sexual punishment. At one point, the narrator/bottom explains, "On the phone it was like a confession to a priest, kneeling in the dark booth recounting my sins. I requested my own punishment in my search for forgiveness."[28] The author constructs the story around an individual woman's desire and the fulfillment of that desire, rather than the power of the top or the power of the "father" (role of the "father" or the "real" father who seems to be in the background). By constructing the story in this way, the reader can engage in a desire seemingly constructed through fantasies of sexual abuse without having to consider seriously the personal and social implications of incestuous abuse.

Similarly, in another story, "Arizona's Most Wanted," which draws upon the roles of a police officer (top) and criminal (bottom), the story is told from the perspective of the so-called criminal. She is handcuffed, thrown in back of a police car, and taken to the police station by her ex-lover where she is strip-searched and fucked. The bottom pleads: "'Please, officer,' I whimpered, 'sexually assault me.'"[29] Again, the story is about the sexual desire of the powerless and her need to be sexually fulfilled through abusive power. Consideration of the sexual power and desire of the top—the police officer—is deflected onto the consent of the bottom.

The sexual arousal and erotic power produced from these stories come from profoundly unequal social realities—incestuous assault and police brutality. While the authors construct the stories as if they naturally serve the bottom's sexual desire and pleasure, in real life, the people who are in the roles of the bottom are powerless (children, prisoners) and are often sexually and physically exploited, beaten, and sometimes murdered. In real life, the public often blames the ones victimized and minimizes our experiences. In this social context, when people are trying to work against these abuses of power, against incredible odds, the use of such inequalities for sexual pleasure seems to reinforce rather than challenge endemic social inequality, abuse, and violence. When confronted with these realities, however, pornographers and their defenders argue that the realities are completely separate from the erotic stories. They claim that the images and stories are separate from the social context and that they are consumed by individuals in the privacy of their own sexual fantasies and practices. And yet, without the existence of these social realities, such eroticism would most likely not exist. The producers of pornography eroticize the brutality that some people experience for the sexual entertainment of others. Sometimes the groups are not different. Some argue that sadomasochistic pornography and the sexual practices on which it is based may benefit individual sexual abuse survivors who, in the context of sexual fantasy, may gain symbolic control over what happened to them as children. Some believe that s/m pornography and consensual sexual practice offer women a safe place to work out personal histories of sexual abuse. It is not our place to deny individual women the sexual paths we decide to explore and take, nor to condemn sexual desires and fantasies. Instead, our argument concerns a cultural industry—lesbian pornography—that profits from the existence of sexual abuse by eroticizing it and reproducing it. The industry does not seem to be engaged in critical analysis of the ways that these stories may simply reproduce dynamics of sexual abuse and assault. We believe the stories merit a discussion of their social implications in terms of lesbian sexual cultures and communities in broader social and political contexts.

Sex radicals distinguish sadomasochism from violence on the grounds of individual consent. According to lesbian sexual sadomasochists, each participating partner consents to the predetermined sexual practices and the sexual scenarios. Each has the capacity to stop the sexual action at any moment and thus each has the power to control the direction of the scene. The s/m stories in *On Our Backs* often illustrate the negotiation of individual consent. One sign of a bottom's consent to be dominated is described as fearful sexual excitement. For instance, in "The Strength of Trees," the bottom's fear and mixed feelings in relation to the sexual acts become part of the sexual turn-on—she longs for the strength to refuse participation. She begins to cry when she receives the orders for the scene from her ex-lover, an internationally known dominant, but her fear and confusion, according to the narrator, simply increase her sexual excitement and inability to call off the scene. In many ways, this seems like the typical "no-really-means-yes" scenario which is a common staple in heterosexual men's pornography. What is different is that the negotiation of consent is actually addressed in the story: "Lena knew that with a single word she could bring the proceedings to a close. . . . Despite her confused emotions, she sighed and said 'Yes.'"[30]

Similarly "The Shower" explicitly addresses how the acting out of dominant and submissive roles is negotiated between the sexual partners and the roles are unstable rather than fixed. In the middle of a sex scene in the story, the two women characters start to giggle. The narrative presents their efforts to keep their roles intact and clear as comical and fun. At the same time, the narrator makes clear that ultimately the role of the top is to figure out how to sustain an air of control and power. She does this through language and physical grip, "letting [the bottom] know I could hurt her if her submission was not to my liking."[31] Only one of the stories, "The Mistress of Iron," involves an exchange or alternation of power positions between the participants.[32]

A central component of the sexual turn-on in sexual sadomasochism is the connection between pain and pleasure. According to Califia (1980), there is no objective definition of pain because it is a subjective sensation that is interpreted within a particular context. While anything can stimulate feelings of pleasure or pain and while the sensations of pleasure may be the same, the interpretation of the sensation as pain or pleasure is dependent on the context. Califia argues that sexual arousal alters a person's ability to perceive pain as pain. As an individual approaches orgasm, she is less sensitive to pain, and for some people, discomfort, stress, or actual pain may contribute to sexual pleasure.

The stories with sadomasochistic themes connect the sensations of pain with sexual pleasure. In the story that builds upon father-daughter incest, the "daddy" hits the "little girl" hard with a riding crop and slaps her repeatedly. According to the story, the level of pain determines the extent of the bottom's pleasure. Upon being slapped hard, the bottom says, "And I start to cry, not because it hurts, but because being slapped gets to me more than anything else. It's so intimate; it's my face. I'm scared and caught up in the fantasy and she's still fucking me hard, wild, and I want to touch her . . . She leaps off me, flips me over and starts hitting me with her belt, hard. . . . I try to get away, but I can't. She holds me down with one hand and flogs me with the belt. . . ."[33] In "The Strength of Trees," the author constructs fear and pain as integral to the sexual pleasure of the bottom. The top repeatedly slaps the bottom's breast, so hard that the breast is described as "speckled dark red" and this is what gives the bottom the most pleasure.[34]

Bondage is integral to the practice of sexual sadomasochism. In the *On Our Backs* short stories, the use of bondage ranges from a woman being blindfolded, tied to a tree, and brutalized,[35] to a woman using rosary beads to "whip" her girlfriend in a Catholic church in Italy as an experience of exorcism from the Church.[36] The former seems to be constructed as a more serious practice of sexual sadomasochism, whereas the latter is a seemingly playful rebellion against the dictates of the Church and its repressive attitudes toward women's sexuality.

Humiliation is another staple. According to Califia, humiliation involves "the deliberate lowering of the bottom's status," treating her as if she were "an object, an animal, a slave, or the top's inferior."[37] The purpose of humiliation is sexual excitement, not permanent injury. As Califia explains, "Humiliation is the emotional or psychological counterpart of physical discomfort or pain. . . . The bottom who derives pleasure from being shamed or abused is triumphing over that degradation" (that is, over feelings in real life of worthlessness). In a few of the stories, humiliation certainly is a component of the sexual turn-on. In the incest story, the "daddy" makes the girl tell "his" friends who are watching them about how he anally fucks her and prods her with fingers, sticks, and dildos. Humiliation, in this story, is also about the top's pleasure, the power and pleasure of being like a man. Again it seems relevant to critically look at the ways that the stories capitalize on the feelings of humiliation and worthlessness, common for sexual-abuse survivors, in order to create sexual pleasure for a market of consumers. The dynamics central to sexual abuse are also central to the sexual turn-on, and thus not fully separate from the realities of abuse and its effects. Again, some argue that the sexual playing out of humiliation can be a valuable facilitator for survivors to work through the damage of sexual abuse. This may be true, however, it seems more complicated on a social level in the context of an industry profiting from the existence of endemic abuse that often combines physical, psychological, and sexual strategies to establish control and power.

The line between the use and abuse of humiliation is not clear in the stories, nor is the demarcation of control necessarily stable. Humiliation is integral to battering and sexual abuse. What are the social implications of a lesbian-created pornography using abusive language and interaction for sexual entertainment? Do the images and stories contribute to the apathy of lesbian communities in relation to domestic abuse and battery within lesbian relationships?[38] These questions are not meant to be rhetorical with obvious and simplistic answers. The questions are asked in a context of cultural confusions around sexual desire and power in intimate relationships. These confusions are readily apparent at many lesbian cultural and social events. Recently, we attended a set of lesbian performances. One of the performances addressed lesbian domestic violence, and yet most lesbians in the audience laughed at the unequal power dynamics and the abusive acts of one of the characters. This laughter may indicate a variety of responses on the part of individual audience members, including discomfort; yet it seemed clear that there was little consensus on what constitutes abusiveness in lesbian sexual dynamics. Open discussion of these issues might help clarify some of these confusions without simply polarizing our positions.

The question remains whether the pleasure of sexual sadomasochism is ultimately linked to liberatory and radical politics. While the stories may feel personally liberating and they may provide sexual pleasure to individual writers and readers, the stories do not exist in isolation from the broader culture and society. The social question must be asked in addition to the individual one. Do the stories and their construction of sexual relations contribute to the cultural confusion in this society between sex and violence? This is a confusion that often leads judges and juries to acquit rapists, it allows many people to deny the severity of sexual or physical assault, and it makes it difficult for women to label and understand their own experiences of sexual abuse. For example, this confusion is evident in the court decisions of two publicized assault cases. In both, the juries seemed to have difficulty recognizing physical assault or rape as "nonconsensual." In one case, the videotape of Rodney King being beaten by police officers was played over and over again to the jury; the defense sought to demonstrate his resistance to arrest and therefore his need to be controlled and beaten. The first jury acquitted the police officers. In the other case, a man had videotaped the rape of his wife in North Carolina. She reported the rape to the police and the case went to court. During the trial, the videotape was allowed to serve as evidence of his story of a consensual sadomasochistic relationship, to discredit her story of rape and battery. He was acquitted. The lines between sex, violence, consent, pleasure, and force in this society are blurred; the confusion is fueled by pornographic and media industries that connect sexual pleasure with force and violence. The question to be posed is how lesbian pornography contributes to and/or challenges these confusions. While the purpose of lesbian pornography is to produce sexual pleasure, like other culture industries, it must also be open to social critique and discussion.

LESBIAN LANGUAGE OF DESIRE

We analyzed the language used in the stories' dialogues in order to explore the relationship dynamics that were being constructed and eroticized. Sexual dynamics were most often constructed along the lines of power—dominance and submission. While a broad range of conversational interaction is reflected in the stories, we found that the dialogic language used immediately before and during the sex acts in most stories became increasingly harsh and hostile: "Lick me til I come, you fuck"[39]; "Piss on me goddamn it Sabrina!"[40]; "I begin frantically whispering in her ear, telling her what a sweet whore she was . . . Now suck my cock and make sure you suck it good, bitch"[41]; "Let me fuck you baby, in the fucking street, I'm fucking you"[42]; "Now shut up and drown in my wetness."[43] After the sexual encounter the story is usually brought to a rapid conclusion. In the descriptions of sexual encounters, the stories often associate sex with force. For example—"I tormented her rigid sudsy nipples until I felt faint with arousal, caught somewhere between tenderness and fury. . . . As soon as we got inside I grabbed her, calling her a bitch. . . . I mauled her tits with my hands and mouth"[44]; "I held her in my arms and slammed it in and out just the way she's asked for it"[45]; "I was painfully aware that some part of me wanted to root around inside her like a troglodyte, to plunder her delicacy with a hard barbaric thrust. . . . I began my excruciatingly slow assault."[46] In the stories, lesbian desire is consistently represented as functioning within an unequal power dynamic connected to hierarchical social relations.

In analyzing the language in the stories, we found a broad range of terms were used to refer to women. While humorous terms (e.g., stringbean, wimp, sisters in iron, no nonsense girl, gentlewoman) and terms emanating from lesbian culture (e.g., bulldagger, amazon woman, goddess, fierce woman) appear, many terms which refer to women reflect the framework of dominance and submission promoted in the stories. There are a plethora of sexualizing and objectifying terms (e.g., hooker, high-class twat, bitch, whore, merchandise, piece, slut, cocksucker), as well as infantilizing terms (e.g., bad/good little girl, daddy's girl) which figure in the narratives of sexualized power relations.

The vagina is referred to in the stories by a variety of names: *gash, pussy, wet prison*. By far the most common term is *cunt*. These terms are also staples of male-oriented pornography from which lesbian pornography borrows heavily. The clitoris is also often referred to in a way that creates an analogy, explicitly or implicitly, with the penis: "My clit was so stiff I was afraid everyone could see it poking through my tights"[47]; "she gave my clit an instant hard-on."[48] Rather than creating newly formed sexual dynamics, the languages and imagery in lesbian pornography seem highly derivative.

LESBIAN REBELLION ISN'T REVOLUTIONARY

We found that the lesbian pornography of *On Our Backs* short stories may be rebellious but not revolutionary. Because lesbians (and women in general) have not had the opportunities to explore, discuss, or celebrate sexual identities, sexual desires, and sexual practices, lesbian pornography seems to be rebellious. It is openly sexual, it attempts to use the sexual language that has been used against women and lesbians, and in some respects, it seems to try to challenge the ideology of women solely as victims, sexually passive, and repressed. It also provides a forum for information and resources about sexual identities, desires, and practices. On the other hand, it is derivative and not transformative. It does not seem to push the boundaries of mainstream pornographic constructions of sexual desire and practice. The language of sexual desire, the central dynamics of dominance and submission, and the one-way forms of objectification are not explored, challenged, or revisioned. Terms like *slut*, *whore*, and *bitch* remain negative and often disempowering terms in the stories—they are not redefined or reclaimed to challenge sexism. The sexual practices grounded in dominance and submission are simply used by women in relationship with other women. While the stories may challenge the sexual emptiness of much lesbian-feminist culture, they lack imagination in terms of a broader vision of sexual and social transformation. Also, while consumers of lesbian pornography may describe it as a form of resistance to men's control over women's sexuality, the fact that it is rebellious does not make it revolutionary.[49]

As lesbian sex industries grow, it seems an opportune time to be reflective of what they are in fact accomplishing. If lesbian-created culture industries uncritically accept the incorporation of social inequalities, exploitation, and sexual abuse into its fantasy commodities, what impact will this have on lesbian perspectives on social justice and transformation? It seems imperative to explore the social ramifications of using such exploitative real world relations as grounds for creating sexual entertainment and profit. At the very least, the assumption that this is a liberating cultural and sexual commodity that will guide us toward freedom might be further explored, rather than simply defended or condemned outright. From a feminist social justice perspective, it behooves us to ask always—Whose liberation? At whose expense? Whose freedom? On the backs of whose lives?

Perhaps Kitzinger and Kitzinger are correct to suggest that producing lesbian erotic material that is substantially different in form and substance is difficult in the current context. They suggest that "changing the political and social conditions within which images of lesbian sex are produced is an essential prerequisite to the creation of more liberatory images. Then, and perhaps only then, can we create and view representations of lesbian passion and desire, which are affirmative, challenging, and truly transgressive."[50]

6

SEXUAL CONFLICTS AND CONTRADICTIONS:
Violence, Desire, Autonomy, Freedom[1]

The sex debates among feminists continue to be volatile. Since the early 1980s, they have created a polarized separation between feminists committed to stopping violence against women and those challenging sexual repression and restrictions. The result is truncated analyses that emphasize one set of issues to the exclusion of the other set. This polarization often reproduces itself in my classes where those who focus on sexual violence tend to minimize the impact of sexual repression, and those who defend women's rights to sex, including participation in the sex industry, marginalize discussions of violence and social inequality. And yet in many women's lives, social inequalities, the threat and experience of sexual violence, and sexual repression are connected. Many women experience sexualized and racialized mistreatment, coercion, abuse, and violence and most of us have been sexually restricted, repressed, stigmatized, and punished. For most neither "side" of the sex debates speaks to the full complexities and contradictions in our lives. Through my experiences in the women's movement and as a feminist educator, I know that many women, including myself, have deep and contradictory responses to the pornography industry and to sexual issues in general. These responses may be connected to experiences both of sexual abuse and of sexual restriction and punishment. They are also connected to our identities and locations within interlocking systems of oppression and privilege.

For years I sought to reconcile myself to one side or the other in the polarized "sex war" debates over sexuality, violence, and pornography. For every attempt to ground myself solely in the antipornography movement, I would return to the recognition that sexual repression, the sexual double standard, and the criminalization of some sexual identities and practices were significantly connected as well to endemic inequality. The either/or framework in which debates get lodged is limited, counterproductive, and for the most part destructive. I disagree with feminists who simply defend the multibillion dollar pornography industry under the guise of individual rights and freedom, and who refuse to recognize how gender and racial inequalities and violence are intricately connected with social constructions of sexual identities and practices. I also disagree with feminists who do not critically analyze the stigmatization of women's sexual identities and practices or value the quest for sexual freedom. As a survivor and resister of both sexual violence and sexual stigmatization, I need the wisdom and passion of multiple voices and perspectives of women involved in the struggles for equality, mutual respect, dignity, and social justice. Writers and theorists on both sides of the debates have had a significant impact on my personal, social, and political life. The works of Andrea Dworkin,[2] Audre Lorde,[3] Kathleen Barry,[4] bell hooks,[5] and Catharine MacKinnon[6] contribute to my knowledge of sexualized violence, racism, and misogyny, and the reproductions of inequalities through mass culture industries, including pornography. The works of Dorothy Allison,[7] Chrystos,[8] Amber Hollibaugh,[9] Cherríe Moraga,[10] and Joan Nestle[11] contribute to my understanding of stigma, shame, and punishment of women's sexual and social identities, and the importance of women's sexual exploration and autonomy. Their works sit side by side on my bookshelf. Each has had a deep impact on my thinking about endemic sexual violence and sexual repression.

It is my belief that pervasive sexual violence cannot fully be addressed without considering the impact of the sexual double standard and its connection to sexual stigmatization and punishment, particularly in terms of the personal, social, and institutional responses to that violence. These often are compounded in the experience of sexual violence, not separated. My personal history of dealing with the impact of sexualized violence, for instance, has not been limited to addressing coercion and violence, although this was a first step. It has been equally important to claim a sense of sexual and bodily integrity and autonomy without carrying the burdens of shame and stigma. Women's experiences of violence are shaped by systems of sexism, racism, classism, xenophobia, and antisemitism, among other forms of oppression and privilege, and these shape our responses and resistance as well. To create a broad-based social movement for change that speaks to the complexities of women's lives and hopes for the future, we must link the struggle for sexual freedom and autonomy with the struggle for freedom from sexual and physical coercion and violence. As Dorothy Allison writes in relation to her own history of sexual violence and its impact, "As deeply as I wanted safety or freedom, I wanted desire, hope, and joy. What, after all, was the worth of one without the other?"[12] Moreover, neither of these is truly possible unless our vision is a society grounded in social and economic justice.

VIOLENCE AGAINST WOMEN—WHAT DOES SEX HAVE TO DO WITH IT?

The feminist movement against sexual violence saves many women's lives, including my own. It provides analyses that name, analyze, resist, and confront sexualized violence. For me, this feminist resistance to violence creates a clarity that make drugs, alcohol, and depression much less necessary in the routines of my everyday life. Andrea Dworkin is someone who speaks to the anger as well as to the grief about the endemic sexual abuse and exploitation in women's lives. Dworkin's analysis of the mass industry of pornography compels me to participate in the critical movement against it. Her work illuminates how sexualized and racialized mistreatment, abuse, and violence are socially legitimated and perpetuated by culture industries, including pornography. She shows how women are made into sexualized objects that are stigmatized and treated as inferior human beings. Her work demonstrates for me that the process of stigmatization is not separate from the violence, but integrally related.

Through my involvement in feminist activism against sexual violence, I learn to link endemic violence with social constructions of (hetero)sexuality grounded in the power dynamics of domination and subordination that are then made to seem natural through cultural discourses. Pornographic discourses construct sexual desire grounded in sexual, racial, and class inequalities; the erotic pleasure comes through dynamics of power and powerlessness. These constructions are connected to broader cultural discourses as well. Together they couch pervasive sexual and racial discrimination, inequality, and violence as natural, inevitable, and erotically entertaining (at least for those who identify with the ones in power). This analysis helps me to understand why women's stories of rape and sexual assault are often denied or minimized. Cultural discourses of heterosexual sex and relationships make it difficult to distinguish sex from rape. From within the culture of heterosexuality, consent may be difficult to decipher since "normal sexual relations" are constructed along the lines of masculine dominance and feminine submission. Moreover, the cultural discourses often blame women for sexual assault. Women are assumed to be the regulators of men's sexuality, and thus if we are raped, we must have somehow asked for it, provoked it, deserved it. The degree of belief in our "innocence" often rests with our racial, ethnic, and class identities. Sex and rape are thus linked in the cultural and social imagination such that women's stories of rape are often not considered legitimate. The only time when rape is distinguished from sex seems to be in cases of interracial stranger rape of "innocent" women (typically defined by age, race, class) where the reigning ideology assumes, for instance, that white women would not consent to sexual relations with Black men; or heterosexual women would never consent to sex with lesbians. The lines between sex and rape seem dependent on external factors connected to constructions of gender, race, class, and sexual orientation.

From another direction, while feminists have argued that violence against women is about power, not sex, the realities for many women are that our experiences of sexual harassment and rape (as adults and children) impact the constructions of sexual identity, desire, and dynamics in practice.[13] Sexual assault survivors often experience sexual shame and feel stigmatized by rape—interpret the sexual assault as something having to do with who we are. The connections made above illustrate for me that sexuality and violence must be analyzed together if we want to end sexualized violence. As MacKinnon writes:

> So long as we say that [sexual violations] are abuses of violence, not sex, we fail to criticize what has been made of *sex*, what has been done to us *through* sex, because we leave the line between rape and intercourse, sexual harassment and sex roles, pornography and eroticism, right where it is.[14]

While some take MacKinnon's argument to mean that all sex is rape, I believe that MacKinnon is simply arguing that rape is *sexual* violence and power, not simply physical dominance and power. Given the pervasiveness of sexual assault, if our goal is to end it, we must consider the social construction of sexual relations that allow assault to look like consent. MacKinnon, Dworkin, and others argue that a feminist theory of sexuality must be grounded in knowledge about male sexual violence. This theoretical approach would elucidate the relationships between gender and sexual relations, locating "sexuality within a theory of gender inequality, meaning the social hierarchy of man over woman . . . "[15] They argue that the *sexual* subordination of women is invisible as inequality because it is experienced as sexual, and heterosexuality, assumed to be natural and biological, constructs men as dominant over women. Sexualized gender inequality, then, is supported and maintained by an ideology of biological determinism which naturalizes *sexual* hierarchy. In Dworkin's terms, "In the subordination of women, inequality itself is sexualized: made into the experience of sexual pleasure, essential to sexual desire." The task of feminism with regard to sexual violence, accordingly, is to isolate and analyze how sexual ideology and practice participate in social structures of domination and subordination.[16]

This perspective makes sense to me and informs my critical analysis of media and popular culture, including pornography. The mass industry of heterosexual men's pornography is an important site for critical analysis and activism because it is a multibillion dollar business that commodifies women's bodies into sexual objects. It is a major source of sexualized discourses that justifies and perpetuates sexualized and racialized mistreatment, abuse, and violence. One can see in its processes of production, consumption, and distribution the material and ideological connections between the sexualized objectification of women in pornography and the structural inequalities and sexually violent practices women experience in our lives.

At the same time, I also find compelling some of the arguments of feminists who call themselves sex radicals. This group of feminists organized in opposition to the growing feminist antipornography movement of the late 1970s. They perceived the feminist critique of pornography to be problematic because they felt it attacked and further stigmatized women's individual sexual identities, practices, and dynamics. Thus, a growing group of women who referred to themselves as "pro-sex" and/or sex radicals began to associate the feminist antipornography movement with broader reactionary forces of sexual repression. Their analysis focuses on the impact of sexual repression and inhibition, not violence, on women's sexual identities, desires, and practices. They critique the sexual double standard and the unfair stigmatization and punishment of women who are sexually active outside of heterosexual monogamous marriage. Pro-sex feminists suggest that this stigmatization creates a situation where women are fearful and ignorant about sexual practices, desires, and power. They suggest that the structure and dynamics of sexual relations are less related to gender hierarchy and violence, and more connected to sexual repressiveness. For instance, Carole Vance suggests that "Despite the many interrelationships of sexuality and gender, sexuality is not a residual category, a subcategory of gender; nor are theories of gender fully adequate to account for sexuality."[17] Instead, as Gayle Rubin argues, theorists and activists organized around sex need a political analysis of sexuality that is conceptually and practically different from a feminist politics of gender inequality:

> A radical theory of sex must identify, describe, explain and denounce erotic injustice and sexual oppression . . . must build rich descriptions of sexuality as it exists in society and history. It requires a convincing critical language that can convey the barbarity of sexual persecution.[18]

Pro-sex feminists argue that sexual stigma and persecution impact sexual identities, desires, and practices more than gender hierarchy. For instance, while lesbian oppression can be explained in part by men's control over women's sexuality, lesbians are also oppressed as "queers and perverts, by the operation of sexual, not gender stratification" which makes the social penalties on lesbians similar to "gay men, sadomasochists, transvestites, and prostitutes."[19]

The sexual hierarchy, Rubin argues, has a separate history and organization from gender. The sexual value system institutionalized in law, religion, and psychiatry, valorizes, condones, and accepts certain sexual practices and discriminates against others. Accordingly she proposes a sex hierarchy in which she juxtaposes the "Charmed Circle: Good, Normal, Natural, Blessed Sexuality" with what she calls the "Outer Limits: Bad, Abnormal, Unnatural, Damned Sexuality." The dichotomies line up as follows: heterosexual v. homosexual, married v. unmarried, monogomous v. nonmonogomous, noncommercial v. commercial, in pairs v. alone or in groups, same generation v. cross-generational, in private v. in public, no pornography v. pornography, bodies only v. with manufactured objects, vanilla v. sadomasochistic.[20] Rubin assumes that the sexual practices listed in opposition to the "conventional" ones are "deviant" and thus set up for social persecution.

Emanating from this political approach to sexuality, considered separate and distinct from gender hierarchy, pro-sex feminists defend women's rights to individual choice regarding sexual identities and practices. Similar to sexual libertarian politics, they conceptualize women's sexual identities and practices as matters of individual choice protected by the right to privacy. This accounts for why many interpret the feminist antipornography analysis to be an attack leveled against individual women, rather than at the broader systems and institutions of inequality, including the mass industry of pornography. From their perspective, sexual injustice stems from the societal intolerance that negatively labels, stigmatizes, and/or criminalizes individual sexual practices as deviant.

SEXUAL REPRESSION AND THE POLITICS OF FEAR AND IGNORANCE

The pro-sex feminists argue that feminist explorations of sexuality should be kept separate from analyses of sexual violence. They fear that the focus on sexual violence promotes repressive ideas about women and sexuality; for instance, Duggan, Hunter, and Vance interpret the movement against sexual assault and pornography to be promoting ideas like

> . . . sex is degrading to women, but not to men; that men are raving beasts; that sex is dangerous for women; that sexuality is male, not female; that women are victims, not sexual actors; that men inflict "it' on women; that penetration is submission; that heterosexual sexuality, rather than the institution of heterosexuality, is sexist.[21]

They seem to fear that documenting endemic sexual violence may minimize women's sexual desire, autonomy, and subjectivity, and magnify women's sense of male domination and misogyny. For them, talking about *sexual* violence somehow diminishes women's sexual choices, power, and pleasures; as Ann Snitow expresses, "To bring sex and violence together is to deny that heterosexual women have a sexual interest in men. It denies women any place in the long history of heterosexuality."[22] In part, some worry that implicit in the feminist analysis of sexual violence is a construction of the "good girl" who is not sexual. The result, Paula Webster envisions, may be that women will accept minimal sexual activity, with "few partners, fewer positions, less pleasure, and no changing of preference," for fear of being labeled "bad girls" or of being punished for actively pursuing sexual pleasure.[23]

Separating sexual violence from sexual desire, pro-sex feminists generalize women's relationship to sex to be one of inexperience, unfounded fears, and moralistic biases. Webster, for instance, reasons that the group Women Against Pornography attracts a lot of women because sex is taboo for women. She says, women are "ready to swear that they find none of that sleazy, pornography sex interesting." She continues:

> Denying their curiosity like the Oedipal daughter, they insist that they could never do anything like that or want anything like that. They assume that women who like talking dirty, anal sex, voyeurism, or even vibrators are suspect, certainly not feminists. But women are feminism's constituency. How do we understand the difference between ourselves and the women who send their photos to *Hustler*, or write letters to *Penthouse Forum*, or buy sex toys, split-crotch panties, and dream of being dominated or becoming dominatrixes? We cannot remain indifferent to the sexual texts and subtexts of women's lives if we are to create a feminist discourse on female sexuality that will replace the familiar one of commiseration.[24]

Given the idea that women are relatively inexperienced with pornography because of the sexual double standard, some argue that women should be encouraged to explore it as a sexual arena.[25] Webster suggests that pornography can challenge "the sacramental character of our sexual desires."[26] It represents a freedom from the double standard that constrains women to be "good girls." Upon touring 42nd Street in New York with the Women Against Pornography, she claims that far from outrage, for her "the tour evoked complex reactions, including envy, fear, and sexual arousal. The social and psychic repression of my female desire was giving way, ever so slightly, under the barrage of sexual imagery. I was a fascinated tourist in an exotic, erotic, and forbidden land." She criticizes the tour guides for not acknowledging the excitement, delight, and terror evoked.[27] Similarly, Lisa Orlando reports that pornography helped her in her adolescent "search for validation and pleasure and sexual autonomy." She claims that

> . . . what pornography gave me years ago was a set of models antithetical to those offered by the Catholic Church, romantic fiction, and my mother. The 'bad girls' it portrayed *liked* sex, even sex with women. Fear-

less and sensual, they scoffed at respectability and were often as independent and aggressive as men. These images not only affirmed my budding desire but also gave me a first glimpse of freedom.[28]

Pro-sex feminists seek to demystify "taboo" sexual practices believing that women benefit from surveying, reading, and using pornography: "With the clues we gather here about our own fantasies, we can begin to map out the zones of cerebral and fleshly arousal."[29]

Pro-sex feminists give voice to the ways that women have been restricted from sexual exploration and sexual agency. Their stories interest me because they speak to the cultural and social contradictions women must negotiate in a context where, on the one hand, our bodies are commodified into sexual objects and bought, sold, and consumed everyday in advertisements, film, television, and many forms of popular culture, and on the other hand, we are criticized, condemned, and punished for sexual expressiveness and exploration outside of the confines of heterosexual monogamy. These contradictions in many ways seem to be at the heart of these debates.

While it is true that sexual repressiveness and antisexual dogma directed against women significantly impact women's lack of sexual autonomy, these forces cannot be disconnected from the experience of gender inequality, sexual harassment, and violence. For instance, it seems that sexual repressiveness actually intensifies the eroticism of inequality by making it seem taboo (particularly in terms of extreme power differences along age or race lines) and yet it is pervasive. By restricting women's freedom to openly express, explore, and celebrate sexuality, the harms of forced sexuality also are made invisible. These restrictions create secrecy, shame, and stigma around sexual activity, forced and consensual. The eroticism of pornography in many ways seems dependent on repression and its consequent secrecy, shame, and stigma:

> The pornographers no less than the puritans have a stake in sexual repression; there is nothing more furtive or repressed than the customers in a back-room peep-show, and peep-shows are the most profitable component of many bookstores' business. By defining sex (and sex equals women) as something evil, dirty, and forbidden, the Moral Majority creates a demand for precisely the kind of misogynist material that pornographers are selling. Repression and pornography are merely two sides of the same coin: sex is dirty, the puritans say—so have nothing to do with women; sex is dirty, the pornographers say—so do anything you want to women.[30]

Repression functions to stigmatize sexual activity and thus encourage secrecy and hiding; it does not simply inhibit sexual activity. The sexual double standard and the stigmatization of women's sexual autonomy control women's public talk and analysis of sex (both forced and consensual), but they do not protect women from sexual coercion and assault. For instance, many young girls are sexually abused by family or near-family members despite the "incest taboo." The taboo however silences women and children by defining it as "bad" and "dirty" and "shameful" for the women and children involved.[31] Similarly, pornography may have an aura of taboo for women because of the stigma against women who express sexual autonomy and agency. The so-called taboo, however, hides the fact that thousands of women are concurrently involved in its production and increasingly in consumption, and are impacted by its discourses, products, and services. Andrea Dworkin suggests that pornography can be considered taboo only if we refuse "to face what the content of pornography actually is and how the forced acts of sex in it correspond to women's lives."[32] Through teaching courses on violence against women and presenting educational programs on the pornography industry, I have learned how significant women's participation in the production and consumption of pornography is. I find that many women are variously hurt, confused, upset, and curious about their relationship to pornography, and their experiences with it, both forced and consensual. The question is how to create a space for women to express and explore this complex web of issues without feeling judged, attacked, or shamed for doing so. In this sense, I am in agreement with the goals of sex radicals to create honest, open, and nonjudgmental arenas for women to discuss as well as analyze our sexual desires and practices.

Sexual repressiveness contributes to the impact of sexual violence. Women survivors of sexual violence are often shamed, stigmatized, and punished for their involvement in the sexualized acts, despite the fact that they are forced.[33] Survivors of sexual violence experience sexual shame and stigma as do women who are sexually active and adventurous. A feminist analysis of sexuality cannot ignore the ways that sexual repression operates in conjunction with sexual violence. In tandem, they control women's sexual choices. Sexual repression and oppression function interdependently to maintain the system of sexual subordination. While it is important for feminists to stress the inequality, coercion, and violence involved in sexual relations and in pornography, we must address processes of shame, stigmatization, and punishment that unjustly target women's individual identities, sexual desires, and sexual practices as inherently problematic.

One of the contradictions I experience in this debate is that I know that sexual ignorance, inexperience, and even violence do create situations where women may reject sexual practices out of fear, rather than knowledge. In this regard, increasing women's fears and judging women's questions and curiosities are harmful and counterproductive. On the other hand, labeling feminists critical of sexualized inequality and pornography as prudes, antisex, and puritanical seems just as punitive and restrictive. I disagree with feminists who automatically are suspicious of women's criticisms of sexual images and practices and who label the critiques as veiled puritanism and/or simply indicative of women's sexual repression. Since women are victimized through sexuality because of its enmeshment with violence and social inequality, many women have legitimate reasons to be critical of sexualized dominance. The sexual ideology and dynamics of mass produced pornography, along with many other cultural media, are a focus of feminist analysis, not because it is sexually explicit, but because it looks like, justifies, condones, and encourages abuse and violence, and the systems of interlocking oppressions that support it.

Pro-sex feminists often speak to the silence and shame women experience around sexual desire and activity, and in so doing, they offer an arena for discussion and exploration without judgment. Forums for women to express and explore contradictory feelings and ideas with regard to sex and pornography, particularly our feelings of complicity and sexual arousal, as well as our fantasies involving sexual power dynamics, are essential. Because women's sexual desires are socially constructed through culture and experience, many of us find ourselves attached to and implicated in the sexual relations of dominance and subordination. In the face of antipornography arguments, individual women may feel bad (i.e., guilty, shameful, ridiculous, stupid) for our participation in sexual dynamics of dominance and subordination and for being sexually stimulated by pornography's use of sexualized inequalities. Pro-sex feminists recognize and sometimes celebrate our attachments to dynamics of sexual domination and submission. They encourage women to claim power in these dynamics, rather than powerlessness. This is an appealing rhetoric, but not necessarily one oriented toward social transformation.

ANTIPORNOGRAPHY AND THE POLITICS OF WOMEN'S SEXUALITY

The critical analysis of pornography is a structural one focused on the oppression of women through sexualized mistreatment, abuse, and violence. Many antipornography feminists have argued that the industry of pornography involves harm to women through its production, consumption, and mass distribution. This harm justifies a critical analysis and politics of public exposure and social change. From within this framework, an individual woman's struggle with sexual desire and practice in relation to pornography has not been the focus.

Mostly the contradictions and complexities of women's relationship to pornographic images and stories are denied or labeled as products of false consciousness. For instance, in my work in the feminist antipornography movement, I have run up against a fairly rigid, though often unspoken, orthodoxy around sexual behavior and attitudes. Efforts to explore and challenge this orthodoxy often are unwelcome, especially because of the polarized debates. As an activist involved in feminist antipornography politics, I have been accused of siding with "the enemy" simply for raising questions about women's desires and their relationship to pornographic constructions. While I disagree with many of the anticensorship feminists for the defense of the industry, I find some of the arguments of sex radicals around the connections between women's sexual desires and pornography intriguing. I believe it is essential to have open dialogues about the complexities of sexual desire, particularly as desire is shaped in social, political, and historical contexts, and is not essential. Included in these dialogues would be a conversation about the contradictions we experience in our own lives and that I see among those working against the pornography industry. I observe serious contradictions between individual women's sexual desire and their social political analysis. For instance, I have known women who objectify women's bodies in their daily lives, and yet who are also known to socially condemn lesbians who make and/or consume pornography. I know women who criticize lesbian sadomasochism and sexualized power dynamics as abusive, and yet who are abusive in their interactions with other women.

I question the usefulness of a politics against the pornography industry that discourages questions and concerns about women's contradictory relationships with sexual desire and dynamics, based on our own confusions given sexual violence, repression, and punishment. Given the negative and sometimes hostile responses to many of my questions in the feminist movement, I began to feel like there must be something wrong with me since my life didn't live up to feminist ideals. Given a history of both Catholicism and sexual abuse within and outside the family over many years, my sexual, emotional, and intellectual responses to the sexual identities, dynamics, and relations constructed in the pornography industry's products are complicated and not always well defined according to strict political categories. I know that I am not alone. If our interest is building a critical mass to confront and challenge a mass culture industry, we need more effective emotional, analytic, and political strategies to deal with these complexities.

Feminists critically organizing to protest, confront, and hold accountable the pornography industry must be open to discuss these complexities to ensure that more voices can be heard and the analysis deepened. Instead in my experience the atmosphere in some parts of the movement remind me of the staunch and unrelenting Catholicism of my childhood—a dogma that had extraordinarily narrow and rigid boundaries about thought and action, and which rarely gave human beings room for complexity or contradiction. It is a dogma that is set up for transgression and failure, because no one can live up to it. As in other parts of the women's movement, the struggle for change often gets translated into demands for conformity where strict standards of behavior are used to judge and exclude people. As Andrea Dworkin suggests:

> People become slaves to theory because people are used to meeting expectations they have not originated—to doing what they are told, to having everything mapped out, to having reality prepackaged. The deepest struggle is to root out of us and the institutions in which we participate the requirement that we slavishly conform.[34]

The sexual orthodoxy that seems implicit in much of the analysis often does not address the complexities and contradictions inevitable in a society rife with discrimination and repression. We must do better. We must work to address the confusions, ambivalences, and fears of many women who are seeking to address the sexual violence and repression within their own lives and the lives of others. One of the effects of sexual abuse in sexually repressive atmospheres is an intense confusion as well as fear and terror around sexuality.

If one of our feminist goals is to create a broad-based movement for social justice, it is incumbent upon all of us to listen to the fullness of women's stories. We might do better to create spaces in which women can explore the contradictions between our feelings, political beliefs, and actions that are inevitable for people who live in a society rife with sexual, racial and economic bigotry, inequality, exploitation, and abuse. In this way the voices and experiences of many women would make up the movement, not only those women who have the same perspective or who experience oppression in the same way.

DISMANTLING SEXUAL SHAME AND STIGMA

Dorothy Allison eloquently asks us to consider "how our lives might be different if we were not constantly subjected to the fear and contempt of being sexually different, sexually dangerous, sexually endangered. What kind of women might we be if we did not have to worry about being too sexual, or not sexual enough, or the wrong kind of sexual for the company we keep, the convictions we hold? . . . Not addressing the basic issues of sexual fear, stereotyping, and stigmatization reinforces the rage and terror we all hide, while maintaining the status quo in a new guise."[35] Her recognition of the fear and contempt toward sexual difference speaks to the heart of the need to address sexual freedom as well as violence.

In my own life, the experience of sexual abuse and violence is intermixed with the experience of stigmatization and punishment. A major obstacle to my own recognition of violence and abuse in my family is directly attributable to having grown up in a staunchly Roman Catholic context with very strict standards of behavior which, in my case, were continually transgressed within and outside of the family. Disentangling the deception and betrayal is the work of a lifetime. Self-blame and shame were central to my Catholic white middle-class woman's experience of sexuality—both consensual as well as forced. Being raised in a very rigid Catholicism that restricted and stigmatized women's sexual desire and autonomy confounded the experience of sexual abuse and violence. It was very difficult to label what was happening to me as anything but my fault and deserved because of the sexual transgressions. The sexual double standard was something I rebelled against from an early age; but the fear and terror around sexual relations, arising both from the abuse as well as the repression, only served to entrench me in their dynamics.

While the movement against violence has helped women to name and recognize the problem, less attention has been paid to offering positive and forward-moving personal and/or social options. Feminists need to be careful in our analysis of the conditions of women's lives that we do not reduce ourselves, and women generally, to these conditions. For instance, from the perspective of the feminist antipornography analysis, women's participation in pornography is often constructed in terms of histories of sexual violence, poverty, racism, and lack of social options. While such a description is accurate in terms of the social conditions of many women's lives, it is problematic as a description of the women. In feminist efforts to draw attention to the violence, feminists must respect women for their work, decisions, efforts, and abilities to create lives for themselves (often against great odds), and not reduce them to what others have done to them. Otherwise, feminists reinforce the stigmatization of the women who inevitably get socially constructed in terms of deviance and pathology. These constructions must be challenged, resisted, and transformed, particularly if the goal is to build a movement and a politics based on mutual respect and dignity of all involved. The language of victimization does not include women's individual and collective hopes and struggles for survival, for food, for friendships, for love, for family, for sex, for community, for meaning. In "Survival is the Least of My Desires," Dorothy Allison writes:

> If we are forced to talk about our lives, our sexuality, and our work only in the language and categories of a society that despises us, eventually we will be unable to speak past our own griefs. We will disappear into those categories. What I have tried to do in my own life is refuse the language and categories that would reduce me to less than my whole complicated experience. At the same time I have tried to look at people different from me with the kind of compassion I would like to have directed toward me.[36]

Feminists on all sides of the volatile feminist debates over sexuality, pornography, and violence might benefit from a compassionate and determined listening in the service of personal and social change.

MOVING BEYOND EITHER/OR FRAMEWORKS

As a lesbian, feminist, outspoken survivor of sexual violence, I have not succumbed to the rigidity of the Catholicism that I grew up with, nor the rigid tenets of the radical feminism that helped change my life, nor the allure of a sexual politics separate from social and economic justice. As well, I have not been destroyed by the sexual abuse and violence so much a part of my life for many years. For me the goal of the women's movement is not to enforce conformity, nor to construct sameness across our many differences, nor to create monolithic standards to be used to judge everyone's attitudes and behaviors. As Dorothy Allison writes:

> Throughout my life somebody has always tried to set the boundaries of who and what I will be allowed to be. . . . What is common to these boundary lines is that their most destructive power lies in what I can be persuaded to do to myself—the walls of fear, shame, and guilt I can be encouraged to build in my mind. . . . I have learned through great sorrow that all systems of oppression feed on public silence and private terrorization.[37]

This means that repressiveness in response to confusion, anger, contradictions, and conflicts is not an answer. Both "sides" of the debate have challenged public silences. The antipornography movement has created a public discussion of the endemic sexualized violence in women's lives; and some sex radicals have created a public discussion of women's sexual desires and yearnings. It is time that feminists break the silences implicit within each of the two positions.

When the discourses are brought together, it seems clear that accepting the exclusivity of either framework does not account for women's experiences, struggles, and hopes; and it should help feminist activists to recognize that pitting one woman's story against another's, as if one can necessarily cancel out the other, does not represent a successful strategy for the women's movement. Women's lives are complex; they are not simple cut-outs to be fit into ideological boxes. As Andrea Dworkin writes, "The search for freedom has to be a struggle toward integrity defined in every possible sphere of reality —sexual integrity, economic integrity, psychological integrity, integrity of expression, integrity of faith and loyalty and heart."[38]

PART III

BRINGING THEORIES INTO PRACTICE

7

NECESSARY VOICES:
A Battered Lesbian Fights for Recognition[1]

In 1992, Debra Reid, an African-American woman incarcerated for killing her lesbian partner, petitioned the Massachusetts Advisory Board of Pardons to have her prison sentence commuted. She was a member of the "Framingham Eight," a group of incarcerated women who were convicted of killing their husbands or lovers, and who felt that their experiences of battering had not been given a fair hearing in the courts that convicted them. Debra's petition argued that she did not receive a fair trial in part because she was not allowed to introduce evidence of a prior relationship of battering with the woman she was convicted of killing. Debra was the only lesbian in the group and she pursued the petition process, despite the many obstacles she faced. She had first to convince the other incarcerated women that the battering she suffered from her lover was as serious as theirs, even though the batterer was a woman. Many advocates in the domestic violence and gay and lesbian legal communities did not want to get involved in her case—it made things more complicated both because she was a woman who had killed another woman and because she was a lesbian. With the support of the Network for Battered Lesbians in Boston, she secured the services of Sandra Lundy, a lawyer in the Boston area who is a lesbian and who has done pro-bono domestic violence advocacy. At the request of Lundy and the Network, I wrote the following essay for Sojourner in order to publicize Debra Reid's case and to bring attention to the issues of lesbian battering. It is based on an interview with her while she was in Framingham Prison in Massachusetts.

After a two year delay, the Board rejected her petition. I believe that the Board failed to consider the overwhelming evidence that Debra Reid had been battered by Jackie Gary, they failed to consider how this battering significantly contributed to her death, and they failed to consider that Debra Reid did not have the opportunity to present a full defense at her trial. Instead, they claimed that there was "insufficient evidence that Ms. Reid was a battered woman suffering from battered women's syndrome at the time of the offense," and while "The Board acknowledges that there appears to be some evidence of a battering relationship. . . . *it appears that both the victim and the petitioner participated in a mutual battering relationship." This rationale was given despite the fact that no evidence of Reid's abusiveness was offered at the hearings. It is noteworthy that this was the only case of the Framingham Eight where the Board used the myth of mutual battery to deny her petition. In the words of the one dissenting opinion on the Board, ". . . it is very easy to dismiss it as a fight between two women which ended tragically—to see it as a battle between two equals. However, the reality is that batterers are not always men and not always heterosexual."*

Despite the efforts of Reid and her attorney to focus the Board's attention on the battering Reid experienced by her lover, including on the night of the stabbing, the Board kept returning to the narratives of her childhood, her previous marriage, her relationship with her family, and her lesbianism to explain her actions on the night of the killing. Despite their refusal to recognize her case as one of lesbian battering, this same board required Reid to attend a weekly group for battered women as a condition of her parole.

Debra Reid's story continues to be compelling in its demonstration of the interlocking oppressions that shape a woman's experience of battering. Sexism, racism, homophobia, heterosexism, and classism shaped Debra Reid's experience of lesbian identity and relationship, lesbian battering, and the culminating death of her lesbian partner Jackie Gary. Living in a small town in rural Massachusetts as a newcomer from Virginia, Debra Reid had no knowledge of public lesbian life. She did not know of any resources, services, and/or organizations that welcomed lesbians. She did not know about services and shelters for battered women, and even if she did, the domestic violence services in her area did not welcome battered lesbians into their programs. The one medical doctor she visited did not have a protocol to assess for abuse and violence, and she allowed Debra's partner to attend their sessions. Racism, classism, sexism, and homophobia further shaped the criminal justice system's response to her once she was arrested, incarcerated, and convicted. They shaped, as well, her experience in prison and the failure to obtain her commutation petition.

I urge readers to consider the full complexity of Debra Reid's story and not to compartmentalize it into a story only about a woman, or a poor woman, or a lesbian, or an African-American woman. Her story is shaped by multiple and interpenetrating layers of oppressive systems—all of which would need to be addressed to prevent the mistreatment, discrimination, and violence she faced before and during the relationship, and as someone subject to the dictates of the criminal (in)justice system and the prison system. It is also the story of a woman who struggled to fight this system as she was simultaneously trying to survive it. Her persistent resilience in the face of many obstacles and opposition is to be honored and celebrated.

□ □ □

"It is our belief/experience that when a woman defends
herself against the deadly assault of her abuser and kills,
this is self-defense."
—Battered Women Fighting Back!: Battered Women
Incarcerated for Self-Defense.

On February 14, 1992, eight incarcerated women in Massachusetts submitted pe-
titions to Governor William Weld for commutation of their prison sentences. The
women, all of whom were battered by their spouses or partners, argue that they
had been unjustly imprisoned for defending themselves, for fighting back to save
their own lives. Each case is being heard by the Advisory Board of Pardons, which
then makes recommendations to Governor Weld about whether to reduce the
women's sentences.[2]

Like the seven other women, Debra Reid is a formerly battered woman who
killed her lover in self-defense; but unlike the others, Debra is a lesbian and so
was her batterer. Against all odds, including the ignorance and homophobia of our
criminal (in)justice system, Debra has persisted in trying to tell her story from a
lesbian perspective, and it is finally being heard. Her story speaks to the incredible
isolation, loneliness, and powerlessness of battered lesbians, particularly lesbians
like Debra who are African American and poor. From the beginning of the criminal (in)justice process, Debra believed that if the lawyers, judges, and/or juries understood that she and her lover Jacqueline ("Jackie") Gary had been in a five-year
lesbian relationship, then they would understand that Jackie's death was not a case
of malice, but completely unintentional, and, if anything, a case of self-defense.
Unfortunately, for a variety of not uncommon reasons—that she is an African-
American lesbian who faced an all-white jury, that she was originally from Virginia
and so was an outsider to the community in which she was living, that she had few
monetary and social resources, and that she had no contact with lesbian or gay organizations or with battered women's groups—her story wasn't heard. On May 1,
1990, Debra was convicted of manslaughter in the death of Jacqueline Gary and
sentenced to nine to fourteen years in prison.

I interviewed Debra on March 2, 1992 at MCI-Lancaster where she is currently serving her sentence. What follows is an abbreviated version of her story as
I have pieced it together from that interview and from her commutation petition.

THE SETUP

In 1984, Debra moved to Gardner, Massachusetts from Norfolk, Virginia where
she was born and raised. She came here to live with her brother Robert and to try

to create a new life for herself. At the time, she was escaping an abusive husband and trying to establish some economic and social independence. After she arrived, she says, "I found a good job making molds for computers. I was able to afford things for myself, like a car. I had my own credit cards and made a good living. I could send money home to my daughter, Yolanda (who was living with Debra's mother), and save some for myself. I shared an apartment with my brother and took care of my own life."

In the fall of 1985, she met Jackie at a bar called "Charlie's" in Fitchburg, and they soon became friends and eventually lovers. Like many women (heterosexual and lesbian) who are battered or formerly battered, Debra got involved with Jackie because she was nice to her. Jackie showered her with attention and love, something Debra had not experienced much in her life. "She was the nicest person I had met in Massachusetts since I got there. She was always around when I needed a shoulder to cry on or just to talk. . . . Jackie knew how to make things feel better for me." After a while, however, Debra's life with Jackie became "a living nightmare."

This was Debra's first lesbian relationship and so she looked to Jackie for a definition and understanding of what lesbian relationships were like. Being a lesbian, she was told, means that few people understand or accept you. Jackie exploited societal heterosexism and homophobia to control Debra. She would tell her that "people don't understand, people don't want you around when you like that, you not straight." As a result, Debra felt she could only be herself around Jackie and Jackie's friends and family, who seemed to accept their relationship and the way Jackie treated Debra. "They knew that Jackie and I was going together when I first met them. Eventually they made me feel like I was welcome in the family, and I could tell that she had probably done it before because of the way that they accepted me."

So began Debra's isolation and Jackie's control over her identity and life. Soon after they got involved, Jackie moved in with her and basically took over. As Debra says, "Because I didn't know anything about being in a lesbian relationship, once I got into it with her, and I let her start changing me, I guess she see that she could do that. I guess I fell right into her trap." Debra rationalized Jackie's control by thinking that it was how lesbians were, coupled with the fact that she was used to such treatment from her family and former husband. "I thought that Jackie was supposed to tell me how to wear the clothes, I thought Jackie was supposed to tell me where to go, I thought Jackie was supposed to be in the car with me at all times. I thought it was all right. I was used to being told [what to do] all my life, somebody always running my life: Debra do this, Debra do that. So her telling me, Debra do this, Debra do that, was all right, because I never knew different. Now is the first time that I'm standing on my own ground. I don't have nobody to tell me, Debra do this, Debra do that."

A classic strategy of batterers is to keep a woman all to themselves, separate from everyone else. Jackie was no different. "She turned away all the people I knew before I met her. She wanted no one around me. I couldn't go anywhere unless she was there with me, which was all the time. I built my world around her. I lived for her, not for myself, but for her. So when it came down to having friends, to keep an argument down, I wouldn't. I didn't like her embarrassing me around my friends, so I cut them off." If Debra talked with or showed any interest in anyone, Jackie would warn people, "She belongs to me." In recalling the loss of her friendships, Debra says, "It's so hard to explain the pain that was in my heart, trying to deal with myself and keep her happy."

Over time, Debra's relationship with her family also deteriorated; her family didn't accept their lesbian relationship, and they didn't like the way that Jackie was treating her. It was difficult, however, to separate the two. After two years, Jackie convinced Debra to move to Fitchburg where Jackie's family and friends lived. She recalls, "Here I isolated myself even more from my family. My mother told me if I didn't let (Jackie) go that I couldn't come back [to Virginia]. And my brother, he hated the idea of it; he didn't want his sister to be seen with a woman. Also I guess he hated her, because of the abuse he listened to [when we lived with him]. Yet he never showed me that he would help me if I wanted out of it."

This separation from her family made Debra even more dependent on Jackie and her family and friends, who made up the neighborhood in which Jackie and Debra now lived. Jackie's family and friends were all very much a part of Debra's life, but they were completely loyal to Jackie. They would tell Debra that she had better not do anything to hurt Jackie, even when they could see that Jackie was emotionally and physically abusing her. They accepted and even reinforced Jackie's authority over Debra's life. "I couldn't get out of the apartment building. I could not get out of that building. I'd go down to Charlie's, and by the time I got back to the house, somebody had called her and told her I was looking at all kinds of dudes' faces. She told me, 'I got eyeballs all over,' and she did . . . people would call her and tell her anything I did." Jackie was incredibly jealous and possessive. She was constantly accusing Debra of being sexually involved with various members of her family or with friends and would provoke fights with Debra or with anyone who tried to make personal contact with Debra.

Debra's every behavior was under scrutiny by Jackie. Clothing was a major arena of control, and it still haunts Debra today. "I thought that I had to change my clothes because I was in a lesbian relationship. I just thought it was what I had to do and I was willing to do that [to please Jackie]. I used to wear a lot of silk. I wore clothes sheer to me. I am small so I wore clothes that fit me." But Jackie told her, "You can't wear that, somebody going to be looking at you, you don't wear stuff like that when you're in a relationship."

One of the difficulties Debra now faces is regaining control over her self-definition. If someone compliments her clothes or appearances, she still hears Jackie in her mind telling her it's wrong: "Like for my trial, I needed a dress to wear, so I told my brother to buy me one, but he didn't. He went and got some of my clothes that I had put in a box before I met Jackie. The dress fit, but it split up on the sides, and I was like, 'Oh my God, I can't go to court like this.' But I had no choice because it was the only thing I had. I kept thinking, 'Oh God, Jackie going to kill me if she saw me with this one.' Stuff like that flashes back, and it's very hard for me to wear something that fits because she didn't like it and we would get into fights."

Jackie's underlying method to maintain control and power was physical violence. "The first time I remember Jackie hitting me was when I went to Charlie's to meet a friend without telling her. When I got back home, Jackie tore off my shirt and pinned my hands down with her legs. She began hitting me all over with her fists. She hit me really hard in the face and my jaw was very sore." Like other batterers, Jackie apologized and promised to never do it again, but the abuse became an everyday event. "She hit me lots of times, sometimes when she was drunk or high on cocaine, or if anybody even noticed me when we went out together. The thing Jackie did most was to choke me until I began to black out. A couple of times, Jackie wrapped a telephone cord around my neck and threatened to strangle me. She slapped me all the time. One time, Jackie pushed me up against a wall. She had a knife in her hand and threatened that she would 'cut my box out.' Another time, Jackie hit me so hard with her fist that I flew across the room, because she was mad at me because she didn't have any money to buy cocaine. Another time, she pushed me so hard against a table that I had a big gash in my leg. I was afraid to go to the hospital because I was afraid to tell them what had really happened to me."

Debra tried to leave the relationship a number of times, and, in a number of ways, she tried to get help. But each of her attempts failed—and each failure reinforced her sense of difference from the heterosexual world, the lack of support from her immediate "friends and family" (who were loyal to Jackie), and her feeling of defeat in the face of Jackie's emotional and physical abuse. "A couple of times I tried to leave Jackie, but she would cry and threaten to kill herself and I would feel sorry for her. I felt guilty myself because I thought she probably wouldn't be doing this if it wasn't for me. I blamed myself so much. And if she killed herself, it was going to be on my conscience. [Another time] I tried to leave; she grabbed hold of me and refused to let me go. I had no idea that I could take out a restraining order against Jackie. I was also afraid to go to the police because I didn't want to tell them that I was beaten by a woman. I said to myself, 'Who is going to listen to me as a gay person?'" Jackie reinforced Debra's fears by telling her that no one would believe her and so she'd better stay.

A few times when Debra did manage to escape, Jackie followed her; once she followed her all the way to Virginia. Jackie would promise to change, and Debra wanted to believe her because she loved Jackie; she also felt that since she was a lesbian, she didn't have a lot of other relationship choices. "One time I was in a club, and she had started one of her acts, when my brother came in. I just took my chance; I got in the car and went to my brother and his girlfriend's house. [But] when we got there, she started calling me every five minutes telling me my dog missed me, telling me she was sorry, please come back, and telling me she can't live without me. And I was like, 'this house [where her brother, his girlfriend, and her four kids lived] is not right for me, maybe I can go back, maybe she be all right.' Well, everything was fine for about a week. And then, she started all over again, right from the beginning."

Debra tried other methods of ending the relationship as well. "At one point I cut off all my hair so that Jackie would think I was ugly and wouldn't want me anymore. I tried so many things to turn her off. At another point I tried to commit suicide by taking sleeping pills." She also went to a counselor once because she was depressed, anxious, and unsettled. But Jackie went with her and made sure she had the last word in defining the problem. After Debra told the counselor how "I was scared to go outside, everything was getting on my nerves; I couldn't function with people being around; I didn't know what was happening, but I couldn't go to the store to shop, I couldn't do anything," Jackie informed the counselor that Debra's problems stemmed from a prior car accident. Debra felt defeated once again in trying to get help. "I just told the lady, 'I'll talk to you another time,' and I left and never went back. I would have told her [about the abuse], but I didn't get a chance."

In the fight that led to Jackie's death, Debra was again trying to leave. "The night that we started the argument, I was on the verge of killing myself. That's how much I wanted out. And for the first time in my life with her, I told her that. I told her so much. I told her I was going to leave her. She tried to get me to shake her hand, and I said, 'No, I'm not going to shake your hand because I know when I walk out that door, I'm gonna have to fight you before I get out.' I knew that." And that's what happened.

For Debra, the night of August 12, 1989, began no differently than many other nights—throughout the afternoon, Jackie was accusing her of wanting to sleep with her nephew and screaming at her out on the street in front of the neighbors and inside their apartment. The only difference Debra felt was that Jackie seemed even more angry and hostile than usual, possibly due to bad cocaine. The incident began when Jackie returned to their apartment, and Debra was at the stove preparing a dinner of corned beef and cabbage. Sandra, a mutual friend, was there and she was drinking a glass of wine.

"She was very angry at me for giving some wine to Sandra. She said that I was giving her things away, but it was really my money that had bought the wine. Jackie grabbed the bottle of wine and began to drink it straight from the bottle. She had never done that before. I was cutting up cabbage, and I took the cabbage and the knife to the stove to cut up the pieces to put in the pot. . . . When I was still at the stove, I had a feeling that Jackie was coming toward my back to attack me. I turned around and there she was. She had the bottle of wine in her hand, which was raised, above her head. She grabbed me by the shirtfront. She seemed stronger than she ever seemed before. I tried to get her off me. She held me by the throat. She yelled at me, 'I'm going to fuck you up.' I had the knife in my hand when I turned to see where Jackie was. The floor was very slippery because the wine had spilled and I was afraid that Jackie or I would trip and that we would get hurt. I tried to take off my shoes when we were struggling, but I was afraid to look down and take my eyes off Jackie. I was afraid to let go of the knife."

Another roommate, their friend Sandra, and Jackie's nephew Junie were in the kitchen at the time and watched the fight. "I kept yelling for them to get Jackie off of me. At one point Junie tried to pull us apart, but he didn't try very hard. The others didn't do anything. I remember thinking to myself, 'They're going to let this girl hurt me.' I was afraid for my life. I knew that if Jackie hurt or killed me, no one in that room would ever tell the truth about it. I pushed Jackie away, and she stepped back. That was the last time I remember touching Jackie."

"After I pushed Jackie away, I went back to the stove to continue making dinner. I heard Jackie fall down and yell for help. I turned around and saw that she was down on the floor and that she was bleeding. That's when I realized that I must have stabbed her. The only way that I knew that I stabbed Jackie was that Jackie had a stab wound and I had a knife in my hand, but I don't actually remember stabbing her. I said over and over again, 'I stabbed her,' because I couldn't understand any other way that she might have been hurt."

When the police came, Debra, in shock, was still murmuring that she had stabbed Jackie. They arrested her on charges of assault and battery, and assault and battery with a deadly weapon. In jail that night, she kept waiting for Jackie to come and get her. "I kept thinking that Jackie was just fooling around like she always did when she wanted me to forgive her for hitting me or talking bad things to me." She also remembers telling herself that "If she did come and get me, I was leaving her because someone was going to get seriously hurt. I was so confused I think I cried myself to sleep."

When she woke up, a policeman told her that she had better get used to the cell because Jackie had taken a turn for the worse. "He said that I had better hope she didn't die, and that if he was Hitler, he would put me in front of a firing squad. I was so frightened that I was afraid to sleep because I thought the police were going to kill me." Afraid for her life, Debra kept imagining herself being lynched by the police. It wasn't until she went before the judge that she found out that Jackie had indeed died.

"When I went to prison, my heart hurt so bad that she was dead, and I had no one who wanted to listen to my cry for help. I'm really sorry that Jackie died, and sorry that she made it so hard for me to feel good about me and about us." Debra wishes that people would recognize that she had no intention of killing Jackie, even the label "self-defense," she feels, is inaccurate. She had no idea at the time that she had stabbed Jackie; it was completely unintentional. She did not want Jackie dead, no matter how much Jackie had hurt her. "No one hurts like I do. I loved her and cared for her. I took what she offered. I didn't know no different. So I've lost a friend. I've lost more than anyone can give me back. And I never even got to say goodbye. No one can give me my life back."

When Debra looks back now and realizes how bad it was—that she was being abused, that she didn't deserve to be treated in the ways that she was, and that being a lesbian doesn't mean you have to accept abuse—she is sad and angry about all of the years she lost—the years with Jackie, and the years in prison.

THE JUDICIAL PROCESS

Throughout the judicial process, Debra wanted her court-appointed attorney to help the judge and jury to understand that she was in a lesbian relationship with Jacqueline Gary and that the conflicts and abusiveness in that relationship, rather than malice, were what led to Jackie's death. Her defense attorney, accepting the homophobia of the judge and jury, downplayed the fact that they were lesbians and he left out the history of domestic violence. "He told the jury to disregard the fact that Jackie and I were lovers. I felt like I was on trial not for the death of Jackie but for just being a lesbian. The trial made me feel like I had not only no right to defend myself but had no rights to be gay."

She disagreed with his tactic from the beginning; as she says, "nobody's gonna hear anything that went on." By opting to leave the details about their relationship out of the defense's argument, the trial focused only on the events of the night in question. As a result, the fight that led to Jackie's death was given no context from which to evaluate Debra's behavior. She recalls, "They only asking me what happened that night. Nothing about what happened in the past. . . . If she wasn't doing one of her violent acts, then she would probably be here right now today. They never asked me anything about what had been done to me, how we had five years of going together, and that you don't just let it go down the drain like that." When she would press her attorney on this issue, he would tell her "they [the judge, jury] could judge you because of that." But as Debra says, "Well they doing that anyway." She was right. "When the judge heard the word [lesbian], the expression on his face showed that his mind was already made up. I knew I was going to get some time but how much I didn't know."

The prosecution, on the other hand, used Jackie's family to discredit Debra, and to blame her for Jackie's lesbianism, playing on the judge and jury's homophobia. "They said I turned her into a lesbian, [that] I was the man, and she was the woman . . . [that] I was the one who told her what to do, where to go, and I had nobody to say different because I had no friends." Debra had no one from the neighborhood to testify on her behalf, in part because of the way Jackie had isolated her from her friends and controlled her contact with others, but also because she had no money to get out on bail to try to gather potential support. Moreover, she didn't know about lesbian and gay organizations or battered women's shelters, places where she might have sought support and/or legal assistance, and her attorney did not pursue these possibilities either.

Even if Debra had tried to seek support from the battered women's shelters in her area, she would not have gotten what she needed.[3] While battered lesbians and their allies have been pressuring the battered women's movement to deal with lesbian battering by addressing homophobia, making shelters open and safe for lesbians, and doing outreach to lesbians, the movement has been slow to respond. As a consequence, Debra was left totally alone. She recalls, "It [the trial] was the hardest thing to do, 'cause I had nobody that I could turn to in the courtroom for support. I had nobody to help me say, this is what lesbians do, I had nobody there to even recognize that it was that."

The all-white jury and judge that Debra faced heard all about her lesbianism from the prosecution's standpoint, but they were told nothing positive about lesbian relationships; nothing about the pervasiveness of homophobia and the isolation that that creates; nothing about battered women, the battered women's syndrome, or the existence and context of lesbian battering. Not surprisingly, Debra was convicted of voluntary manslaughter. Her attorney told her that it would do no good to appeal, that she would be getting the same judge and two more just like them, and that it was very possible that they could increase her sentence. On this advice, she felt she didn't have a chance.

PRISON: A BATTERED LESBIAN FIGHTS BACK

In prison, "I isolated myself from everybody. I didn't want to be bothered. I didn't want to talk. I got out on comp time and started working at a store. And one day, I was telling this girl what had happened to me, and she was saying, 'Why don't you go to this battered women's group?' And I was like, "What would I be doing in a battered women group? I'm not in here for battered women, I'm in here because these people say I killed this girl with malice.' You know my mind was not together. So when I go to it, I was listening to the other girls talk about what had happened to them, and I thought, 'Oh my God, that happened to me.' And I just said [out loud], 'that happened to me, but it happened to me with a woman.' And everybody turned around and looked at me. I closed myself up again, because of the way they looked at me."

The facilitator of the group encouraged Debra to find other lesbians, including members of the Boston-based Network for Battered Lesbians, but it was hard for her to trust that anyone would listen. "I just couldn't, because of the way that everybody was treating me. . . . They [the other inmates] wasn't listening to me; when I said a woman, I was shut out, just like that. I get comments like, 'How could you let a woman do that to you?' or 'I would have dogged that girl,' but they don't understand. [The articles on lesbian battering] wouldn't sink in; it was like it hadn't happened to nobody but me. I was the only one in the world that this had happened to. At that point, I was like that."

Despite the resistance and denial of Debra's truths, she continued to fight for the recognition of her life experience. After getting involved with the other (heterosexual) battered women in prison, she helped found Battered Women Fighting Back (BWFB), a facilitated self-help group for women who have been incarcerated for defending their lives against their batterers. "When BWFB said that we was going up for the commutation petition, I was like, 'Yeah right. Who you gonna find for me?' I just felt like I wasn't going to find anybody to ever hear me. I felt that I had to hold this in for the rest of my life, and nobody's gonna ever get a chance to hear what they really done to me."

But they did find someone: Sandra Lundy, who was with the law firm Testa, Hurwitz, and Thibeault, agreed to take on the case and wrote a powerful legal brief on Debra's behalf. Active in the battered women's movement, she is a member of the Domestic Violence Council and a member of the Massachusetts Lesbian and Gay Bar Association. Sandra is committed to seeing the issue of lesbian battering dealt with in both communities. Debra says, "At first, when I met Sandy, I didn't know what to do. I was scared. I had put up my wall. My abuse wouldn't allow me to trust. But she sent me a letter [she had sent out] finding some people to send me a letter of support, and I was like, 'Oh, wow, she gets it.' I believed that she was helping me. That really did it. It's like, now that I'm learning about the abuse, it's allowed me to let people in; it's allowed me to have felt that there is someone else out there that's been through what I've been through."

Debra remains very isolated in prison as a lesbian because prison regulations prohibit any support groups or meetings that specifically address lesbian issues. As a result, her contact with the Network for Battered Lesbians has been crucial in helping to break down her isolation. "My purpose is to stop the court system on a lesbian situation from doing what they did to me. I don't want anybody to go through what happened to me. I need the Network for Battered Lesbians to help me stay strong. But it is hard, because if I get one little push, I'm the type of person who will close up. 'Cause if anybody back off to me, it's gonna be like everything all over again. I'm gonna hear that voice say, 'I told you.' She still in my brain saying, 'Who's gonna believe you?' So she's still torturing me, she still have a hold, but I will be able to keep her aside one day, I don't know when, but I will."

I asked Debra what might have helped her at the time, and she told me, "I looked in the telephone book. I saw nothing in there for me to get some help. I needed something that said lesbian, that said gay something, 'cause I was not going to anybody straight. [Lesbian services] need to be more public. They say they have shelters, but I bet you if you walked in there and said you're a lesbian and being battered, they wouldn't know what to do. They need to be educated on that, I think they need to put out more pamphlets on lesbians. It just needs to be open to let people know that there is a place to go, because it does happen, regardless of whether it's a man doing it. It happens and I'm tired of them saying that it don't happen. So it need to be out in the open, and that's what I'm trying to do. I'm trying to do that now."

Debra has lots of plans for when she gets released. "I'm going to get my GED, 'cause I have to have a GED before I can get into a college classroom. I want to take up computers. I need computers for when I take up psychology. I'm going for a hard task, I'm not going to educate lesbians that get battered only, I'm going to educate the batterers themselves. That's what I want to do. I got to hit the mind. If you don't know what's going on in the mind, then how can you help somebody? There is something wrong with lesbians who batter. I want to go to them, and if we help them, then we can stop that. Like they try to stop the men from doing it to the women, I want to stop the women from doing it to the women. And I want to tell battered women, 'Don't let anyone tell you that you are a nobody, because we can be anything we want to be.'"

White feminists often add to the polarization, rather than disrupt it. The racist profiling, coding, and targeting of communities of color around sexualized gender issues has gone mostly unremarked by many white feminists despite persistent questions raised by feminists of color. The racism not only goes unchallenged but is often reproduced in the name of challenging sexism and violence against women. I cannot even count the number of recent conversations with white feminists that begin with O.J. Simpson as a key symbol for the struggle against domestic violence. Among many white feminists, the names of white men do not have the same resonance in conversations about sexual harassment, rape, battery, and murder. We do not consistently refer to Bob Packwood, Bill Clinton, John Mack, William Kennedy Smith, Joel Steinberg, Sean Penn, Sean Connery, among others, as known harassers, rapists, and batterers. Some white antiracist feminists are beginning to follow the lead of feminists of color in addressing these discrepancies. Michelle Fine, for instance, notes, "when white men do the same [violence against women] our cultural instinct is to resist voyeurism. Elite white men at least enjoy the dignity of 'privacy.' Not quite as vulnerable to gossip, they are rejected culturally as the site for social surveillance."[3] Bulkin and Thompson suggest, "The fact that these issues have been brought to public consciousness as a result of individual Black men's alleged or proven actions, while no white men have received comparable public attention and censure in relation to these issues, is itself outrageous. This reality underscores some of the ways in which racism and sexism are intertwined."[4] The symbolic uses of Simpson as well as Tyson and Thomas in public mainstream discussions of violence against women serve to fuel racism, to perpetuate the hegemonic myth of Black male criminality, and the racial and class stereotypes that are used to explain violence against women.

During the sensationalized media coverage of the Simpson case, when I would criticize the racism of the media and police response, many white feminists responded with surprise and anger. Many felt that discussing racism in the O.J. Simpson case played into the "race card." Some implied that I lost my commitment to the cause of battered women, and some accused me of betraying Nicole Simpson and battered women in general. I disagree. It is both possible and necessary to develop a progressive, antiracist and feminist analysis of domestic violence that recognizes the interplay of sexism, racism, classism, and homophobia in the incidence of violence and in the social and institutional responses to violence. Feminists of color have been developing this analysis for well over the past century, and certainly since the beginnings of the contemporary women's movement in the United States. As Barbara Schulman, a white antiracist feminist reminds white women, "The unwillingness of many contemporary white feminists to acknowledge the symbiotic relationship between the politics of race and those of gender tragically repeats the mistakes of our nineteenth and early twentieth centuries movements."[5] In opposition to this historical tradition, it seems essential to refuse to exclude a recognition of one oppression for the visibility of another. Challenging racist practices in the classification and response to perpetrators of violence does not mean that I accept some men's abuse of women. Instead, I believe that it is incumbent upon white, middle-class feminists to not allow racism and classism to shape our discourse against woman abuse; we can follow the leadership of women of color doing this work.[6]

In the late 1980s and early 1990s, I lived in Cambridge, Massachusetts. During this time I witnessed sensationalized media coverage of the Charles Stuart case of domestic homicide. Charles Stuart, a white, upper-middle-class man killed his pregnant wife, blamed it on a Black man, created a kind of racialized hysteria, and when it was clear that his hoax was going to be revealed, he killed himself. In 1990, I wrote a short article in *Sojourner* that expressed my outrage about the racist and classist responses of the police and the media both before and after the hoax was revealed.[7] As I watched the unfolding of the O.J. Simpson case, I was struck by the difference between the racial and class coding of the media stories explaining Simpson's violence from that explaining Stuart's violence. I was drawn to compare the ways that race and class assumptions differentially shaped the explanations of the men's violence. The narratives constructed in each case offer racialized explanations that feed white supremacist, class-based, and patriarchical systems of oppression.

Through this coding, media constructions perpetuate ongoing social ignorance and indifference to most interpersonal intimate violence against women. This racialized discourse sensationalizes ideas of Black criminality that feed into white fears regarding interracial relationships and interracial violence against white women, while being indifferent and apathetic in response to intraracial intimate violence within communities of color[8] and to white male violence against people of color and white women. It is essential for feminists to reveal and disrupt this racial and class profiling of men's violence against women if we want to make the system accountable to all women and if our ultimate aims are to end violence against all women and to build a socially just society.

CHARLES STUART AND THE FABRICATED STORY OF WHITE ANOMALY

In the fall of 1989, Carol Stuart, a white, upper-middle-class suburban professional and pregnant woman was murdered in Boston. Her death drew national media attention and the case became a media extravaganza. Her husband, Charles Stuart, provided the initial narrative the police and media accepted as truth. Stuart had called the police from his cell phone on the night of the murder. He claimed that he and his pregnant wife had been returning to their suburban home from a prenatal class at a Boston hospital when the car was hijacked, the couple was robbed, and both were shot. After a thirteen minute frantic phone call where Charles Stuart claimed that he was lost, the police found him with his dying pregnant wife. The couple was taken to the hospital, and thus began the saga. The mother-to-be was pronounced dead a few days later and the baby, seventeen days later. During this time, the police carried out what one news report referred to as "the largest manhunt in recent memory" in Boston.[9] After terrorizing many Black men in the Mission Hill neighborhood while looking for any potential suspect, the police arrested William Bennett, an African-American man. By January 1990, Charles Stuart's story began to crumble. After his brother approached officials with evidence implicating him, Charles Stuart committed suicide by jumping off the Tobin Bridge in Boston. Public officials then had to retrace their steps and reconstruct the story of Carol Stuart's murder.

The media's response to the initial story as well as to the revealed hoax demonstrates white supremacist racial and sexual fears, biases, and hostilities toward men of color in particular. Initially, the press presented the Stuarts as a mythical Camelot couple—the perfect lily-white upper-middle-class heterosexual couple—attacked by a Black man—constructed through the lens of the myth of the inner city Black male criminal. As with similar racial hoaxes, the media sensationalized the initial story beyond belief.[10] Local newspapers offered days and days of coverage, from the exact transcript of Charles Stuart's phone calls to the police, to reports about the fears of white middle-class suburbanites to come to the city, to reports about urban poverty and chaos that were offered as explanation for the crime. As Miller and Levin point out, "The deep public outrage and sympathy that the case triggered was a direct result of the belief, fostered by media coverage, that a menacing black criminal had destroyed the lives of a decent, loving, white, middle-class family."[11]

Living in Boston at the time, I became increasingly angry at the media's sensationalism of this murder, especially in light of their apathy to the deaths of women generally. Along with others, I grew suspicious of Stuart's story, despite the media and police refusal to consider other possibilities. I was especially frustrated as the media began to warn white women and men to beware of the city because of "inner-city" (read: African-American and Latino) violence. These warnings felt like pure propaganda. Most violence against women is not committed by strangers, but is committed by men known to women, such as husbands, boyfriends, other family members, and acquaintances.[12] White women have far more to fear from white men than from African-American and Latino men. More to the point, people of color have far more to fear from white men as well as women in terms of pervasive discrimination, harassment, and violence.[13] Given this knowledge, I was angry at the ongoing indifference and apathetic media response to the many women who were being raped, assaulted, and murdered in all of Boston's neighborhoods.

The sensationalized media coverage of the Stuart case can be attributed to a number of factors emphasized in Charles Stuart's hoax. As mentioned, the media and police accepted his hoax and capitalized on the mythic elements of his story—the story of a young, white upper-middle-class couple from the suburbs who were preparing for the birth of their first child. Media stories described an idealized couple from the suburbs who had come into the city together for a prenatal class—in the *Washington Post* report, "Charles and Carol Stuart, a white couple, were driving home to suburban Reading from a childbirth class. . . . They were expecting their first baby at Christmastime."[14] The timing of the baby's birth at Christmastime garnered significance in each news story, as did the fact that this was their first child. The stories emphasized that the couple was on their way home to their "safe" (read: white and middle-class) suburban home and they contrasted this image of innocence and purity with the image of the supposed criminal assumed to be a Black man from an "inner city" neighborhood.

I wonder if Carol Stuart's death would have even made the news if they had known that her husband was the murderer (although because of her race, class, and occupation, there may have been one or two stories), or if she had been a woman of color or a poor woman. Certainly, the high level of official response would have been different had it not been portrayed as an "inner city" Black Man-on-White Woman crime. For instance, as it was, major public officials attended her funeral, including Massachusetts then Governor Dukakis, Boston Mayor Flynn, and Boston Police Commissioner Francis M. Roache. They would not have attended her funeral had they known from the beginning that Charles Stuart, or even another family member, had killed Carol Stuart.

Charles Stuart was very strategic in his maneuvering of his wife's death. He knew how to manipulate the white middle-class public—those who speak for them (media), and those who protect their interests (police). He could count on the racism of the city to deflect attention away from his actions. He drew upon a deep seated white racism that has at its core the socially constructed fear that African-American men will rape and kill innocent white women. Not long ago, white mobs routinely lynched African-American men; they justified the lynchings to themselves and a broader white public on the grounds that the men were inherently dangerous, bestial, rapists of white women.[15] Stuart's allegations of Black male criminality, thus, served as yet another rationale in a racist and segregated city for white racist police interrogation and terrorism of African-American men in a racially mixed community. This particular community, Mission Hill, was already under siege in some ways by institutionalized racism and economic exploitation, including police harassment, drugs, poverty, and crime. In addition, the .

mainstream media had a pattern of targeting African Americans in the metropolitan Boston area for crime and violence generally. As Kirk Johnson found in his study of Boston newspapers in the mid-1980s, the majority of news reports in the white dominant media that focused on predominantly Black communities concerned crime or violence. He writes, "In the major media, 85 percent of the news items reinforced negative stereotypes about blacks. Blacks were portrayed as drug pushers, thieves, and as victims or perpetrators of violence."[16] Boston's Black community and the man eventually arrested for Carol Stuart's murder are the ones that took the brunt of the fall-out from Charles Stuart's manipulative lie.

White women are also at the center of this discourse; it is white women's bodies that the racist discourse proclaims to protect and to avenge. Charles Stuart called upon a white male racist and classist chivalry that is limited to white middle-class women when the threat is a "stranger" from another social group (defined by race, class, nation). This protective shield is not extended to white middle-class women who are raped and murdered by white middle-class men. In fact, this chivalry may have little to do with white women in and of themselves, but is enmeshed with an ideology that sees white women as the property and possession of white men, to be protected from "other" men, not from white men themselves.[17]

Charles Stuart's story, of course, was eventually revealed for the fallacy that it was. After the hoax was revealed to the public, for a brief moment, the racism of the police, the city and state government, and the media were, at least superficially, called into question. The police investigation and media sensationalism were indicative of the low value the city places on the lives and welfare of Black communities, and the high value placed on the credibility of white upper-middle-class men and on the lives of their wives. Ultimately, however, public officials never took responsibility for the role of racism in their response to the crime. Many defended their methods of handling the case and denied that race had anything to do with their responses.

Once Stuart was implicated as the murderer, the analysis of the case changed in the media, in people's discussions, and in investigative insight. In place of social explanations that located the crime in a context of urban poverty, the media now constructed explanations focused on individual psychology. The media had initially constructed the Stuart case as a social crime of great concern to society (i.e., for them, this translates to white men and white women connected to white men, who are potentially the targets of nonwhite people's violence). With the shift from stranger to husband, from Black to White, from interracial to intraracial, from extrafamilial to familial, the explanations shifted as well from social to individual, and from sociological to psychological. In October, the media discussed the pathology of violence and drugs in the "inner city" (read: people of color), in January and February, they analyzed the crime as an individual act of a "normal" man gone awry (read: white middle-class men). In place of urban crime as cause, so-called "reasonable" and individual motives were speculated upon—from insurance money for a restaurant to the role of another woman. For instance, one media story reconstructed the murder as the work of a "sociopathic plotter" who "apparently . . . did it just for the insurance money to open a restaurant. . . . "; another referred to the murder as "a classic yarn of greed and betrayal." One report observed, "It was probably inevitable that there would be a woman in the case: the lovely blond graduate student, figure skater, and part-time fur-store worker, Deborah Jean Allen."[18] Others attributed the murder to Stuart simply not wanting to have a child.[19] As this report explained, "Stuart's apparent lack of remorse fits neatly into the sociopathic profile: a narcissistic personality lacking any conscience but able to mimic conventional emotional responses. In his case, criminologists surmise he felt his primacy threatened by the baby and saw no other option but to destroy it. Stuart came first."

This construction of Stuart's individualistic motives follows a pattern of descriptions attributed to white male criminals. As Miller and Levin suggest, whites who commit crimes are often depicted as "unique—they don't reflect white culture and society more generally." Crimes by whites are never labeled as "white crime" or "white-on-white" crime. In a survey of twenty-four hundred news articles, Russell found "fewer than fifty that used the term 'White crime' or 'White-on-White crime.'"[20] This is in contrast to over one thousand articles referring to Black crime. As Russell points out, "The virtual absence of articles on White crime suggests that in our singular and collective minds 'White' and 'crime' simply do not go together."[21] The stories of white men who are criminals then do not tie the crimes to white criminality; there is no social discourse tying whiteness to criminality.

White male criminals are instead constructed as individuals with specific problems, who are not affected by social forces. The roots of Stuart's violence are minimized and neutralized—as if they need no further analysis. This is a common media strategy when discussing white men's violence against white women. As Meyers points out, "white, middle-class men who batter and/or kill their wives are 'constructed in state and media discourses as the victims of provocation or personal stress, more deserving of mercy and compassion than condemnation and constraint.'"[22] A number of news stories reflect the media's individualization of Stuart's crime. One reporter, Bruning, writes, "If, as now seems likely, he was guilty of killing his pregnant wife and implicating an innocent man, Stuart deserves no further consideration. He simply was a fellow who went terribly awry—a coarse and corrupt individual whose opinion, were he able to offer it, counts for nothing."[23] And in another case, Martz, Starr, and Barrett write, "But in the end, there is no great moral. The story will remain a mystery; the mystery of a seemingly normal man who was incapable of recognizing the humanity of his own wife and child. And if we don't understand how that kind of mind works, we can be grateful that we don't."[24]

Only one news story that I read alluded to a narrative that would link Stuart's crime to social context, and of course in this case, the reporter links his criminal behavior to his working-class background, again deflecting away from a criminological profile of white middle-class and upper-middle-class men. In this article that appeared in the *Boston Globe*, Sally Jacobs and Anthony Flint allude to a fabricated middle-class identity that hid Stuart's working-class roots.[25] These are the roots, they suggest, that might help explain his actions. They write, "For Chuck Stuart spent a lifetime creating himself, molding a polished executive from a working-class boy. The image may have gone no deeper than the cologne brushed across his skin, but it was deep enough. And it worked, at least until the end."[26]

What is wholly missing from all of the news stories was a discussion of Charles Stuart's murder in the context of other men, especially white and/or middle-class and upper-middle-class men, who had murdered their wives, lovers, and ex-wives during this same time period. At the time of Stuart's killing, battered women's networks were trying to draw media attention to the realities that every twenty-two days a woman was killed by her husband or lover in Massachusetts. The media rarely reports these deaths in any detail, particularly in the cases of women of color, poor women, single mothers, or women working in prostitution. As in the case of rape, the media capitalizes upon white racism and its distorted fears of Black violence to sensationalize a case of murder alleged to involve a "stranger" attack on a white middle-class heterosexual married woman. This is despite the fact that women are more likely to be raped and murdered by the men who know and often supposedly love them—i.e., their husbands, lovers, and ex's—than by strangers. Moreover, when nonsensational cases of murder are covered, rarely is there an accompanying social analysis offered, and when it is, it usually has something to do with the particular women killed.[27]

The story of endemic violence against women was not only missing from the media reports, but actively denied. In response to the claim that the hoax was racist, *The Economist*, in "The Killing of Carol Stuart" offered the following commentary:

> The irony is not the 'insidious form of racism in society,' as one black minister has put it. It is that Mr. Stuart's story was more plausible than the truth. The implausible story is the one that emerged and is still emerging. People do not kill their wives in such a premeditated, ingenious and theatrical way (if at all). The murder of a spouse is generally impulsive—done in the heat of the moment. But random violence in in-

ner-city black neighborhoods is an everyday fact. The homicide rate among blacks in the United States is more than ten times that of whites, FBI crime statistics reveal.[28]

In a similar report, Alter and Starr argue, "The hard truth is that murders of middle-class whites (especially pregnant ones) are more rare and thus more newsworthy, and they sell more papers because they strike deeper chords with readers, most of whom are white."[29] First, the authors ignore and summarily dismiss the people of color who read, watch, and partake in the daily news. There is no articulated sense of accountability; this admission alone is evidence of pervasive racism on the part of dominant white media. More to the point, their opinions that are written as facts distort the realities of white crime as well as white middle-class men's abuse and murder of white middle-class women. As Russell points out, "Contrary to popular belief, arrests for crimes involving White offenders are the most common. . . . The public's inaccurate picture of the amount of Black crime is partly media driven. . . . Although each year two-thirds of the people arrested for street crimes are White, Blacks continue to represent the public face of street crime."[30] In Chideya's analysis of crime statistics, she reports that, in fact, "three quarters of white victims of violent crime say their attacker was white; well over 85 percent of African-American victims say their attacker was black. The same is true for murder—fully 80 percent of murdered whites were killed by other white Americans."[31]

The crimes of white middle- and upper-middle-class men are never tied to their race or class in public discourse. Media stories want to make sure that readers understand that Stuart acted as an individual, not as a white upper-middle-class married man who holds, with other white men, social economic, political, and personal power. Readers are to see him as an individual, not as someone who holds such power that he could create a situation in which a whole community could be terrorized, while he, a white man, collected everyone's sympathy, over the loss of *his* wife. Little media analysis discussed how and why it was so easy for Stuart to feed into racist fears and hostilities in Boston that resulted in terrorizing a Black inner city poor community. Nor did the media feel accountable for their participation in the hoax and its resulting impact on the Black community.

While in a number of news stories, reporters admitted the problem of racial stereotyping, they responded with defensive justifications. For instance, in response to a challenge that the coverage wouldn't be as focused if Carol Stuart had been Black, *Newsweek* writers respond by sidestepping the charges:

But the black leaders who make this point have a logic problem. They attack the double standard whereby black victims are covered less than white ones. Meanwhile, they also are angry at the negative, stigmatizing coverage of black criminals. They can't have it both ways. It would be impossible to cover more black victims without also covering more black killers as well, since most violent crime in urban American is black on black.[32]

The article is referring to two different critical analyses of the media. One addresses the differential coverage given to women who are killed and the other has to do with differential coverage of criminals. In both cases, racism underlies the presentation—underemphasis on women of color as victims and overemphasis on men of color as perpetrators against white women. In neither case does media coverage reflect social realities. For instance, in another report, a reporter defends the racialized media response by suggesting the following:

> The stereotype that he exploited was partly the product of hype—the use of Willie Horton-style scare tactics in politics, the daily 'if it bleeds, it leads' coverage of the drug wars in the local media. But it was also buttressed by some solid facts. As in many big cities, blacks in Boston commit a disproportionate amount of the city's crimes; while making up less than 25 percent of the population, they commit most of its violent crime. Urban youths kill far more readily than in the past, often for seemingly trivial reasons. While such facts may have given more weight to the prejudice in the Stuart case than the crude epithets of the anti-busing mobs, it wasn't anything to be proud of. Rationalized racism is racism all the same.[33]

The reporter here assumes he knows "the facts" about Black-on-Black crime, and does not recognize that these "facts" may be a reflection of racism in media, criminal justice, and reporting mechanisms. Chideya in *Don't Believe the Hype,* challenges such assumptions. With regard to crime in Boston, for instance, she reports from a study done by the Massachusetts Department of Public Health that found that

> poverty, not race, is the biggest factor in who turns to violence. 'South Boston, the most exclusively white neighborhood in Boston, has a homicide rate equal to that of South Dorchester/Mattapan, a poor community that is nearly 50 percent black,' the report read. But of course it is Mattapan and Roxbury, another black Boston neighborhood, that are constantly written up in the pages of Boston's homicide news.[34]

Chideya also points out that while statistics show that "black Americans are more likely to commit crimes than whites, the statistics are too often left unanalyzed." She suggests that "the numbers are skewed by a pattern of race-based treatment in the judicial system" with disproportionate arrest, conviction, and sentencing rates related to racial bias and discrimination, including in the case of domestic violence.[35] Moreover, the assumption is often made in these news articles that whites from the suburbs do not commit crimes; yet, as Russell points out, "Whites account for approximately two-thirds of the suburbanites who are arrested for murder, rape, robbery, arson, DUI, and vagrancy."[36] Moreover, with respect to the differentiations constructed between victims of crimes, Chideya further points out: "White victims are much more likely to be the beneficiaries of profiles and 'follow-ups' with their friends and families, humanizing their pain. Black victims are quick statistics. . . . While whites are cast as martyrs of crime, blacks are often cast as 'deserving' victims."[37]

To build upon Chideya's argument, it is revealing that even after Stuart's hoax was revealed, the press continued to vilify William Bennett, the young African-American man who was originally arrested for the crime. In an article in *Newsweek*, after the author considers how unjust it would have been had Bennett gotten the death penalty, he continues to attack William Bennett; he ends the essay—"Bennett has spent years victimizing those who live in his community. He is hardly alone. One of the saddest dimensions of this case is that the people who need police protection the most have been given another powerful reason to distrust it."[38] The reporters insist again that the public return its gaze to assumptions about Black criminality and away from the realities of white-on-white domestic violence as well as other violent crimes. In a similar vein, *Boston Globe* columnist Mike Barnacle continued to prosecute Bennett in his columns. He claimed that even though Bennett may not have been involved in Stuart's death, he was still a criminal. As Russell notes, the Stuart hoax follows a standard pattern in racial hoaxes where "even after the hoax is uncovered, the image of the *criminalblackman* lingers and becomes more embedded in our collective racial consciousness."[39] In this case, it not only lingers, but is reinforced in the defensive responses to charges of racist media and police practices.

The white dominant media did not ever discuss the impact of the racial hoax on the Black community. There was little to no discussion of how the police harassment affected the many Black men pulled over and interrogated. These effects are continuously minimized or absent. The social and psychological costs in people's lives, however, are significant. As Russell argues, "Numerous costs are associated with race-related police abuse. Blacks individually and as a community are psychologically harmed. . . . The impact of police harassment is cumulative.

Each negative experience creates another building block in the Black folklore about police."[40]

The myth of the Black male criminal and the myth of the white male anomaly keeps racism alive. These myths keep white women dependent on and loyal to white men (despite the public and private abuse to which these men subject "their" women). They keep the hegemonic focus on the Black community as the source of danger and criminality to whites, while remaining indifferent to violence against women of color. They deflect attention away from institutionalized racism and white supremacy as social causes for racial division, inequality, police harassment, and brutality. The myths protect white male criminals, especially those of the middle and upper classes, and it endangers white middle-class women victimized by them. Finally, they protect whiteness and white supremacist patriarchy from public scrutiny and accountability for the perpetuation of inequality and violence.

O.J. SIMPSON AND THE FABRICATED STORY OF BLACK CRIMINALITY

When Nicole Simpson and Ronald Goldman were murdered in 1995, I, like many others, became engrossed in the media spectacle. During the initial news coverage, I was struck by the decided contrast in the media stories that offered explanations for O.J. Simpson's battering and alleged murder of Nicole Brown Simpson and Ronald Goldman. In this chapter, I limit myself to some of the initial media stories, in particular the ones that sought to explain O.J. Simpson's actions as a male batterer who may have murdered his ex-wife (although most of the essays presumed he was guilty from the beginning). I am interested in drawing out the striking contrasts with the news narratives that explained Stuart's killing. This contrast exemplifies the racialized coding that I perceive underlying many discussions of the sources of men's violence against women. The news narratives that explain Simpson's violence reveal how mainstream white public discourse locates the roots of domestic violence in racial, ethnic, and class contexts—a racialization with roots in white supremacist patriarchal discourse.

As Simpson was a celebrity of stature and recognition in the public eye, and because the media mostly denies domestic violence and its link to the killing of women, the dominant mainstream media needed to make sense of his potential for violent murder. Evidently, the media and the police were less concerned when he was simply battering Nicole Brown Simpson, as many news reports noted that his battering of Nicole was common knowledge. Murder in this case escalated their interest. The media mostly downplays and individualizes domestic violence with no consistent social tradition of linking such violence to middle-class and upper-middle-class culture and families.[41] Thus, the media reporters sought to find the roots of Simpson's violence either in his psychology or in his racial identity and social class background. Given the ongoing hegemonic constructions of Black male criminality, most reporters chose the latter. The news stories often created a framework that encouraged an understanding of a man with two sides. This construction helped explain the behavior of someone who was a hero to many and yet who was now linked to battering and murder. The stories characterized O.J. Simpson as someone with a dual persona—one constructed as "white" and one constructed as "black." For instance, the headline on the cover of *People* reads— "THE MAN WITH TWO FACES" with the subheading, "One week after O.J. Simpson is accused of murder, a darkening portrait emerges of a man of infinite charm who was also willful, possessive and given to frightening rages." *Time* took this a step further by darkening the actual cover photograph of Simpson for their June 27, 1994 issue.

O.J. Simpson, the media stories suggest, created the "white" persona as a façade to cover up his true character, associated in the articles with his Blackness and his childhood experiences of growing up poor. Media stories suggest that Simpson had purposefully constructed a false self since he was a young child in order to succeed. His success in the stories is linked to his ability to present himself as "white" and as someone from a higher social class. The stories trace his "true self" to his childhood growing up in the projects in San Francisco without a father, with a violent mother, and with a history of involvement in gangs and petty criminal activity. For instance, Evan Thomas in *Newsweek* constructs the following contrast out of Simpson's life story; he writes:

> As a child in the Potrero Hill housing project of San Francisco, he learned the importance of disguising his inner life, and it was a lesson he never forgot. . . . Simpson set out to create a more pleasing self. He was gracious, warm, congenial. . . . To an extraordinary degree, Simpson convinced friends, colleagues and admirers—even, at times, himself—that this was his true character.[42]

The two selves are both implicitly and explicitly racialized in many of the initial articles that attempt to explain Simpson's domestic violence and potential for murder.

Given the media's fabricated construction of a man who portrayed a false self to the public in order to cover over the true self, the news stories link the escalation of Simpson's violence against Nicole Brown Simpson to a breakdown of the falsely constructed self. News stories in *People* and *Newsweek* allude to a "crack" in Simpson's supposed façade; in the words of Thomas, "At some point, a double life can become too much to bear. It is amazing, given the story that follows, how long Simpson kept up the façade."[43] And in the words of Schindehette, "As for O.J., he may for years have fooled himself and the world, but in retrospect it is clear that recently, even in public, cracks were beginning to emerge in his carefully constructed façade."[44]

The news stories developed their construction of his "true self" by collecting anecdotes from Simpson's childhood that supposedly reveal his inherent criminality and a history of manipulating his image so as to appear noncriminal. In some cases, they use stories from Simpson's autobiography to bolster their construction—the story of a young boy and man who, they say, created a false self to hide a manipulative, criminal, and violent self. For instance, Thomas writes, "'The ghetto,' he wrote in his autobiography in 1970, made 'you want to hide your real identity—from cops, from teachers, and even from yourself. And it forces you to build up false images.'"[45] In an article in *People,* the autobiography was also drawn upon. The article describes, "as a youth in San Francisco's Potrero Hill Projects, Orenthal James Simpson was hauled into a local police station for a minor offense."[46] O.J. Simpson had told the story that he had given his name as Burt Lancaster and that the police had believed him. The authors then quote from his autobiography—"I was really putting one over, a teenage black kid fooling the Establishment into accepting a fake identity. . . . I can understand how others got the same feeling of achievement and kept right on fooling people—and themselves—for the rest of their lives."[47]

In these stories, his racial identity and working-class background are constructed to be the root of his violence and his propensity to manipulate others so that they would see him as a "good man." Again, as Thomas constructs, "Despite his effort to rise above race, he wound up in a kind of gilded no man's land. To many whites, he was not so much enviable as safe, and to some blacks, particularly his brothers in the sports and entertainment world, he was too white."[48] Rachel Jones astutely questions the racism of these two-sided constructions; she writes:

> Was the charming affable, articulate Simpson white and the druggie sexual predator black? . . . Painting American success as a white attribute smacks of white supremacy. It's another not-so-subtle message to blacks that being black, in whatever guise, will never be good enough in this country and that the only way to even approach the pinnacle of success is to strip away that blackness and mimic the ultimate standard—white people.[49]

Moreover, as Bulkin and Thompson point out, "The O.J. Simpson case reminds us that no matter how successful a Black man becomes, he can be quickly reduced to a racist stereotype: a reverse Superman who, beneath his expensive suit, is ready to burst forth—violent and driven by uncontrollable sexual passion."[50]

Given the link between domestic violence and patriarchal family relations elucidated by feminist theorists, one could argue, as Ann Ducille does, that "If O.J. Simpson treated his wife like property, it might be read as another way in which he functioned *like a white man*. It has been easier, however, to claim his behavior as part of a black syndrome rather than a patriarchal one—as a 'black thing,' rather than a 'man thing.' Whatever else black men may be guilty of, such interpretations make their original sin blackness itself."[51] As with other crimes, domestic violence becomes associated with Blackness rather than masculinity, with roots in poverty and not in men's issues with social control and power.

Interestingly, a few articles generated about the Simpson case do discuss the issue of domestic violence more generally. Here the authors seem to draw upon theories that link battering to education and social class. In *Newsweek*, July 4, 1994, a sidebar lists "Ten Risk Factors." Among the ten were the following— "Male unemployed; male has blue-collar occupation, if employed; male did not graduate from high school; total family income is below the poverty line."[52] This sidebar is developed further in the article through references to the research of Richard Gelles, Director of the Family Violence Research Program at the University of Rhode Island. The article reports that "Richard Gelles says men who have less education and are living close to the poverty line are more likely to be abusers, many white-collar men—doctors, lawyers, and accountants—also beat their partners."[53] Thus, the gaze is refocused on working-class, poor, and/or uneducated men and women, and the violence of the middle- and upper-middle-class is alluded to, but given marked unimportance. Moreover, as in the tradition of most mainstream news articles on domestic violence, the stories focus on women's abilities to detect abusive and battering characteristics and to make individual decisions to leave their husbands or boyfriends, rather than on men's use of violence to establish power and control over women with whom they are involved.

DISRUPTING WHITE SUPREMACIST DISCOURSE ON MEN'S BATTERING OF WOMEN

Feminists need to disrupt the white supremacist patriarchal discourse on violence against women and the ways that it sensationalizes some violence, and ignores, minimizes, and individualizes most violence. The racist and classist constructions of black and brown criminality, in contrast to white individuality, must be spotlighted and challenged. The patterned discourse that defines white men's violence as an "anomaly" must be disrupted. One method of doing this is to label, explore, and explain pervasive white criminal violence against women in terms of white identity, race and class privilege, and white power in conjunction with patriarchy and male dominance. We must publicly criticize white women and men who capitalize on socially constructed white fears of Black male criminality to deflect attention away from their own criminality. The perpetuation of racialized notions of

Black criminality must be challenged in all cases, whether or not the perpetrator of violence is a person of color.

In our efforts to draw attention to violence against women, feminists must move beyond simply saying that violence happens everywhere—among all races, classes, and sexual orientations. We must challenge tendencies to single out specific groups of men for particular scrutiny. We must ask ourselves why African-American men have become symbols of violence against women? Or why Latinas are assumed to be more at risk, or why Latinos are associated with *real* machismo? Or why U.S. feminists call up images of wife killing when talking about India, as if it was wholly different from wife killing in the United States?[54] These questions are important; they must be interrogated through critical contextual analysis.

White feminists in the United States tend to perceive differences in sexism and violence against women across groups of women and attribute these perceptions to *cultural* differences. Underlying these perceptions is a belief that U.S. culture—supposedly specific to the white, middle-class, heterosexual, and Christian majority—is less sexist, more "civilized" and superior. Of course such ideas are formulated through a white eurocentric and ethnocentric lens, defining "culture" as something "different" and "other" to the so-called norm. In such formulations, white middle-class Christian culture in the United States is unspecified and often by implication in these narratives "better" for women. Uma Narayan offers an insightful contrast in her book *Dislocating Cultures*. She suggests that were an Indian journalist to come to the United States to discover the cultural roots of violence against women, she might be very frustrated with the lack of analysis of "American culture" in contrast to the many reports linking "Indian culture" to wife murder. She describes the dilemma—"She might come to see that while Indian women repeatedly suffer 'death by culture' in a range of scholarly and popular works, even as the elements of 'culture' proffered do little to explain their deaths, American women seem relatively immune to such analyses of 'death or injury by culture' even as they are victimized by the fairly distinctive American phenomenon of wide-spread gun-related violence."[55]

Similarly, in response to the stories I tell about violence in my family, listeners often project the violence onto my father's ethnicity, or to his assumed working-class background. No one has ever suggested that his professional status as a medical doctor was linked to his propensity to power and control, the central dynamics in domestic violence. And yet such an analysis might yield some important results. Interestingly, as I write this chapter, three domestic violence murders have grabbed the public's attention for a brief moment. Three doctors in Massachusetts face charges of murder. As predicted, the news stories refer to the murders by doctors as "anomalies" and as a "sad coincidence."[56] One reporter, Kay Lazar, pushes the analysis a bit further, and yet not enough. With the headline, "Deadly docs—3 accused shared power, privilege," she explores the workings of power in the three cases.[57] She notes that while the public may worry that these reports suggest that doctors are more prone to violence, experts are asking more about whether or not their odd and difficult behavior is overlooked because of their status and privilege. She alludes to a connection between the medical profession and violence, although she emphasizes that doctors are more likely victims of violence, rather than recipients. The connection she says is the motivation to have power and control—and that it is an "excessive need for power" that may motivate a few doctors to be violent. Again, however, the analysis is about individual anomalies, rather than an analysis that links the incidents to a broader social system of power.

It is incumbent upon feminists to challenge racial and class profiling of domestic violence perpetrators in order to speak to the roots of all violence and the power, control, and hierarchical systems from which it stems. Feminists need to be more critical in our analytic responses to the murders of women we read about and those that don't make the news. We must be more outspokenly critical about the way the media treats these murders and the racial and class bigotry that may inform them. In so doing, we must not allow ourselves to create social indifference and apathy to some cases and racialized hysteria to others. Barbara Schulman directs us to the social implications of our decisions in this regard; she writes:

> When we fail to acknowledge the inextricability of racism and violence against women, we contravene this country's long and sordid history of the deployment of sexual violence to advance dominant race and class, as well as gender, interests. By so doing, we inflame longstanding racial and class divisions between women. Even worse, we become unwitting accomplices in facilitating continued assaults on people of color and the economically disinherited, including the women who comprise the majorities of these groups. How can that be feminist?[58]

We must continue, in louder and more aggressive ways, to demand for ourselves and all the women who are being raped, beaten, and murdered, that our social institutions—media, criminal justice, healthcare—take all of our lives seriously.

9

TAKING BACK OUR LIVES:
Expanding Campus Efforts
to End Sexual Violence

Take Back the Night marches and speak outs are powerful events. They create a space for survivors and allies to name our experiences, to speak truth to power, to hold accountable perpetrators and the social institutions that protect them, to reclaim bodies, souls, and minds, and to take back our lives. A survivor myself, Take Back the Night marches have been enormously healing. Speaking out breaks the isolation of victimization, removes another layer of shame and self-blame, and renews my passionate commitment to continue to fight for social and institutional change. Take Back the Night reminds me that the abuse and violence I experienced was not my fault, that I was not the cause, and that it was not "just life." Over the past twenty years, I have had the honor of witnessing the stories of hundreds of different women and some men and marching with thousands to protest this violence and call for an end to it. This collective storytelling often is unsettling, enraging, and life-changing. When the stories become collective, when the violence is named as undeserved and unjust, and when it is linked to social and political institutional contexts, Take Back the Night can be transformative for those of us involved. Morales's description of healing in collective contexts speaks to the power of such events; she writes, "Healing takes place in community, in the telling and the bearing witness, in the naming of trauma and in the grief and rage and defiance that follow."[1] Transformation happens when we are compelled to action—to commit our lives to ending violence against women and to creating social and economic justice.

I have participated in Take Back the Night rallies on college campuses since the late 1970s. Until recently, I attended these rallies thinking of myself primarily as a survivor of men's violence. Sometimes I muster up the courage to tell my stories. I tend to tell my stories differently each time—sometimes I tell stories about the neighbor down the street who sexually abused me when I was five and six years old. Other times, though much less often, I tell the stories of my father's sexual and

physical abuse, and the ways I felt the Catholic Church and the medical establishment protected him. Sometimes I tell the story of when I was raped during my first
year of college and how it took me years to call it rape despite the fact that he
knocked me unconscious to accomplish his goal. Other times, though less often, I'll
tell the story of being only one of many women sexually abused by a college professor and how many in the university knew of his behaviors, but chose to stand by
and do nothing. In telling my stories, I seek to offer a feminist analysis locating the
roots of violence in a patriarchal society with social institutions that condoned, justified, and/or ignored endemic violence against women. The purpose of my storytelling is not simply for my own healing, however. Speaking out for me has always
been for the purpose of analysis in the service of social and institutional change.

I actively participate in campus efforts to create support services for survivors,
to build institutional accountability for the prevalence of sexual assault, and to
help prevent sexual assault because it has a major impact on many women college
students. Koss's study in the early 1990s found that one out of four women college
students is a victim of rape or attempted rape. Each year women tell me stories—
in my classes, in the hallways, and in my office. The mere mention of the issue in a
class often brings on stories and requests for support, information, and resources.
I know that I only hear a small fraction of the stories. I continue to be surprised at
the level of isolation, confusion, and fear among students in the aftermath of harassment, rape, and battery—surprised because I assume that most young university women have the tools and resources to label, understand, and address their
experiences. I am reminded always of my unrealistic optimism; this sustains my
passionate commitment to education and advocacy whenever the opportunities
arise.

The impact of sexual assault on a survivor's college education cannot be minimized. It contributes to students' decisions about whether to stay in school, where
to live, and what classes to take. Sexual assault can contribute to a student's sense
of safety and security on and off campus. It is often linked to their choices of social
activities and friendship networks. The experience of rape often contributes to
survivors' decisions about academic interests and career planning. The experience
often makes it difficult for survivors to focus on their academic studies and to per-
form effectively. The impact is compounded when they are isolated, when they do
not tell anyone, and when they do not seek out support and resources. In my experience, most blame themselves in some way or another. Even those who do seek
support from friends often do not attain the support they need. I know countless
stories of women who meet with minimization, denial, and blame when they tell
their friends. I will never forget a student who was drugged and raped by a man
she met at a bar. Her best friend responded by telling her that since she did not
remember it, she should not be upset by it. Many students tell me that they do not

know how to respond to friends, family members, and acquaintances who tell them they have been harassed and/or assaulted. The pervasiveness of ignorance, apathy, and minimization in response to these issues only compounds the negative impact of harassment, abuse, and violence.

These realities underscore the significance of Take Back the Night events and educational sexual assault programming on college campuses. Each program gives voice to the need to challenge the endemic threat and reality of rape in women's lives and to provide women with tools to analyze their experiences and to take action for self-determination. The efforts also force social institutions to be more responsive to survivors of violence and accountable for the extent of sexual assault on campuses. Most of the educational programs, support services, and educational policies regarding sexual assault developed in response to student protest.[2] The existence of such programs is essential. It makes a significant difference in many students' lives. Yet, as they develop within the university administrations, they become more institutionalized and less tied to the voices and perspectives of survivors and activists. Like the broader feminist movement against violence, they are more limited and narrow in scope and vision. The main cause of this narrowness, I believe, is the exclusive focus on sexual assault from within a gender-exclusive and often depoliticized framework. What this means is that the issue of sexual assault is often disconnected from social issues of discrimination and inequality, and the focus of programs is on education and support services, not institutional change. This is not to say that education and support services are not essential. Rather, in isolation they do not serve a vision of creating a socially just society which should be at the heart of feminist efforts to end violence against women.

Rape does not occur in isolation and its impact is conditioned by many other factors connected with our social identities and locations and our previous life experiences. The personal experience of and response to sexual assault is often shaped by the broader campus environment and social context. With an exclusive focus on gender roles and expectations, many programs and events marginalize explicit stories of racism, classism, and homophobia that are central to women's experiences of violence. Until the early 1990s, I mostly followed the lead and focused on men's violence against women. In so doing, often I left out the stories of abuse and violence by women in my life. I left out stories of sexual coercion in my lesbian relationships, and the stories of homophobic harassment by peers and by people on the street. When I was asked to speak more broadly as an activist and advocate, I usually left out the stories of racist, antisemitic, and xenophobic mistreatment, harassment, and abuse I've witnessed against those I know and love and those I don't. Even when I included the multidimensionality of many women's stories, they did not seem integral to the broader narrative constructed at the Take Back the Night marches and in campus sexual assault programming. As a result, the multiple sources of oppression and resistance remained less noticed and visible even when the stories were told.

Similar to the women's movement against violence in the United States, campus efforts are increasingly depoliticized and decontextualized. The dominant framework of campus sexual assault programming is heterosexual men's rape of heterosexual women. Programs honor the experience of individual survivors, but the roots of the violence are often left invisible and unspoken, beyond appeals to education and awareness. Campus organizers often conceptualize women as a monolithic group of potential and actual victims and survivors of sexual assault. In many cases, sexual assault is the sole issue; it is seen mostly in terms of individuals, and its existence is not connected to broader structures of sexism, racism, and homophobia, issues of discrimination and harassment, and experiences of intimate relationship violence. The programs rarely address women's differential experiences of violence. The way that women are often complicit in violence against women other than themselves is also mostly invisible. Many organizers seem unaware of the racialized indifference to violence against women of color and of how this indifference might be perpetuated in campus programs, services, and resources. Homophobia, racism, and xenophobia are rarely linked to campus sexual assault and to the reasons that women might not feel comfortable reporting their cases. Instead, the sole focus of campus efforts is on women as individual victims of men's violence and on gender roles and expectations as the cause of sexual assault.

Increasingly on college campuses, attention is given to the experiences of a few male rape survivors. Mostly, however, men are viewed as a monolithic group of potential and actual rapists. Programs approach men mostly as individuals who are impacted by gender roles and expectations; the broader structural inequalities and ideologies of sexism and male dominance are rarely addressed directly. When men are included in campus sexual assault educational programming, the focus is on heterosexual acquaintance rape with alcohol and miscommunication as the central causes. The harassment and assault of gay men, and the social context of homophobia, are mostly invisible. Programs generally do not address the racist profiling of Black and Latino men as perpetrators of violence, and the ways that white men are often let off the hook for sexual assault. I have never seen the racialized mistreatment and harassment by the city police or campus security addressed, nor a discussion of how this might impact campus organizing against sexual assault. Moreover, most campus sexual assault literature does not link the specific protection of white men under the guise of "boys will be boys" to white men's social privilege and power. The historical underpinning of racialized rape thus proceeds unquestioned.

The more I learn about the systems of racism, antisemitism, ethnocentrism, xenophobia, and homophobia, and their relationship to violence against women, the more critical I am when they are marginalized or minimized in feminist education and activism. Often, when some of us raise these issues, one common response is to say that we are moving away from the *real* issues—*rape* and *sexual assault*. Yet, the complexities around the incidence and response to sexual violence are integral, rather than peripheral, to building a community that does not tolerate discrimination, harassment, and violence. Another set of responses is to enlist a "diversity" of speakers for programs and to do "outreach" to underrepresented groups. However these responses are often ineffective. The first one leads to mere token participation, and the second fails because the basic approach to sexual assault remains unchanged. One result of the failure to address racism may be that women of color come to perceive sexual assault as a "white woman's issue" or as another example of the unfair racist targeting of men of color.[3] The problem is not simply "outreach" but is a substantive question of approach and strategy. When women of color and their allies (including myself) continue to critically challenge the mainstream approach, the response of mostly white women returns to "yes, but how?" and "yes, maybe, but we do not want to lose focus on the *real issue* which is *rape*?" This chapter is one effort to respond to these questions and to make some suggestions that might contribute to building a broader based campus movement against sexual violence.

FROM DIVERSITY TO ANTIOPPRESSION

In much feminist antiviolence work organized by white women, we are trained to focus on gender roles and expectations, sexism, and male dominance as the primary sources of violence against women in this society. We are not trained to analyze and strategize the multiple sources of oppression and privilege that impact women's experiences of and responses to violence. When educators and activists seek to address race or ethnicity or sexual orientation in programming, the tendency is to approach the issues as ones of "cultural" differences. Some campus sexual assault organizations create programs for specific groups of women—lesbian, African-American, Latina, Asian-American, Muslim, Jewish, bisexual women—or educational programs that include a diversity of cultural perspectives on sexual assault. On the one hand such programs are essential. They provide forums for multiple voices, stories, and perspectives for women in the audiences to find their own stories. They also help provide safer spaces for groups of women and men to talk about the particular ways that our experiences of sexual assault are shaped and impacted by racial, ethnic, class, and/or sexual identities and cultures. Events like these are opportunities for women to get validation and seek support for our own stories and lives.

For instance, events that give particular voice to the stories of lesbian and bi-

sexual women who are survivors of both same-sex and heterosexual rape are absolutely essential for lesbian and bisexual survivors. Every year I teach courses on
violence against women, and every year students tell me stories of women's violence—by mothers, lovers, friends, professors, employers, and classmates.
Women who experience women's violence feel isolated and invalidated in feminist
work against violence that only names and validates men's sexual assault of women
and that only discusses men's participation in sexism, and not women's participation in multiple systems of oppression. I am reminded all the time of the importance of giving particular voice to women's diverse experiences and perspectives.
African-American, Latina, Native-American, Asian-American, lesbian, bisexual,
disabled, Jewish, Muslim, and all women on college campuses need to be able to
tell our unique stories, to hear stories of women like ourselves, and to have access
to analysis and interpretation that allow us to change and improve our lives.
Everyone needs to have trustworthy support and validation in order to address
and heal from sexual assault, to prevent sexual assault, and to create safer lives for
ourselves, our families, and our communities. The stories are essential to building
inclusive and accessible campus services for women and men in all of their diversity. A broad range of voices and perspectives is essential to education, support
services, and activism.

Focusing on cultural diversity, however, does not necessarily challenge
racism, homophobia, classism, xenophobia, antisemitism, ableism, or any other
oppression that shapes the experience of and response to sexual assault. While
programs focused on particular groups of women and those that include a broad
range of voices and perspectives are essential, in isolation they are inadequate. As
many feminists and womanists of color argue, feminists must address the interlocking structural inequalities that shape every aspect of rape from the incidence
of rape, to the experience, to the ways that families and social institutions (including school, media, health care, and criminal justice systems) respond to rape. We
need programs that acknowledge, analyze, and seek to dismantle white and heterosexual privilege, including the integral historical and contemporary connections between rape, racism, and homophobia. As Janelle White argues, we must
connect antirape work with antioppression work. Acknowledging cultural diversity
is not an answer to racism. We need to address the ways that multiple oppressions
feed into rape, rape culture, as well as feminist movements seeking to address and
end rape. White suggests, "Movements that fail to take this into account cannot
fully succeed and may cause more harm."[4]

The inadequacy of such programs was once again made evident to me a few
years back. I was asked to present a program on sexual assault within the lesbian,
bisexual, and gay campus student communities. A few lesbian students attended
the event, no gay men attended, and none of the heterosexual women from the

campus sexual assault organizing committee attended. The lack of participation by the fuller committee communicated to lesbian students (and to me) that lesbian and gay issues are marginal and peripheral to the campus antirape agenda. While some lesbians participate in antirape organizing, the agenda rarely encompasses explicit reference to intralesbian and bisexual women's sexual assault, to rape motivated by homophobia, or to the impact of homophobia and heterosexism on lesbigay students and to their relationship to campus services and administration. When lesbian and bisexual women's identities are addressed, racial, ethnic, and national identities are often invisible. Campus organizers against sexual assault often assume white middle-class heterosexuality to be the normative identity of "most students" and they do not connect homophobia and heterosexism to (heterosexual) rape. The assumption is that heterosexuality is an identity, rather than an institution, and that it needs no interrogation. Queer students do not have a significant voice in the programs, the homophobia and heterosexism of campus services remain unchallenged, and the issue of sexual assault continues to be associated with heterosexuals.

In order to change these dynamics, campus educators, activists, and support providers need to analyze white and heterosexual privilege as they impact their understanding of sexual assault and the concerns of a broad range of students. Part of this analysis must include a look at how institutionalized heterosexism and racism create limited campus resources and services. We also need to recognize the impact of these inequalities on the experiences of queer survivors and survivors of color. Out of this analysis might come a more effective approach to developing broader participation of women and men whose needs are being unmet, ignored, and dismissed by these exclusions and limitations.

If educators, activists, and service providers do not dismantle the reproduction of white, middle-class and heterosexual privilege in campus efforts, the programs will simply continue to privilege the already privileged, and marginalize the already marginalized. One way to change this situation is to have ongoing trainings that explicitly address how racism, classism, xenophobia, antisemitism, and homophobia shape the experience of and response to sexual assault. If this is done consistently, these connections can be addressed in mission statements, in publicity, and in educational literature. Take Back the Night events may feel more welcoming to survivors of lesbian and bisexual women's violence if heterosexism and homophobia are explicitly recognized as significant campus issues connected to sexual assault, and students of color might feel more welcomed if racism and xenophobia are explicitly addressed. In addition, campus sexual assault activists might embrace and include broader campus struggles against sexist, racist, homophobic, xenophobic discrimination and harassment of queer students, students of color, disabled students, and international students, among others in their public speak out events. If the goal is to end sexual assault, we must include discrimination, harassment, and assault by a multitude of sources—by classmates, by professors, by colleagues, by staff, by administrators, by police and campus security. We need to hear the stories of faculty, students, and staff who experience homophobic, racist, and xenophobic bigotry in the dorms, classrooms, and at public events. Discrimination and bigotry significantly impact the experience of sexual assault and/or battery, and they impact how survivors perceive and enlist the resources of the university in addressing their experiences. These issues could easily be addressed by expanding Take Back the Night events, or those like them, to include multiple forms of discrimination, harassment, and assault. In efforts to make support and advocacy systems more accountable, the multidimensionality of survivors' identities and experiences must be explicit and central to the agenda.

THE DIFFERENCES BETWEEN US—
INTERROGATING WHITE HETEROSEXUAL PRIVILEGE

The mainstream campus antirape efforts tend to be white and middle-class in composition, approach, and strategy.[5] Even when a broader range of women is involved, the approach tends to remain white, heterosexual, and middle-class. This is evident in the documented resistance to addressing racism and homophobia within the national movement to address rape on college campuses.[6] What do I mean by a white and middle-class and heterosexual framework? This is a framework that assumes that women are similarly situated with regard to the experience and threat of sexual assault, as well as to the criminal justice system, support services, health care industry, and advocacy resources. Gender is the primary analytic framework. Racism, classism, homophobia, and other systems of opression are invisible or marginalized as peripheral to sexual assault. Campus activists mostly assume that rape is heterosexual and is tied exclusively to gender roles, expectations, and inequalities. Its incidence is connected with sexism, but the impact of racism, classism, xenophobia, or homophobia, for example, on the threat and incidence of rape, on the experience of rape, and on the social responses to rape is often neglected. Many feminists assume that society's inadequate, apathetic, and sometimes hostile response to rape victims/survivors is exclusively connected to systemic sexism. Many assume that the primary barrier to speaking out about rape and sexual assault is internalized sexism and sexual shame/stigma. While culture is used sometimes as an explanatory framework for some women's lack of involvement in campus organizing against sexual assault, many campus activists do not consider how hostile environments created by racism, homophobia, and xenophobia make it difficult for some women to speak out about experiences of sexual assault. Given racial discrimination generally, for instance, as McNair and Neville report, "African-American women are less likely than White women to disclose the incident to significant others and report the assault to public-service agencies."[7] The reluctance to report is most likely a result of a history of the dominant culture's indifference to the rape of African-American women and institutional hostility toward African Americans in general. Given the racism on many white dominant campuses, women of color are less likely to disclose, report, or feel safe speaking out about their experiences. Similarly, queer students are often not open about their sexual identities and would not rely on campus services for support or protection. Many perceive these agencies to be indifferent, unsafe, and/or hostile.[8] This may be compounded in situations of same-sex rape and domestic violence. Moreover, the assumptions about culture made by organizers often emanate from ethnocentric frameworks. As Dasgupta points out with regard to immigrant women in the U.S., often "they are viewed as backward, subservient, and quietly accepting of male domination and patriarchal control. . . . Such ethnocentrism contributes grievously to the culture of violence that surrounds immigrant women of color in the United States."[9] If campus activists make ethnocentric and/or racist assumptions about students of color (immigrant and nonimmigrant), we perpetuate the violence itself as well as the individual isolation of survivors.

The whiteness of sexual assault programs is never questioned, the white and heterosexual privilege of those who disconnect the issues is never interrogated, and the ways that white privilege frames the approach and strategy are never discussed. When I say "whiteness" I mean that most white students, staff, and faculty involved in campus organizing against sexual assault do not talk about, analyze, or interrogate the ways that being white as well as middle-class and heterosexual shape our understanding of rape. This would include an understanding of the roots of rape culture, the needs of rape survivors, the differences in various communities' relationship to rape and thus needs for particular approaches to rape education, among other issues. By not addressing the racial contours of "whiteness," the experiences of whites retain an aura of normativity and generality that is, in fact, particular and exclusive.

The unmarked whiteness allows white educators and advocates to argue that rape, not racism or homophobia, is the primary issue; whereas, many women of color, lesbians, bisexuals, and gay men may recognize the importance of addressing racism and homophobia in the incidence, personal experience, and social response to rape. It is white and/or heterosexual privilege that allows white heterosexual women to ignore the connections between rape and homophobia and racism. White privilege must be interrogated as part of the campus programs so that the burden of antiracism does not continue to be placed on women of color. Those of us who are white antiracist educators, service providers, and activists need to publicize and educate about how white supremacy and privilege shape the dominant social responses to sexual assault. We need to make visible the whiteness of antisexual assault agendas, literature, and programming by interrogating how race frames white women's experience, interpretation, and response to rape and the threat of rape. This is not always easy to do.

One strategy is to pay attention to the ways that racism and classism permeates discourses about violence against women, to make the whiteness visible, and to challenge its claim to normativity. For instance, I often notice that in antirape literature and in many conversations, the discourse about rape, especially on college campuses, implies whiteness, although it is not directly named. The literature emphasizes that rape can happen to *anyone*, without regard to race or class, and yet much of the literature about acquaintance rape on college campuses seems to make an implicit reference to white middle-class heterosexual women. In educational literature about sexual assault, the "good victim" is often one who is assumed to be white, middle-class, and heterosexual. Such a characterization is illustrated by the use of "The Perfect Victim" as a title to Katie Koestner's essay in *Just Sex*. While I respect Koestner's national efforts to address rape on college campuses, her use of this terminology is problematic. In the essay, she does make one reference to the racial, class, and sexual implications of her designation; she writes:

> Of course, I must acknowledge that white skin, virginity, Christianity, a prestigious college (William and Mary), good grades (I did eventually graduate magna cum laude and Phi Beta Kappa), an upper-middle-class socioeconomic status, heterosexuality, an alcohol-free date (almost—he persuaded me to have two sips of champagne), youth, and innocence had something to do with the fact that it was a 'perfect victim' image, rather than some otherwise equally 'qualified' victim, on the cover of Time.[10]

Beyond this acknowledgment, Koestner offers no further analysis. She does not use this as an opportunity to analyze the social privileges that permeate her story; moreover, she chooses to use the phrase the "perfect victim" as her title and thereby reinforces the race- and class-based system that produces it. Miriam's discussion of the "nice girl" construction ties in with Koestner's assumptions about the "perfect victim." Miriam points out, "The history of the 'nice girl' in our culture is buried in assumptions of class and race (as well as of gender)—the angel in the house, the gatekeeper of morality, the chaste, domesticated 'lady,' are all deeply coded as white and bourgeois."[11] "Innocence" has historically been tied to whiteness, heterosexuality, and middle-class status, especially in the ways that rape has been socially and legally interpreted and enforced. This system of racial and class differentiations for women, however, perpetuates rape and rape culture, because it perpetuates the idea that some women are "less perfect" and thus less deserving of attention, respect, comfort, support, and advocacy.

Teaching courses on Violence Against Women at the Massachusetts Institute of Technology for nine years was an eye-opening experience about the operation of such status designations. Students, as well as staff and faculty, considered it common knowledge at MIT that some men's fraternities organized their social life and parties along class lines (although I am one of the few that named it "class"). There was actually a common saying attributed to fraternity men at MIT—it went something like "Katie Gibbs[12] women to f___, Wellesley women to marry, and MIT women to talk to." Dating choices and parties were organized along these social lines. A white fraternity brother described his fraternity's approach to social life to one of my classes in the late 1980s. He told us that his fraternity, among others, organized separate parties for designated groups of women. For parties designed for the women from Katherine Gibbs, they served grain alcohol punch (a very potent drink) with pretzels and chips, and they played very loud music to diminish the possibilities for real conversation between the women and men. The men approached the women from Katherine Gibbs as sexual objects and prey, not as social or intellectual equals. By contrast, the parties designed for the women from Wellesley included fancier hors d'oeuvres with wine or champagne, accompanied by soft romantic music. The women from Wellesley were viewed as potential marital partners, and thus required better treatment. This student admitted what many of the MIT women already knew—fraternities often did not organize parties with MIT women in mind. MIT women were not considered appropriate for socializing purposes because they were perceived as too smart (subtext: unattractive, threatening, and possibly lesbian). In many of my classes, we analyzed the social implications of this system. When we discussed rumors about gang rape and sexual assault of women at some of these parties, especially when the rumors were about women from other schools, the women students rarely had empathy for the women from other schools. They labeled the women from Katherine Gibbs and similar schools as "sluts" and "bimbos" and thus seemingly unworthy of MIT women's concern. According to some of the students, this group of women set themselves up for abuse.

This social-class and gendered system was set up by groups of men at MIT, and yet many women reinforced it. In addressing sexual assault at MIT, I felt we needed to directly address this class-based system, otherwise, our efforts simply reinforced it. The interlocking systems of oppression and privilege that we live within continually differentiate and polarize women. Unless we directly challenge such differentiations and recognize that they privilege some women while oppressing others, our efforts to end sexual assault are limited and inadequate. When I taught at MIT and tried to raise the issues, I tended to focus on how the women from Katie Gibbs were being set up for rape; I did not talk about the privilege of the women at MIT who benefited from these social distinctions. In saying this, I do not mean to imply that women at MIT were not raped, because they were, and they too did not receive much support from one another. I do mean to imply that their privilege of being MIT students was connected to their indifference to the women from the business schools, and thus served to perpetuate a rape culture that designates some women rapeable. Moreover, the sexual assault programs and support services were benefiting only some of the women raped on the MIT campus. It is this social privilege that I would now include in my efforts to interrogate and dismantle this system.

One strategy I use to make visible white and middle-class privilege of survivors and activists is to recognize the unearned advantages I myself have experienced as a white middle-class rape survivor. Through the telling of my own stories, I label the ways that white middle-class privilege shaped my experiences of violence, survival, and healing, and my involvement in feminist activism. One obvious benefit of unearned privilege has been my ability to assume that racism and classism are disconnected from my experiences of rape. I work daily to challenge this assumption. White privilege impacts my experience in the feminist movement to end violence; I do not face racism or classism; I am not usually afraid that my stories will be truncated to fit someone else's political perspective. As a white middle-class woman survivor of rape, when I speak out against the white men who have raped and sexually abused me, I have not had to be concerned about the racial and class implications of my statements. Increasingly I label the perpetrators as white and middle-class, rather than refer generically to "men." This labeling challenges the racist and classist mythology that white and middle-class men don't harass, rape, and batter. When I speak of the feelings of shame, self-blame, and worthlessness emanating from the ongoing levels of mistreatment and abuse I've experienced, they are not automatically attached to my racial or class identity. Given the unmarked and yet entrenched class- and race-based context, I need to be mindful of the ways that my unearned privilege may render me more "deserving" of protection and to challenge this interpretation. The only times I have felt protective of my identity communities has been when my experiences of sexual abuse have been negatively connected by others to Catholicism, Italian men, and lesbians. For instance, my protectiveness arises when some people interpret my stories as if "Italian" and "Italian-American" men's sexism is somehow "worse" than the sexism of other white men. I am defensive against those who seem "titillated" by my stories and their connection to the mythologies about the sexuality of Catholic girls. Finally, it angers me when some friends and family members assume that I am a lesbian because of my experiences of child sexual abuse. I use the knowledge gained from my own protectiveness to understand and respect the impulse to protect one's own kind from outside threats, negative stereotypes and controlling images, and social contexts of hostility and bigotry.

Generally, unearned white and middle-class privilege makes me seem to others who are socially privileged like a generic (white, middle-class, heterosexual) woman un"tainted" by particulars of race, class, ethnicity, religion, or sexual orientation, which might specify my experience. This perspective exists despite my openness as an "out" lesbian; my ability to "pass" as heterosexual allows those who wish to ignore or at least minimize my specific sexual orientation to do so. This prescribed identity provides me with unearned privileges with regard to my work against sexual assault on college campuses. I am allowed to coexist in the "normative" category of rape survivors; I am labeled an "expert" because of my college education even when I'm designated a survivor; I am encouraged to speak for all survivors even though I can only truly represent myself. Most importantly, the ways that white middle-class privilege shapes my ability to speak, to survive and thrive, as well as to speak as an "expert" are often unmarked and invisible to whites. I make these specifics of my identity more visible so that social privilege is recognized for its specific contribution to my stories, and so that my stories are seen as limited in their historic and social specificity.

The strategy of making visible white and middle-class privilege challenges the so-called normativity of sexual assault support services, educational programs, and advocacy projects that are often based on the experiences of white, middle-class, heterosexual women. It can help to highlight the limitations of a gender-exclusive framework and approach. By recognizing the specificity of our own experiences, we recognize the necessity for multiple voices and perspectives in the development of programs and policies. Accepting unearned and unfair advantage with respect to a movement to end sexual harassment, assault, and battery is inimical to social justice; it means that some of us benefit and others do not. This is contrary to the vision of a feminism that seeks to free all women, not just socially privileged women.

Acknowledgment of privilege, however, is not enough. It must be linked to a committed practice of interrupting and dismantling institutionalized discrimination and the unearned privileging of only some groups of women and men in programs addressing sexual assault. For white women, this means disrupting racist, heterosexist, homophobic, and xenophobic practices that may contribute to rape culture, incidence of rape, and response to rape. It means actively working to improve and expand support services, educational programs, and institutional responses to be more inclusive and multifaceted. It means creating safer spaces for all survivors to speak out, seek support, access resources, and advocate for social justice on campus.

RACIST AND CLASSIST CODING OF SEXUAL ASSAULT ON COLLEGE CAMPUSES

In my experience, college and university administrations seem to recognize most consistently "stranger" sexual assaults by male perpetrators who are not connected to the campus community, not students, staff, or faculty. This has been a consistent pattern I've noted while teaching at the University of Illinois, Massachusetts Institute of Technology, Tufts University, Clark University, and DePaul University. In the rare cases of stranger rape or assault on these campuses, flyers are pasted all over campus with brief descriptions and sketches of the men. In most of the cases, the sketches identify the perpetrators as men of color (African American or Latino). The flyers warn women students, staff, and faculty of these "dangerous" men who are marked as outsiders to our supposedly "safe" campus community.

These isolated flyers stand in stark contrast to my knowledge of sexual assault on these very same campuses. Over the years, I have heard hundreds and hundreds of stories of sexual harassment, sexual assault, and physical violence against women. As well, I have heard stories of racist, homophobic, and xenophobic harassment and rape, and in a few cases physical assault. In most of the cases where students have sought redress for these assaults, campus administraters have not responded with a comparable outcry. I have never seen posters or warning signs indicating areas of campus known for sexual harassment or sexual assault. There is no hostile environment for campus-based rapists and harassers; there is a hostile environment for those who speak out about harassment and rape on campus, however. Similarly, I have heard no comparable outcry to the plethora of stories I hear about racial harassment of students of color—by roommates, by faculty and staff, by the staff of local stores, and by the police. I hear no comparable outcry to the stories of homophobic harassment—by students in the dorms, by heterosexual faculty and staff, and by people on the street. And yet I hear the individual stories much more often than stories of "stranger" rape and assault. When the rapes occur off campus, they are also not given the media spotlight and the campus administrations are not involved.

In the early 1990s, in response to institutional indifference to campus sexual assault, a group of women students at Brown University took control over their own stories. They began to list names of men who had raped them on a bathroom wall in the main library at the university. The list began with just a few men's names, but quickly grew to around thirty names. When efforts were made to erase and wash over their words, the women rewrote the names; they were not going to allow anyone to "wipe out their experiences." Of course, the university, media, and public were appalled! The women were assumed to be accusing "innocent men." Their actions were labeled as divisive, unfair, and disrespectful. Never mind that each of the women involved had attempted to bring charges against these same men through official channels. In fact, four of the women had attempted to work with administrators over the previous spring and summer to make the system work better for women. Their input was ignored and dismissed. Their experience is a common one across the country despite pressures to the contrary.

The writing on the bathroom wall did elicit a response from Brown's administration. A forum was held and hundreds of women attended. Many wore red to make themselves a visible and strong presence. The Brown students' grievances parallel those of women at most colleges and universities. Insensitive, ignorant, and inconsistent responses on the part of administrators were high on the list. Placards quoted some of their responses—"your rape can be boiled down to a case of bad chemistry," and "sometimes he forced you, sometimes he didn't. You can't have it both ways." Another read, "You really need to find it in your heart to be more forgiving," and yet another, "I met with the men, and they seem like fine, upstanding young gentlemen." The women's stories documented the indifference, minimization, and trivialization of women's experiences of sexual assault. In many of these cases, the men were white and middle-class students.

These responses, again, stand in stark contrast to the response to "stranger" rape. When "stranger rapist" flyers are the only ones given sanction as "official warnings" to the campus community about rape, while the ongoing intracampus and intragroup rapes are ignored, the flyers feed racist and classist myths that men of color and working-class/poor men are the ones more prone to rape. These flyers work in conjunction with campus security efforts that focus on safety lighting across campus, safe-rides, and self-defense training for women (mostly oriented toward stranger assaults). I am not disregarding the potential for "stranger" assault nor for assaults on the street; I am questioning the exclusive focus on these given that most sexual assaults of women students are by men that women know— friends, boyfriends, acquaintances, and co-workers, not "strangers."

The flyers warning women of "stranger" rapists also contribute to an already existing hostile environment for male students, staff, and faculty of color who work and/or live on campus. Many experience the feeling of being held suspect as members of the campus community. Over the years, I have heard many stories of African-American and Latino students being stopped on campus by campus security and city police, asked for identification, and interrogated about their activities. Many students tell me about the emotional impact of these interactions and the toll it takes on their education as well as their own sense of security on campus. When a man of color is identified as a rapist, the tendency is for all men of color in the vicinity to be held suspect. This has led to increased racial tensions on college campuses. Flyers like these also contribute to the multiple binds facing women of color who experience and witness the hostile environment created by racism in relation to rape and yet who have been raped and need to address their own experiences as well. Many may not want to report rape for fear of reinforcing and contributing to racism.

None of the intracampus violations get the necessary attention to stop their perpetuation. Again, I never see signs up to identify acquaintance rapists, racists, or homophobes. At all of the universities that I have attended and taught, I have seen little to no public attention given to homophobic, racial, and antisemitic harassment. Students who experience having the words "die dyke die" across their dorm doors, or who try to pursue charges of acquaintance rape against male students, or who are harassed by security are not given the same public recognition as "stranger" assaults. And so, the ongoing harms of sexism, racism, and homophobia in campus communities continue to create an often hostile, negative, and defeating environment for those targeted.

The more I've learned about racism and rape, the more I challenge the racism of white officials and institutions who try to lure me into their camp by appealing to the "protection" of my supposed "innocent" white femininity. One illustrative example happened a few years ago when I was walking down the street near DePaul University's campus. An older African-American man approached me to ask directions and to chat about my coat. Minutes after we parted ways, and I continued walking to campus, an unmarked police car zoomed up to the side of me. Two white men jumped out of the car, showed me their police badges, and began to interrogate me about my conversation with this African-American man. They insisted that he was standing too close, that he was threatening, and that he was dangerous. I disagreed and refused to participate in the targeting of this man for their racist agenda. These white police officers were trying to scare me into asking them for "protection" by drawing on racist fears and they were doing so at the expense of a fellow human being. Had I not known the historical connections between racism, the myth of the Black rapist, its unjust targeting of African-American men, and the so-called white supremacist claim to "protect" white women from "other" men, I may not have seen through their racist actions masked by protective gestures. While I mentioned this history to them, they simply responded with the insinuation that I was simply a naïve white woman liberal.

Feminist efforts addressing sexual assault must label and challenge these racialized constructions. If we do not, we contribute to unabashed racial harassment and to institutionalized racism within our universities and in the criminal justice system. We can do this by educating ourselves and our college campuses about the link between racism and rape. We can draw attention to differential treatment when it occurs and protest it. We can encourage students to speak out against racialized discrimination, harassment, and assault at Take Back the Night marches. We can encourage alliances between groups addressing sexual assault and those addressing racism and homophobia. We can create joint educational programming and collaborate when working for institutional change so that our efforts do not inadvertently serve to hurt one group in the service of helping another.

TAKING BACK ALL OF OUR LIVES

Multiple and interlocking systems of oppression and privilege must become integral to the agenda of educators, activists, and service providers who are committed to addressing sexual assault on college campuses. This means that they become essential ingredients in the overall analysis, in speak outs, in programs, in support services, in advocacy, and in policy-making. Sexual assault is not an isolated issue that impacts generic individuals with unidimensional histories, identities, and experiences. The existence of sexual assault is connected to broader structures and ideologies. In students' lives, it is connected with our social locations and our relative experiences within the broader campus community and society. Take Back the Night must be multidimensional and complex in order to address the realities of everyone in the community. We cannot support, advocate, and serve one group of people at the expense of another. In addressing one layer of oppression, our efforts must not ignore or reinforce another. If the overall goal is to create a community that takes all of our lives equally seriously, we must create approaches that value each and every one of us in all of our complexity.

PART IV

TRANSFORMING FEMINIST RESISTANCE THROUGH STORYTELLING

10

THE STRUGGLE FOR INTEGRITY IN AN UNJUST WORLD:
Feminist Resistance Through Storytelling

"[A]s powerful as the wielders of death appear, in the end life is stronger."
—Aurora Levins Morales, *Medicine Stories*

"The mind struggling toward integrity does not accept someone else's version of the story of life: this mind demands that life itself must be confronted, over and over, by all who live it. The mind struggling toward integrity confronts the evidence and respects experience."
—Andrea Dworkin, *Letters from a War Zone*

Throughout my life I have constructed stories to understand myself and to come to terms with the contradictions inherent in my historical realities. The stories changed and evolved over time, as stories do. Through these stories, I have shifted through the interlocking layers of victimization, surviving, thriving, and fighting the abuse and violence in my life. In *Letters from a War Zone*, Andrea Dworkin aptly describes a woman's struggle to decolonize her mind; she writes:

> The mind struggling toward integrity will fight for the significance of her own life and will not give up that significance for any reason. Rooted in the reality of her own experience—which includes all that has happened to her faced squarely and all that she has seen, heard, learned, and done—a woman who understands that integrity is the first necessity will find the courage not to defend herself from pain. The colonized mind will use ideology to defend itself from both pain and knowledge.[1]

From an early age, questions of reality and illusion haunted me. It wasn't a philosophical issue for me, it was based in my conflicting material, linguistic, emotional, and bodily experiences. I grew up in the confines of an idealized Catholic, upwardly mobile middle-class family with a strong sense of ethnic identifications in Italian- and Irish-American cultures. I am college educated, currently a professor in Women's Studies, and I experience on a daily basis the *unearned* privileges and benefits of being white and middle-class in the United States. This description of my identity is coupled with my multiple and layered experiences of mistreatment, harassment, rape, and battery throughout much of my life. My father's sexualized misogyny resulted in sexual, physical, and emotional abuse and violence against me and other members of my family; my mother's internalized misogyny resulted in passivity in relation to my father and in physical and emotional abuse against her children. My father's social power and privilege afforded him a veneer of privacy and protection from state intrusion such that the violence was minimized and/or blamed on the "rebellious" kids and/or excused through projection onto his Italian-American ethnicity. A neighbor's sexual abuse of me contributed to the confusion and chaos of childhood. The multiple experiences of abuse throughout my childhood laid the groundwork for ongoing mistreatment, sexual abuses, and rapes in the contexts of my personal and social networks as a young adult.

The socially constructed stories that I have drawn upon throughout my life have been contradictory, with my experiences often directly conflicting with the available and popular narratives of the time. Our experiences are shaped by the socially constructed stories that we tell about our lives. The stories are different depending on who we are—our experiences, our social positionalities, our historical and political contexts, and the available social narratives, as well as from whose perspective the stories are told.

Storytelling is a way to make sense of life as well as to live life. In the context of narratives and their involvement in healing from abuse, Freedman and Combs write, "the narratives we are talking about are the stories that people *live*. They are not 'about' life; they *are* life as we know it, life as we experience it. Since, as far as meaning, hope, fear, understanding, motivations, plans and the like are concerned, our life narratives are our lives, it makes all the difference in the world what sort of narrative is available to a person." [2] In this chapter, I explore the available and changing stories that have shaped and continue to shape my memories, experiences, understandings, and responses to the sexualized abuse and violence that I experienced in my life. Throughout the last forty years of my life, I have challenged parts of the "realities" offered in available narratives. My abilities to truly reconceptualize myself, to reclaim my soul and body, to resist oppression, to acknowledge and take responsibility for privilege, have been deeply connected to whether or not the narratives subverted, rather than justified and perpetuated, injustice and inequality. Aurora Levins Morales makes clear the interconnections between storytelling and the experiences of and responses to abuse when she writes, "However the abuse is perpetrated, the result is the same: abuse does not make sense in the context of our humanity, so when we are abused, we must either find an explanation that restores our dignity or we will at some level accept that we are less than human and lose ourselves and our capacity to resist, in the experience of victimhood." [3]

CATHOLICISM

"Two or three things I know for sure, and one of them is the way you can both hate and love something you are not sure you understand."

—Dorothy Allison,
Two or Three Things I Know for Sure (1995)

Catholicism shaped my early girlhood. Being born into a Roman Catholic, upwardly-mobile, middle-class family meant that I, along with other members of my family, relied on the Church for identity and life understanding. I attended Catholic schools from first grade through eighth grade. The nuns and priests of the Parish were part of our extended family. They would often come over for Sunday dinner and they were central to our lives. I felt that the nuns and priests, as well as the broader community of friends, idealized my father and *his* family, and proceeded to overlook or to minimize his abusiveness, or to justify it by blaming it on the kids. I experienced my father as a tyrant—an angry frustrated man who had the power to control us through his physical, sexual, and verbal violence, his emotional manipulations of our identities and actions, and his social power in the extended family and in the community. My mother was a passive recipient of my father's disrespect and abuse; she took her repressed anger out on her children both through denial of my father's abuse and her own brand of physical and verbal aggressions. Family relations were tense and volatile; as kids, we were always on alert for the next explosion. My memories of the explosions included being hit, beaten, ridiculed and chastised for the smallest of infractions, and being sexually abused.[4] Because of the difficulties of my childhood—specifically sexual, physical, and emotional abuse within the family as well as in the neighborhood—I looked to God and to the Church for understanding and for redemption. I often thought that if I prayed loud enough and often enough that the abuse, the misdirected rage, the dysfunction, the pain, and the sadness would end.

The Catholic narratives that I grew up with deeply shaped my experiences of abuse and consequently the construction of my identity. First of all, the prevailing Catholic patriarchal ideology was key to understanding myself and my role in the family. As Tish Langlois, for instance, suggests, a Catholic framework includes "the disparagement of women's sexuality in historical and theological writings; a theology of ownership that has historically protected men's proprietorship over women and children, including the right to violate women's and children's physical, sexual, and emotional boundaries; the exclusion of women from positions of leadership and authority within the church; . . . and Catholicism's emphasis on suffering and self-sacrifice."[5] Taken collectively, the Catholic Church taught young girls like myself to be ashamed of our bodies and of our sexual desires, to submit to male authority despite its cost to our own integrity, and to minimize if not deny our own needs and desires. My struggle to understand, let alone to validate, my own reality was compounded in this context; Sumrall and Vecchione describe, "Although the Church demands truth from its faithful, we learn early that the word of God, the priests, and the nuns have more credibility than our own experience. The Church instills in us a belief that we are in essence born scarred and must atone for the Original sin that we inherited from Eve. We must repent, silence ourselves, submit. For Catholic girls the need to define one's truth is crucial."[6] One of the key stories that I learned from Catholicism was the one about disobedient, disappointing, and ungrateful children who need discipline and punishment to purge their flaws.

The Catholic Church of my white, upwardly-mobile, middle-class childhood supported an idealized family and social structure that enforced white patriarchal authority and white men's power over women and children. Women and children were treated as subordinate to men; the Church, in collusion with broader social institutions (media, law, education), granted white husbands and fathers the authority to control and dominate the lives of their family members. As Tish Langlois explains, the church's teachings officially and consistently promote "a hierarchy of social privilege within the ideal Catholic family: children defer to parents, women defer to men and men assume a natural and rightful position as the head of the family."[7] No one outside this legally and socially protected private upwardly-mobile white Catholic family was to question the father's authority; moreover, women and children were to remain loyal to the father and to *his* family no matter what the circumstances.[8] In this context, my mother and we kids deferred to my father. The mandate of Catholicism was to be obedient, to follow the rules no matter how arbitrary, and to not question authority. As kids, we tried to follow the dictates, but the rules often changed and their arbitrariness made it hard to predict outcomes. Instead, we simply felt guilty for making our parents lives miserable, and then we set about scrutinizing and patrolling one another's flaws and disobedience.

Growing up in this conflicted context of idealized family values entangled with sexual abuse, chaos, and explosive anger and violence, I felt confused and angry, yet I also had a kind of loyalty to my father and the family he created. On the one hand, my father's dominance seemed grandiose and charismatic—he seemed to be loved by many people and the extended family treated him as a kind of "God" figure because of his upward mobility and his medical knowledge. From a patriarchal upwardly-mobile middle-class family framework, it seemed like I was quite fortunate. My father and his friends, as well as my mother and our extended family, seemed to celebrate this idealized version of paternalistic authority and dominance as exemplified by my father. He seemed to be an emerging leader in the community, and certainly in his family, and so how lucky I must be to have him as a father. On the other hand, his attitudes and actions were often unjust, sexist and misogynistic, irrational, and full of an unexplained rage. The glorification of his paternalism in the face of his explosive rages and violence seemed contradictory to say the least, and at the most mind numbing. I remember the confusion of my seven-year-old self when I was confronted at the local bowling alley with a community member's praise of my father's kindness, gentleness, and generosity; I stood in awed silence wondering how her story fit into my own experience of his explosive temper, his unending disappointment in who we were, and his lack of tolerance for our many imperfections. In retrospect, my experiential reality was "gaslighted" by his social power and charismatic authority, as Rich describes when she writes, "Women have been driven mad, 'gaslighted,' for centuries by the refutation of our experience and our instincts in a culture which validates only male experience."[9] The discrepancy between the idealized version of my father and the material reality experienced as a daughter under his power and control created a major faultline in my Catholic narrated girlhood identity.[10]

The Catholic churches and schools of my childhood encouraged self-sacrifice and invisibility for girls and women. Martyrdom was the order of the day; the priests, nuns, and lay teachers rewarded us with praise for higher and higher levels of commitment to it. The community I grew up in required self-sacrifice of women and girls and submission to the needs, desires, and dictates of the white middle-class men in the family and in the community. Loyalty was always to men, not to women. As Tish Langlois describes, "The dominant forms of consciousness meant, quite simply, that the desires and needs of males were 'respected' while females were expected to sacrifice their own."[11] Our extended family and the community of friends seemed to expect my mother to erase her needs, desires, hopes, and dreams and to accept the substance and structure of my father's control and dominance. The Catholic community expected women to serve men, to accept male authority, and to be silent. All of this despite my mother's growing sadness and disconnectedness. She swallowed her anger and resentment, packed away her own needs and often those of her children when it came to safety and bodily integrity, and accepted the dictates of the male dominance in her midst. In some ways I followed in my mother's self-sacrificing footsteps, despite my anger at her passivity. The story of self-sacrifice, while tempered, remains to this day. Self-sacrifice, however, must not be mistaken with complete powerlessness nor passivity, as I have been rewarded with praise for the sacrifices I have made for family and friends. As a "dutiful daughter," I moved home in 1981 to help my mother when my father became sick and died; I continued to live with her and my youngest brother for another two years as a way of helping the family. While my feminist friends often critiqued my family's expectations and my compliance with them, my family appreciated my efforts. I too felt good about my choices as they relieved some of the residual guilt that might have haunted me later and they fed into my selfless, self-sacrificing story. Even when I am not explicitly rewarded, I have elevated my self-worth by stories of self-sacrifice. I can still boost my self-image through my stories of selflessness and giving unto others; such a story can be about a saintly and heroic role, even though often thankless, devalued, and self-destructive.

The Catholicism of my childhood also mandated that women and girls be virgins until married into monogamous heterosexual unions. Sexual purity was high on the list of criteria for self-worth, although many of the Catholic girls that I knew were not virgins. As Langlois describes, "Catholic sexual ideology's rigid regulation of sexuality, along with the profound repercussions for 'immoral' sexual behavior, worked against the survivors by creating a culture of *erotophobia*—a culture in which fear, denial of, and punishment for sexuality were the norm."[12] Catholicism offered scripts of self-blame, shame, and worthlessness to women and girls who were sexually impure whether we chose to be sexually active or whether we were forced. In speaking of the survivors that she interviewed, Langlois reflects, "the very act of incest, which constituted a serious breach of Catholic sexual ideology, compounded the survivors' feelings of unworthiness, guilt, and self-blame."[13] This script led to an inability to articulate sexual abuse and further entrenched the shame that attended it. Within the narratives of my Catholic girlhood, no language existed to discuss sexual activity, violated bodies, or family sexual transgressions. The only framework I had to work with was the virgin/whore dichotomy. Within this frame, I most certainly fit into the category of slut and whore. This was reconfirmed by family and authority figures in the schools I attended. As a result, I felt like I deserved whatever mistreatment I received. This script is inherently gendered within Catholicism; the heterosexual men I have known in and outside of my family have never been held accountable for their sexual activity outside or within the context of marriage and family.

In contrast to the Catholic narratives of self-sacrifice, self-blame, and shame, there was also one about gratefulness. The Catholic priests, nuns, and teachers encouraged me to be grateful for what I had been given in this life. They considered complaining and asking questions as selfish and ungrateful. In the face of the serious breaches of bodily integrity and attacks on my personhood, I remember clinging to a song I learned in the schools that taught me to be grateful for having eyes to see, hands to hold, legs to walk, and ears to hear, and to recognize how very lucky I was indeed. The church, schools, network of friends and family encouraged me to be grateful for the accumulating class privilege that my family was gaining as a result of my father's profession as a medical doctor. The mandate to be grateful created a context where I felt I had to be passive, to accept injustice, and to somehow recognize that I had it made. The nuns, priests, teachers, as well as my parents discouraged and often punished me for asking critical questions about the discrepancies between discourses and realities. They did not like it when I drew attention to the conflicts seething underneath the publicly constructed ideal family, and when I challenged the personal and social injustices seemingly condoned by the community at large. On the contrary, they rewarded me when I seemed grateful and obedient, even if self-destructive and withdrawn.

RUNNING AND DISAPPEARING INTO THE FOG

> "Women run away because they must. I ran because if I
> had not, I would have died. No one told me that you take
> your world with you, that running becomes a habit, that
> the secret to running is to know why you run and where
> you are going—and to leave behind the reason you run."
> —Dorothy Allison,
> *Two or Three Things I Know for Sure* (1995)

By the seventh grade, I gave up on the idea of God and on the integrity of the Catholic Church. God didn't seem to be listening to my prayers. I was sent to the principal's office for asking questions, including one time when I asked about reincarnation (hoping for a better life) and didn't understand the refusal to explain why it wasn't possible. The nuns seemed deadset against me and colluded with my father in silencing me. I began to voice the contradictions making up my life experience; I confronted my father at twelve with my newly formed belief that there was no God. I had learned the definition of "hypocrisy" in school and I found it a refreshing one word response to the chaotic contradictions surrounding me. The word aptly seemed to describe the discrepancies between Catholic moral proclamations and actual behavior. I confronted my father and the teachers in the schools about some of these discrepancies. For instance, I was most troubled by the discrepancy between the rhetoric of service to others and yet the active disassociation and condemnation of anyone who was not Catholic; the discrepancy between proclaiming love for all of your neighbors and yet excluding people on the basis of race from the Parish and its neighborhoods; and the discrepancy between moral dictates against the use of drugs and alcohol and yet the unquestioned presence of alcoholic adults within and outside our families.

I began to seek out alternative frameworks to guide my life and construct my identity, although the narratives of Catholicism continued to simmer below the surface. I turned to the high school youth culture of "sex, drugs, and rock and roll" for both rebellion and escape—rebellion against the standards of white middle-class Catholic girlhood and a hoped-for-escape from the pain of its labels and shame. If I couldn't change reality, I'd simply escape it, at least that's what I told myself at the time. This was the early 1970s—a time of social tension as well as change. I heard vague references from the conservative white-dominant media and schools in Central Illinois about the counterculture movement, hippies, and the civil rights and women's movements. I had no direct reference point at the time, but change was in the air and I gravitated toward what I perceived to be a more rebellious youth culture with the hope of constructing a new identity and a different life. What I found was a subculture that ultimately was just as conservative, repressive, and bigoted as what I was trying to run from. Both groups shared a commitment to denial as well as acceptance of mistreatment and abuse, both enforced the feminine virtues of passive conformity to the dictates of men, both policed the boundaries of racial segregation in personal and social relationships, and both reveled in the (ab)use of drugs and alcohol to numb discomfort and unhappiness.

I constructed myself against my family's conservative attitudes and practices, but only through a process of numbing and making myself absent, a process actually supported by my immediate as well as extended family. Contradictions filled my daily existence. On the one hand, I had been taught that using alcohol and drugs was wrong; on the other hand, my extended family and broad network of familial friends were involved in alcoholism and hidden drug addictions. As an adolescent and young adult, I found a kind of glamour in the parties and the chaos. The conflicts enacted in the family amid the big parties to celebrate loved ones whether in marriage or death felt melodramatic and surreal. I remember loving the Godfather films as they captured the essential dynamics in my family—the high melodrama in the extended family and network of close relationships involving betrayal, grief, guilt, shame, and loss, the demand for family loyalty amid incredible dysfunction, the glamorized mistreatment and abuse of women, and the celebrations of patriarchal dominance and power. It was all there; unfortunately my life wasn't a movie and living it wasn't quite as glamorous as I would have liked. The Godfather motif, however, provided me with a framework to explain my family to others and my melodramatic tales kept all my friends intrigued and laughing.

The subculture of drugs and alcohol provided a mental fog into which I ran. This fog supported my desire to numb out the difficulties and contradictions in my life, to repress my anger and rage, and to keep my conflicting realities from crashing into one another. Yet, the fog created the conditions for the perpetuation of sexual abuse. It made it difficult to name what was happening to me. I ended up experiencing and being subject to ongoing incidents of abusive mistreatment, rape, and battery in my heterosexual relationships with men and eventually in my relationships with women. Consuming whatever I could find to dull the heartache, I had an active and often conscious resignation to what I perceived to be the narrative of my life.

And yet despite the mental fog layering my experiences, I continued to read and to observe the world around me in search of escape routes. The stories I sought out were ones of middle-class rebellion against and escape from unjust authorities. One of the TV shows I liked was Perry Mason; sometimes I would imagine myself as a daughter lawyer who would fight against injustice. In my friendships, I fashioned myself an ally to those who were being mistreated and hurt by people in authority, be it social or institutional. I felt contempt toward those with illusions of "superiority" and I distanced myself from them as far as possible.

As a young college student, I began to hear different narratives about families. I met other kids my age who had never been hit, who got along with their families, and who didn't consume drugs to blot out their lives. I was surprised and intrigued. I began to take psychology courses; I found my own flaws in most of the books and actively began a process of seeking out labels for myself as I downed more beers and any drugs I could get my hands on. Luckily, I was repulsed by the mandate to conduct experiments with mice, and I decided to pursue a different major. However, my short time in psychology, in conjunction with meeting people with different experiences of family, led me to question the ongoing problems in my family and to seek more answers. It was this growing knowledge and my physical separation from home that enabled me to more actively challenge my father's white patriarchal class authority.

As an undergraduate, I did not live in the same town as my family, and yet I tried to stay connected with my younger sisters. I had high hopes of helping them to navigate more safely through my father's anger, control, and violence. Both were trapped in my family—the older three kids were gone and so the realm of control and dominance narrowed. I watched as my sisters retreated into a similar world of drugs and alcohol. The family tensions seemed to escalate. My sisters' rebellion against my father seemed more direct than that of the older kids. He felt more threatened and out of control. His response to my sisters rebellious unhappiness was to exert more control over their lives; he used his institutional authority to reign my sisters in through psychiatrists and psychologists. I tried to be my sisters' ally by advocating for them against my father's power and the church and the medical establishments that actively supported his efforts to control them. In my dreams, I was able to convince him of his wrongs and of the need to change; in my fantasies, I was able to stop the narrative of abuse and to prevent my sisters from symbolically losing their lives. My narratives, however, were naïve and unrealistic. In the end, the family as a whole was forced to live under the structural constraints dictated by *his* story, after all, he was the one with socially conferred power to do with us, especially those still under his direct supervision, whatever he wanted. It was his story of my sisters' delinquency along with his status as a medical doctor that built his justification for their submission to medical authority and power. The doctors, the schools, the extended network of friends and family accepted his story as truth and thus accepted his determinations. As a result, both sisters were institutionalized at different times; my youngest sister was sent away more permanently to a behavior modification institution. My dreams and fantasies of heroic intervention lived out by actual attempts were smashed and I felt responsible for the losses. I continued to numb out and to try to cope as best I could; it took me years to untangle the web of responsibility and to rewrite the story of my resistance (but now I'm getting ahead of myself).

FEMINISM: FROM DRUGS TO POLITICS

Drugs served to numb my rage and block out my memories of my childhood that might have helped me to understand what was going on in my life, and yet the effects were devastating. One friend killed himself, several overdosed, and still others became more and more strung out and lost. Due to a series of my own "bad experiences," including close calls with drugs and death, I transferred to a different university. Here I discovered politics. What a blessing this was. Socialist and feminist politics helped me to question the destructive benefits of drug abuse, although it took many more years to pull myself completely away from the comforts of drug and alcoholic numbness and fog. Social activism provided me with an outlet for my anger, directed my rage, and pulled me out of the morass of self-destruction. In many ways, feminism's analysis of sexism and misogyny saved my life. It offered me a space to express righteous anger and rage about injustice; it provided a method of externalizing the pain in my life and it facilitated the beginning of the life-long process of decolonization. Politics began to replace the drugs that were beginning to devastate my life and the lives of many of my friends.

Feminism and socialism gave me a language to understand my place in the world and to name the structures that shaped people's lives, including my own. I began to redirect my grief, anger, and rage and to externalize the location of the problems in the world rather than to internalize them. All of the sudden, things began to make sense. I remember some of the early markers of recognition directly related to my earlier confusions. Mary Daly's *The Church and the Second Sex* and Gena Corea's *The Hidden Malpractice: How American Medicine Mis-*

treats Women particularly come to mind in relation to the story I am constructing in this chapter.[14] Both of these books were eye-openers as to the lies of the patriarchal and misogynist institutions that were particularly responsible for my confusion, my powerlessness, and my vulnerability. The feminist critique fueled at the same time that they clarified my anger at the Catholic Church and at the medical system that had produced my father and had protected his abusive misuse of power and authority. I felt alive!

Through my active participation in the women's movement, women's studies classes, and in rape crisis trainings, I began to reframe the stories of my childhood and young adulthood. Things began to make sense in a very different way. The naming of women's experiences of sexual harassment, incestuous assault, rape, and battery cleared out some of the debris of victim-blaming and misogyny. I began a process of redefining "bad experiences" as "rape" and "child sexual abuse," and I began to locate the problems in male dominance and power, not in my own individual failings. The fortresses of shame and stigma built up over the years began to crack. Much of this was due to the process of hearing women's stories and beginning to tell my own. Aurora Levins Morales writes:

> When individual people are abused, the events themselves become a story of our worthlessness, of our deserving no better. We must struggle to re-create the shattered knowledge of our humanity. It is in retelling the stories of victimization, recasting our roles from subhuman scapegoats to beings full of dignity and courage, that this becomes possible. The struggle we engage in is over whose story will triumph, the rapist's story or the raped woman's, the child abuser's or the child's, the stories of bigoted police officers or those of families of color whose children are being murdered. The stories of perpetrators are full of lies and justifications, full of that same projection that holds the abused responsible for her abuse. The stories of the abused are full of dangerous, subversive revelations that undermine the whole fabric of inequality.[15]

The world began to split open. Feminism shed new light on the stories I'd been telling since childhood. Feminist friends would interrupt my sarcastic and funny stories about my family and my intimate relationships with emphatic statements like—"Ann, it's not funny, it's horrible." A small piercing light would break through the fog and I'd have a glimpse into another story waiting to be told. As Faye, an incest survivor who participated in Langlois's study says, "You have this idea of what you were like as a child and how you grew up and that's your view of reality. But when you start to remember abuse that view just cracks. . . . It's like a fissure goes right through reality and what looked like reality you realized wasn't reality at all. . . . It feels like you're crazy, like you're losing your mind."[16] But as she says, it's the illusions that begin to crack, not the realities.

The feminist stories I first connected to were stories of institutionalized male dominance and misogyny. Stories of family chaos, confusion, and melodrama became stories of male dominance, race and class privilege, and the masking of abuse and violence. My stories became woven into broader more complicated stories of oppression and privilege. The overlapping narratives created renewed identities focused on resistance and social change. The stories of male domination were easy stories for me, at least on the surface. My anger at my father was longstanding and my resentment of his power was not new. In some ways, the analysis of male dominance allowed a kind of depersonalized relationship to my father and to the men in my social networks who were sexual harassers, abusers, and rapists. I simply saw them as "the enemy" and that felt great. Finally I felt I had some clarity—there were victims and there were perpetrators, most perpetrators were men, most victims were women, men were guilty, women were innocent.

The hurt and betrayal I experienced as a child and young adult got translated into raw anger at the injustice of their actions and the larger system that supported them. I participated in Take Back the Night marches, I wrote articles, I taught courses that analyzed the violence in women's lives in terms of sexism and misogyny manifested not only in individuals but in social institutions—in the criminal justice system, the health care system, the Catholic Church (among other religious institutions), the educational system, among others. The more I told the stories, the more I learned about what had happened to me and to many thousands of other women, and this knowledge, as it accumulated in my mind and heart, led to outrage as well as despair. It produced in me a deep commitment to social change and social justice. I dedicated myself to the women's movement against violence, and through this I expanded my horizons to the multitude of efforts and projects whose goal is to challenge and to end all forms of racial, economic, sexual, and international injustices. I will never go back; I am committed to the long haul and to the revolutionary transformations necessary to building a truly human community. The knowledge of violence and its impacts, however, also led to an enormous grief and despair for which I didn't have an outlet.

My intellectual and political storytelling fueled my intellect and helped pull me out of the emotional entanglements of denial and internalized rage. However, the stories did not necessarily soothe my heart and soul, nor help me to build the emotional skills necessary to name ongoing patterns of emotional and sexual abuse in my personal relationships. My political analysis, in other words, did not necessarily sit well with my emotional and experiential realities. I could provide the abstract analysis of women's stories, I could intellectualize the dynamics of oppression, and yet I still had trouble telling my stories, believing my stories, accepting my stories, and restoring my own self. Parts of myself had not caught up with my politics. I still had trouble recognizing and naming abusive mistreatment, especially in my intimate relationships. The old pulls of self-blame, shame, and self-hatred continue to rear their ugly heads, even as I write. The defenses of my life have been to numb, distance, minimize, and deny; in some ways, my political analysis can sometimes serve to distance and minimize as well. My feelings sometimes continue to be in conflict with the narrative I provide as a teacher and advocate against violence against women to the public. The question is how to reconcile my political analysis of my life with my emotional turmoil in the context of that same life. My feminist political analysis and participation have been necessary and yet not sufficient to create a whole self and to build a life of integrity. The internal conflicts have been sharp and steadfast. Simply naming the experience has not been enough and the story of male dominance is limited. The stories did not speak to the grief of violence, of betrayal, of self-blame, of self-loss, of shame; nor did the narratives speak to my privilege, to my resistance, to my strengths and powers.

FEMINISM MODIFIED AND MULTIPLIED

The stories of male dominance trace my life through the lens of oppression and violation, and while the stories provide a much needed clarity, they are limited, narrow, and not necessarily oriented toward addressing the emotional layers of shame, self-blame, and betrayal. I love the clarity of radical feminism, and yet I am increasingly frustrated with the rigidity that often accompanies its analysis and vision. By exclusively focusing on men's violence and male domination, radical feminism often fails to fully account for the interlocking forces of racism, classism, and homophobia, as well as the complexities of power and privilege that shape what I know about life, both my own and other women's. Many of the feminists that I've worked with on issues of violence against women tend to deny, minimize, and even refuse to listen to the differential complexities and contradictions in many women's lives that cannot be accounted for exclusively by male dominance.

For instance, despite my political analysis of male violence and my anger at my father and the line of men who came after him, deep down, feminism didn't initially offer me an analytic voice to frame my anger at my mother. As a feminist, I developed an intellectual understanding, and even an empathy, for abusive and violent mothers (of course in the forefront of my mind and heart, though rarely publicly stated, was my own mother). I attributed mothers' violence to *their* victimization at the hands of husbands and fathers, and to their economic, social, legal, political, and, in relevant cases, racial, class, and ethnic oppression under the larger white-male-dominated system. I began to understand my mother's status and behavior in the family through the feminist lens that constructed her as a victim of the familial as well as societal patriarchy. I began to empathize with her, despite her verbal and physical violence and her allegiance to male dominance. I even felt protective of her against the backdrop of putdowns and condescension she faced in the family.

I was ripe for this analysis in the early 1980s when my father died and I moved home to live with her and my youngest brother; over late night beers, my mother would tell me *her* story of the years of my childhood. She told stories about her loneliness and her powerlessness. She told me about calling her mother, sometimes on a daily basis, to get assistance. Her mother, a very committed Catholic woman, was unsupportive. She told my mother that it was her choice to get married and that divorce was out of the question. My grandmother's solution was for my mother to pray more. My mother told me stories of the many miscarriages she had and my father's lack of empathy for her; she talked about her pregnancies, the lack of control over her life, and her resentment about the life she had created. I grew sad for my mother. We never discussed the violence—not his, not hers—and yet I knew her stories were given as a way of explanation, maybe apology.[17] I fit these stories into my feminist analysis that argued that men were the perpetrators of abuse and violence, not women, and that women's violence was a consequence of men's power. The stories were not enough, though, to soothe my soul. For one, my mother could not live with the stories she told across the kitchen table after too many beers, and so I would wake up, once again, each morning with a mother who would deny the stories and dismiss their implications. The question of reality and illusion continued to be open and volatile.

My mother died seven years after my father, and it was through her death that I began to shift my feminist lens to face the gaps, silences, and contradictions of her stories. I needed a different narrative to reconcile the betrayals of my mother in deferring to my father and his craziness, and also for her own violence against us, the kids. Facing my mother's abusiveness has been a necessary part of finding peace with the various tragedies of my childhood. This has been a struggle because it has meant a further breaking of the strong tradition of family loyalty. I've been able to do this in part because of the courageous voices of the women who have publicly spoken out about their mother's physical, emotional, verbal, *and* sexual abuse; I'm also able to do it because both of my parents are deceased. I still feel that my mother's story is one of victimization, especially by my father and her social surroundings, but I no longer feel the need to excuse her for her behavior, nor the need to always protect her by repressing my anger and sadness about her treatment of me and my sisters and brothers.

THE STORY OF RACE AND CLASS PRIVILEGE

Throughout the 80s and 90s, my feminist politics were radically challenged by feminists of color. I began to rethink my stories in terms of the unearned race and class privilege that have shaped my stories and my feminist analyses, strategies, and visions. I interrogated my stories in an effort to explore and make visible how they are steeped in class and race privilege just as much as they are in gender inequality and misogyny. I became more aware of how my privilege is often invisible, unmarked, and unacknowledged in the stories I've told about my life. What I realized was that I needed to understand how middle-class whiteness shaped my experiences of abuse and violence—the ways that it shaped how I (and others) have labeled and interpreted my experiences, the social and institutional responses I have received, and my experiences in feminist organizations that have been so essential to my processes of healing and resistance.

The men who committed sexual assaults and battery against me, including my father, have been mostly white middle-class men. Yet as a white middle-class girl-child and woman, middle-class and white people always warned me, implicitly and explicitly, of the dangers of men of color and poor men. They encouraged me to look to white middle-class and upper-middle-class men for protection. It has been the very men to whom I was to look to for "protection" who were the harassers, rapists, and batterers in my life. It is very important to name *white professional* and middle-class men as rapists and batterers and to name *white supremacy and a hierarchical class system* as major contributors to their acts of rape and battery and to the ways they are protected from public scrutiny. When I tell my stories from a framework of male dominance, their white and middle-class power and privilege remain unmarked and unanalyzed. Yet their abilities to be protected from institutional scrutiny are as much tied to their race and class as to their gender.

When I tell the stories of the violence against me, listeners often project "otherness" onto the men responsible and/or they minimize and excuse the violations. Rarely do folks link my stories of men's intimate, familial, and interpersonal violence to the social and economic power of middle- and upper-middle-class men. In discussions of men's violence, there is often a displacement onto the men's racial or ethnic identity, or to their "working-class" roots, or to their individual pathologic personalities. There is often a refusal to make middle-class and upper-middle-class white men—as themselves—accountable for the violence perpetuated and to link this violence to class and racial privilege and power.

The various responses to my experiences of sexual harassment and rape confirm this pattern. Listeners often minimize the violence of my father unless they can project it onto his Italian ethnicity or working-class roots. In response to my story of sexual harassment by a white male professor at a major university, feminist professors and support staff minimized not only the extent of the harassment against me, but also its impact. When I reported the incident years later to a sexual harassment administrator, she suggested that I should be grateful since I had indeed finished my Ph.D. In this response, she not only minimized the significant impact the event continued to have on me, but she also erased the other women graduate students who had dropped out of school because of their experiences with this same professor. Another feminist professor responded that since this man had since married, he would be less likely to continue his harassment of women students. I am sure that their reactions would have been much different had the male professor been nonwhite and/or someone who worked in a less prestigious job within the university.

While white skin and class privileges protect white professional men who are abusive and violent, they also benefit me in the ways I have been able to cope with and respond. For instance, I have had access to many resources. I have had the benefits of private individual counseling through health insurance provided by my various jobs in academia and white-collar clerical work. In private counseling and support groups over the years, I have not had to fear racial or class stigmatization by the counselors or other members of support groups. I have presumed that the counselors and support groups' members would be accepting of my background and culture (although I have at times felt defensive of my Catholicism and my lesbian identity). The unearned privileges of being white and middle-class have made my process of addressing these issues less fraught with tension, at least in comparison with women who have experienced ignorance, racism, classism, and other forms of oppressive attitudes by similar services.

The ways that feminism helped to save my life are connected with white and middle-class privilege as well. Because of the dominant race and class interests of many of the organizations, over time, I have gained the label of "authority" and "expert" to speak out and advocate because of my graduate education and my access to venues of authority. The privilege of skin color, class, and education afford me the credibility to speak generally and normatively, despite the limitations of both my experiential knowledge and the knowledge that I have accumulated through my scholarship and activism. Both knowledge bases are limited by the race and class identities and experiences of those central to its research base. In recognizing my white and middle-class privilege, I can own it while undercutting and undermining the ways it makes me into an "authority," or the ways that it would allow me to use my experience as normative and/or representative of women generally. I do this by marking the privilege and its impact on my experiences. I acknowledge that it is unearned privilege and thus unfair when exclusively given. Through my stories, I demonstrate how it has shaped as well as limited my experience and perspective, and I challenge the authority it seems to provide me. These strategies seem essential to a feminist practice that seeks to disrupt privilege and power systems that are responsible for the perpetuation of violence and oppression.

REVISIONING THE SELF

In much of the feminist analysis of intimate interpersonal violence, the identity of survivors that is constructed in the narratives is often one who is powerless, devastated, hurt, and often destroyed. After reading so much of this literature, I found myself constructing stories about my own pathology and pain. Despite the recognition of survival, the emphasis has been on the violence and its effects. We called ourselves survivors, and yet this didn't ultimately feel transformative. In the early 1990s, I found myself in desperate need of another story-line. Living without drugs, with less alcohol, *and* simultaneously confronting the realities of endemic abuse and violence was very difficult to say the least. It became really clear, really fast why I numbed myself out for all those years.

In her book, *Two or Three Things I Know for Sure*, Allison writes, "incest is a coat of many colors, some of them not visible to the human eye, but so vibrant, so powerful, people looking at you wearing it see only the coat. I did not want to wear that coat, to be told what it meant, to be told how it had changed the flesh beneath it, to let myself be made over into the rapist's creation. I will not wear that coat, not even if it is recut to a feminist pattern, a postmodern analysis."[18] Her words resonated with the discomfort I experienced with stories solely of vulnerability, powerlessness, and loss. The prevalence of these stories seemed to reconfirm my victimization and its pathological impacts. The stories did not challenge the underlying shame and self-hatred borne in abuse and violence. I began to question the political effectiveness of such stories in building a social justice movement oriented toward change. Allison's words helped me to question the benefits of women defining themselves in terms of what others had done to us. If I define myself solely through the stories of my father's abuse and violence, or the neighbors, or the men from my young adulthood, then the perpetrators still control my identity and life, and in the process, I am further diminished.

Naming my experiences as sexual harassment, rape, and battery has been absolutely essential to reconstructing the self previously disintegrating in a fog of denial and self-blame, and yet such naming in itself can become deadening to the heart and soul. Like Dorothy Allison, sometimes I tire of the explanations for incest and rape; as she writes, "I've got my own theory. My theory is that rape goes on happening all the time. My theory is that everything said about that act is assumed to say something about me, as if that thing I never wanted to happen and did not know how to stop is the only thing that can be said about my life."[19] I refuse the conclusive judgment that somehow what others did to me define me as a woman, as a lesbian, as a person, and yet I insist that the crimes of rape, battery, and murder against women be made visible and addressed.

I reframe myself as someone who is not simply the sum result of the tragedies of rape and battery. Claiming my rage through the women's movement has saved my life and yet I want more. In her essay, "Survival is the Least of My Desires," Allison claims, "we must aim much higher than just staying alive if we are to begin to approach our true potential."[20] In aiming higher, possibilities emerge and I glimpse a self that is strong, vital, passionate and courageous. With a newly dawned clarity in the mid-1990s, I returned to my life stories and began to re-imagine myself. I didn't necessarily find new stories, but I revised old ones through a new lens. This lens was one of resistance, escape, and subversion. I re-turned to young adult experiences of rape and attempted rape. While I speak out against the rapes, I highlight my resistance. My stories of attempted rape become stories of resistance. For instance, I tell stories about how I borrowed friends' cars to go on "dates" in order to prevent the possibility of being raped; in some cases, my suspicions about this need were accurate, and because I had prepared an es-cape route, I was able to run. Other times, I was less lucky. It took me years to val-idate one experience as a story of "real rape" even though he knocked me unconscious and I woke up with the rape in process.[21] Despite my own denial and minimization, despite the fact that I blamed the incident on my own naïvete, I did fight back by warning women in my social network that he could not be trusted and that they should stay away from him.

I began also to reformulate the struggle with my father over my sister's lives. For many years, I felt responsible for the fates of my younger sisters. I tried as best I could to intervene, to challenge his authority as well as that of the medical and psychiatric establishments, and to recruit other members of the family into a more united front. I did not succeed. I felt like a failure—I assumed that the only story was that my sisters lost, and my father, with the backing of social institutions, won. The story of this loss haunted me for years. Recently, however, I began to re-think the story with the help of my youngest sister, Laura, and with a frame of re-sistance and struggle. Instead of exclusively focusing on my powerlessness and instead of blaming myself for not being able to change the fate of my sisters, I be-gan to appreciate the efforts I did make. For instance, in one case, when my father began the process of sending my sister away to a behavior modification institution, I called a family meeting; I confronted the psychiatrist and psychologist responsi-ble; and I confronted my parents and other siblings about the problems associated with the plan to send her to this institution (which was being referred to euphemistically as a "reform school"). I then made my home available for my sister when she escaped from this institution with a friend of hers and I hid her from my parents for a few months until we felt it was safe to let them know that she was with me. Thus, instead of telling a story of my failed interventions, I tell stories that include resistance and struggle. As a result, I have begun to see myself in part as the radical I had been searching for in early childhood—the one who challenges unjust authority and struggles for freedom and self-determination for all. I embrace Audre Lorde's conception of process as it applies to the contexts of my own life; she reminds me that "I do not have to win in order to know my dreams are valid. I only have to believe in a process of which I am a part."[22] I have become a believer in my own process and in the multiple stories that are always evolving.

MIRACLES

> "Yes, I have been shaped as a lesbian and a writer by miracles. Miracles, as in wonders and marvels and astonishing accidents, fortunate juxtapositions and happy encounters, some resulting from work and luck but others unexplained and unexplainable."
>
> —Dorothy Allison, *Skin* (1994)

It began with my sister Laura who told me to ask for miracles from the universe when I needed a parking place. I ask, and amazingly enough, I often find. I've been encouraged to embrace the miracles of the universe and their impact on my life's journey. I am inspired by Dorothy Allison's conviction that while she "clings to no organized religion," she believes in the constancy of miracles. Once again, I seek to expand my stories, this time naming and appreciating the miracles that have surprised and sustained me over the years. At first I found it hard to break through the cynicism and anger of earlier selves who felt that miracles were only for the naïve. And yet cynicism only prevents movement. Cynicism seems effective only when combined with a lot of alcohol or drugs. One breakthrough has been listening to women friends involved in addiction recovery who talk about gratefulness. It took some effort for me to embrace the concept. Feminist analysis taught me to reject the gratefulness that I had been encouraged to feel as a young girl; I felt that the Catholic Church cultivated a gratefulness in order to erase and mystify women's oppression. Thus, I was highly suspicious. Increasingly, though, I am grateful for the life I've been able to forge for myself with the help of many miracles and twists of fate. As a kid, many miracles helped to sustain me—the miracle of books that allowed me to escape the chaos of my immediate surroundings, the miracle of my Aunt who took time out to sit and talk to me when we would visit her, the miracle of spelling bees that allowed me to believe that once learned, I could mostly predict future spellings, a prospect that gave me much relief in an otherwise very unstable environment. And like Dorothy Allison and many others, the miracle of feminism saved my life—enabling me to believe that it was possible to create a different life for myself, to find true friendship and community, to build enduring relationships, and to be a part of a larger movement for social justice.

> "My stories are not *against* anything; they are *for* the life
> we need."
>
> —Dorothy Allison, *Skin* (1994)

I fashion myself a malcontent; I don't accept the way that the world is structured and I'm continually outraged by the small and large atrocities that humans and human institutions commit. My righteous anger and deeply felt grief, however, are not simply a rebellion against the world but a struggle for a remade one (in the words of Dorothy Allison). This includes a remade family. As a feminist I have been deeply conflicted about the meaning of family—a patriarchal system and a place of potential connection and love. Many feminist friends have challenged my ongoing connection with my family. They see that this connection often has made me anxious, upset, angry, distraught, guilt-ridden, and more. Some have asked, "why bother?" and have encouraged me to create a new family of chosen friends. I would never be who I am today without this chosen family of friends and without the social and political movements that sustain my hope for social justice. At the same time, I have never given up on my biological family. Partly this is because I grew up with a strong sense of family loyalty—family connection, service, and commitment were considered most important in our lives.

Despite all the family dramas and conflicts, the betrayals and the losses, we—my immediate family members—have stayed connected. After my mother died and the stories of abuse and violence became open sites of conflicting interpretations and meanings, it seemed as if our connection was permanently broken. It was through the efforts of my youngest brother, Mark, who had been a latecomer to the family (he was born ten years after my youngest sister), that we came together to face each other's accusations and claims. In the early 1990s, we met as a group of brothers and sisters who were trying to come to terms with the loss of our parents and with the conflicting memories and interpretations of the family. While we did not arrive at an agreed upon set of stories, we created an opening for more honest and direct communication. The melodrama continues—we agree that we enjoy it too much to let it all go. But some of the underlying truths of our experiences—whether completely agreed to or not—have now been openly spoken and addressed even though a continual source of anxiety and tension. This is a miracle and has made possible an ongoing connection between us that while sometimes tense and stressful, remains a constant in my life today.

> "Our Catholic girl selves, like the vigil flame at the altar, live in us always."
> —Amber Coverdale Sumrall and Patrice Vecchione,
> *Catholic Girls* (1992)

Among the many "recovering" Catholics I know, we often commiserate that "once a Catholic, always a Catholic." While I renounced God and the Catholic Church in my early adolescence, I continued to struggle with its impact on my life. Beginning in the late 1980s, I felt forced to confront my conflicted relationship with the Church. When my mother died in 1988, suddenly and without notice, I was sent into a deep shock. It was like the rug had been pulled out from underneath me and everything came loose. I was beside myself. I was so discombobulated that I would find myself automatically reciting the "Hail Mary" whenever thinking about my mother, about my family, and when confronted with painful situations. I began to frequent Catholic churches. Often when I would pass by a church, I would enter and light a candle for my mother and for all the lost souls in the world. I realized that the Catholic girl in me was not dead at all, but alive and even praying, against all my expectations. This disturbed my feminist atheist self to say the least. I began to talk with other Catholic feminists, trying to sort out my confusion. I understood the anger. It was the grief and loss that were more difficult to untangle.

It was in the early 1990s when I began to imagine a confrontation with the Church in the hopes of some resolution. I wanted to be liberated from the Church's hold on me so that I might explore other spiritual possibilities. In the summer of 1999, I had the opportunity to speak with a radical nun about my experiences with the Church as a child and young adult. This was an amazing experience. She listened to my stories, she apologized on behalf of the Church, she helped me to recognize the aspects of Catholicism that continue to speak to me, and she helped me to see beyond the institution of the Church. While I am by no means reconciled with the Catholic Church, she showed me a path out of the morass of betrayal, grief, anger, and loss in relation to it. The bottom line of Catholicism, she said, is to follow your conscience. Another layer of shame and guilt began to peel away through this conversation. New stories are bound to evolve.

My conversation with this radical nun coincided with my participation in an Artist's Way workshop.[23] Central to this workshop is the concept of god defined as a higher power or spirit that is larger than life. I struggled daily with what this would mean for me who did not believe in god and who had renounced Catholicism as a young girl. Through this process, I realized that I could believe in "the universe" and with it the worlds of possibilities it offers. Spirituality can offer hope and possibility, which I find are essential to sustain my activism against the many injustices in the world. A sense of spirit and possibility allow me to see beyond the despair of endemic violence and oppression. As Aurora Levins Morales describes, "The spiritual is whatever allows us to notice the miraculous nature of life, how it keeps coming back, asserting itself in the midst of destruction. Whatever allows us to notice that life is in fact bigger than all the mean-spirited cruelties and brutalities of unjust societies. . . . It doesn't seem to matter what the source is, but without some sense of abundance, people get overwhelmed and lose their compassion and good judgment in urgency." [24]

WHAT IS MY CALLING?

As a kid, I identified with the flowers called weeds. I would ask their names, and demand to know why they were defined as weeds rather than as flowers. I was outraged at the campaign to destroy them. Dandelions were my favorite flower. I loved seeing them defy the odds of pesticides and mowers; I celebrated the way that they would pop up on the carefully manicured lawns of the neighborhoods in which I grew up. They became a metaphor for resistance and struggle, and for the hope and resilience of survivors, thrivers, and fighters. They reassure me that no matter how much people try to silence, to punish, to annihilate, to exterminate those who resist oppression, we continue to blossom, to show up, to announce ourselves and our defiance, and to speak our defiant refusal to be silent or dead. Years ago, I explained to my mother that my friends and I were really just a group of "dogmatic dandelions"—a group of women who refuse to accept the mistreatment, harassment, inequality, abuse, and violence in this society and who are passionately committed to social and economic justice. Andrea Dworkin best describes the contours of an identity that resonates with this resistance; in describing herself in her essay, "A Battered Wife Survives," she writes:

> In her heart she is a mourner for those who have not survived.
> In her soul she is a warrior for those who are now as she was then.
> In her life she is both celebrant and proof of women's capacity and will
> to survive, to become, to act, to change self and society. And each year
> she is stronger and there are more of her.[25]

11

A FEMINIST PRACTICE OF ANTIRACISM:
Strategies to Recognize and Disrupt White Privilege and Power

Barbara Smith offers a profound argument for why feminists must address racism; she writes,

> The reason racism is a feminist issue is easily explained by the inherent definition of feminism. Feminism is the political theory and practice that struggles to free *all* women: women of color, working-class women, poor women, disabled women, lesbians, old women—as well as white, economically privileged, heterosexual women. Anything less than this vision of total freedom is not feminism, but merely female self-aggrandizement.[1]

This definition is foundational to feminism. In the early 1980s, my limited notions of feminism, grounded in my white middle-class identity and privilege, were turned on their head. In a feminist theory class at the University of Illinois, we read Cherríe Moraga and Gloria Anzaldúa's anthology *This Bridge Called My Back: Writings by Radical Women of Color*, Angela Davis's *Women, Race, and Class*, bell hooks's *Ain't I a Woman?*, and Gloria Joseph and Jill Lewis's *Common Differences: Conflicts in Black and White Feminist Perspectives*, all published in 1981.[2] The passion and anger of the writers and activists moved me deeply. Having been involved in feminist activism for the previous five years, I felt variously defensive, guilty, and sad, as well as impassioned, angry, and hopeful about the possibilities for building a multiracial women's movement. I began to rethink my ideas, my strategies, my actions and behaviors.

In this class in 1982, as I read the writings of women of color, I imagined, quite naïvely, that once white middle-class feminists like myself recognized the limitations of our politics, the racism and classism of our organizations, the failures of our so-called "sisterhood," we would change and join in coalition with interested women of color to transform the world. With this hope in mind, another white graduate student and I did a presentation on racism in the women's movement as a wake-up call to ourselves and to the white middle-class members of the class. One of the professors in the course interrupted us early on in the presentation and the class's apparent unity began to unravel. White professors and students alike, during and after the class, charged that our presentation was antifeminist and divisive. I experienced what I came to understand as an active feminist racism of white privileged middle-class feminists communicated through defensive anger and denial. The white women in the class felt threatened by the writers' insistent arguments that radical women of color offered a fundamentally different perspective on feminism. They defended feminist politics from charges of being limited and steeped in racist and classist assumptions. They minimized the privilege we had as white and middle-class students and the power we had in feminist organizing. They denied the ways in which white feminist organizing often excluded, marginalized, and mistreated women of color, including working-class women, poor women, and lesbians. As a white privileged middle-class feminist, I was astounded by the defensive and angry responses. In retrospect, I realize that my surprise was mostly an indicator of my privilege. In any case, in this brief moment, I recognized the necessary significance of making antiracism integral to my feminism.

It has been almost twenty years since this feminist theory class and I have been on an incredible journey of self-realization and self-scrutiny ever since. I continue to be involved in personal and collective antiracist efforts under the broad rubric of feminist movement and politics. An ongoing process of unlearning racism, recognizing and taking responsibility for white privilege and power, and taking actions to challenge and dismantle the structures of white supremacy deepens my hope and vision for a community based in equality and justice. This process continues to be humbling as I realize how much I do not know and how much I continue to need to learn and relearn. In this chapter, I reflect on some of the lessons, strategies, and actions that have been a part of my journey. I write knowing that I am in a continual process of learning and revision, and that this chapter is necessarily incomplete and subject to challenge and change.

LEARNING TO LISTEN

Sometimes it is the simplest lessons that are the most difficult to learn. Learning to listen is a necessary first step in white antiracist practice and politics. Leslie Roman points out that the question of whether or not the subaltern can speak may not be the most significant question, but "Instead, it is whether privileged (European and North American) white groups are willing to listen when the subaltern speaks and how whites can know the difference between occasions for responsive listening and listening as an excuse for silent collusion with the status quo of racial and neocolonial inequalities."[3] The difference between the two is important. Responsive listening requires attention and responsibility. Responsive listening is a skill, it does not come naturally. It requires that I am fully present to the words, experiences, and perspectives of another person. Through responsive listening, I seek understanding without reducing another person's story into the framework of my own, and yet I also seek to include the story and its multidimensional complexities as part of my analysis of the world that I want to change. Responsive listening requires that I not only listen, but also that I act. The second kind of listening requires nothing of the listener; in fact, it can seem as if the speaker hasn't spoken. For instance, it is when white women in white dominant settings listen to perspectives of women of color that may challenge our own, we acknowledge the point, but then we move on with the conversation as if nothing has been said. This is not an antiracist practice of listening and must be challenged and disrupted. Instead, we must cultivate responsive listening with responsible actions.

ANGER AND RACISM—LETTING GO OF DEFENSES

Listening to women's anger, sadness, pain, and rage in response to racism is essential to a transformative politics. Feelings of fear, anger and rage are inevitable in discussions of racism and white supremacy. As Audre Lorde illuminates— "Women responding to racism means women responding to anger; the anger of exclusion, of unquestioned privilege, of racial distortions, of silence, ill-use, stereotyping, defensiveness, misnaming, betrayal, and co-optation."[4]

When called to account, the socially privileged often respond with defensiveness. I know this response from experience as I have been called on racism and white privilege many times over many years. It is always uncomfortable to be called on racist ideas and practices and on unacknowledged white privilege, and it is a learning experience that can result in personal reflection and change if I refuse to move into or remain in a defensive position.

In becoming observant of my own and other white feminists' responses to being challenged on racism, I recognize in our defensiveness a refusal to listen to what is being asked of us and a protectiveness toward our own status. Defensiveness is immobilizing and entrenches me in the status quo. In "The Wonderbreading of Our Country," the author illuminates white middle-class defenses. He writes, "For the middle classes, 'white' identity is based on maintaining their innocence. . . . Therefore the worst epithet that a middle class white person can be given is that s/he is a racist. This calls into play an *unconscious* loyalty that pervades all interactions—a white bonding when racism is charged, the response is

not to look at what happened and the impact of actions, but to defend the innocent intent of the person behind them. White identity here is about protecting
'their own,' not about justice."[5]

The defense of individual intentions is common and insidious among white
privileged feminists. Often, we defend ourselves through reference to our best antiracist intentions, our antiracist "credentials," and our antiracist "commitments."
Defensiveness can only be seen as unreflective, self-absorbed, and sometimes reactionary. Terrence Crowley's exploration of the principle of intentions v. effects is
instructive in this regard. He talks about the process of dismantling his assumptions of entitlement and privilege as a white man in the women's movement. He
explains the principle as follows, "my intentions are not necessarily what gives my
actions their moral value but rather their effects on others—specifically, those
people who are disenfranchised by my privilege, those marginalized by my sense
of entitlement. . . ." He reflects on how his privilege has given him "permission to
frame my perceptions as the Truth," and he suggests that to become an ally he had
to learn to give up notions of his authority. He has learned to refocus his attention
to the effects of sexism as defined from women's perspectives, rather than to assume that he can define sexism by referring to his intentions or his perceptions.
He says, not only were women "the ones to *name* those effects . . . they got to say
what I needed to do to redress the damage."[6]

Crowley's reflections offer guidance to white antiracist feminists as well. We
must learn to replace defensiveness with responsive and responsible listening that
results in active reflection and change. We must move beyond defending our intentions to explore the effects of our ideas and actions. As Audre Lorde writes,
"My anger is a response to racist attitudes and to the actions and presumptions
that arise out of those attitudes. If your dealings with other women reflect those
attitudes, then my anger and your attendant fears are spotlights that can be used
for growth in the same way I have used learning to express anger for my growth."[7]
Growth and change are possible only when we use the challenges as opportunities
for self-scrutiny, reflection, and change.

TRANSFORMING GUILT INTO ACTION

White privileged feminists also often respond to our implicated status in institutionalized racism and white privilege with guilt and shame. Having grown up
Catholic, I am no newcomer to either of these feelings and they are the first to arrive when faced with the realities of racism, class exploitation, antisemitism, and
other forms of discrimination and power in which I reap benefits. Unaddressed
and unanalyzed guilt and shame have mostly immobilized me. The more I learn to
name them and to see them for what they are—barriers to self-reflection and

change located in fear and insecurities—the more I am able to transform the feelings to ones of responsibility and willingness to change. Recognizing my power, I am freer to act. Naming guilt and shame as a way to let go of them allows me to redirect my energy and knowledge into positive action. It is not always an easy process, but a necessary one. One strategy that moves the feelings of guilt and shame along is to enlist what I call the "reality check" in situations where I have been called on my racism. In Audre Lorde's essay "The Uses of Anger," she analytically responds to white women's use of guilt and offers a perspective that challenges us to go beyond it; she writes:

> Guilt is only another way of avoiding informed action, of buying time out of the pressing need to make clear choices, out of the approaching storm that can feed the earth as well as bend the trees. If I speak to you in anger, at least I have spoken to you: I have not put a gun to your head and shot you down in the street; I have not looked at your bleeding sister's body and asked, 'what did she do to deserve it?'[8]

Responding to the charge of racism with fear and guilt as if it was an attack on my personhood does not create the conditions for mutual respect and dignity; responding with reflective willingness to change, on the contrary, offers the opportunity to create a more just community.

Another antiracist strategy to address guilt and shame is to recognize the power I do have and the responsibility I have to use this power in the service of change. With a focus on my white privilege I ask myself what I can do, rather than wallow in who I am and what I represent. As Barbara Smith suggests in reference to conversations with white women dealing with whiteness,

> No one on earth had any say whatsoever about who or what they were born to be. You can't run the tape backward and start from scratch, so the question is, what are you going to do with what you've got? How are you going to deal responsibly with the unalterable facts of who and what you are, of having or not having privilege and power? I don't think anyone's case is inherently hopeless. It depends on what you decide to do once you're here, where you decide to place yourself in relation to the ongoing struggle for freedom.[9]

Some say that when feminists focus on racism in the women's movement it contributes to negative and divisive relations among women. They imply that challenges to racism are just indicators of why we can't move "beyond race" and only lead to feelings of liberal guilt, rather than social action. I disagree. Being challenged on the racist dimensions of my work, behavior, and attitudes are often invitations to change, to take responsibility, and create connection across racial divides. Critical exchange offers me the opportunity to learn more about the insidiousness of racism and how it operates as a barrier that prevents the development of inclusive women's movements. A willingness to listen, to take seriously the charge, and to change creates possibilities for sustaining connections between women. Refusing to listen to charges of racism, responding defensively, and blaming whoever bears the message only bolsters the barriers between us and destroys the possibilities for connection and alliance. Change can be conflictual, difficult, and sometimes painful, and yet also transformative.

When white middle-class feminists recognize our own power in this society and take responsibility for the ongoing production of inequalities, there is less room for denial, guilt, and paternalism in trying to change it. Through self-scrutiny and honest reflection, I can act against racism, create positive change, and seek connection across differences in the pursuit of social justice. From this vantage point, I interpret the active critique of racism and white privilege as an invitation to change, rather than an end to the conversation.

CULTIVATING HUMILITY

Sometimes those of us white middle-class folks who engage in antiracist feminism end up reproducing ourselves as "superior" when our critical engagement with racism becomes an opportunity for self-righteousness. As Jennifer Simpson insightfully admits, "In addressing my privilege, I often trip on my ignorance and silence with my arrogance."[10] In my life I often find the path of self-righteousness to be one that invites my participation. I have definitely taken it at times, but not without regret. Upon reflection, I recognize that it is, in fact, easy for me as a white person to feel self-righteous in my anger toward white people, and white feminists in particular. Ever since I was a kid, I have had a deep anger at the multiple layers of injustice I experienced and witnessed in my family and in my community. This anger continues to save me from depression and despair. When I observe the racist attitudes and actions that stem from white privilege and white supremacist power I often respond with a righteous anger. The problem, however, is when I use this righteous anger to distance and differentiate myself from other whites and from white privilege and power. Disassociating myself from other white feminists is not an effective antiracist strategy, although at times it is my impulse. If I distance myself from other white people, I can delude myself into thinking that I am an exception and that that is enough to end racism and white supremacy. I can pretend that I am not implicated in white privilege and power and that I am somehow different from my white feminist friends, co-workers, and comrades. This strategy does not build an antiracist feminist movement, it simply operates to make me feel a little better about myself which ultimately is self-centered. Its effect on others is minimal and its impact on institutional structures nonexistent.

The move to self-righteousness among antiracist white feminists is worth exploring and disrupting. In part, it seems to stem from a harshly critical place within myself, a harshness that I project onto others. It may more accurately reflect my own sense of failure. In its place, I now try to build a sense of compassion and humility with regard to antiracist education and activism. The purpose of antiracist action is not to prove I am a better person—more innocent, less tainted— but to disrupt oppressive practices and create possibilities for individual, collective, and structural change. I find the words of Aurora Levins Morales profoundly provocative when she writes about the desire in antioppression work to distance ourselves from perpetrators of violence; she writes, "All of us have had failures of integrity. I believe part of what makes it so hard to consider perpetrators as part of our constituency is that we cannot bear to examine the ways in which we resemble them."[11] Morales challenges my disassociation from white racist practices and institutions; and she encourages me to engage with "the enemy" in all of its many guises, within and outside of myself. I have learned that antiracist feminist practice is about recognizing myself in others, and refusing the invitation to distance myself from the system of white privilege and supremacy and from those who perpetuate and benefit from it.

MOVING BEYOND SHARED VICTIMIZATION

White and middle-class feminists sometimes ingore or minimize the social differences between women by focusing on what we perceive to be shared victimization among women. Many feminists, especially in the 1970s, believed that through sharing stories, women would recognize our common experiences of gender-based oppression and violence and from that shared experience join together in a unified feminist movement. When I first began to listen to survivor stories of discrimination, abuse, and violence in order to build a theory and politics to resist that violence, I agreed. I focused on the common elements I heard in women's stories and used these in my efforts to connect and collaborate with other women. I believed that a unified sisterhood depended on our having shared a common experience of oppression. In retrospect, I realize that such a notion of sisterhood accomplished just the opposite because it reduced the complexities of many women's stories and it erased our historical, social, and cultural differences and divisions. A feminist commitment to shared victimization as a road to solidarity often means that we do not listen to the fullness of women's stories; we truncate them. In listening for commonality, we minimize women's different histories, cultures, contexts, experiences, and perspectives. What becomes known as "common" is based only on a very limited range of elements that the stories seem to generate. The stories often are not heard in their complexity, only for their relevance to the common gender-based oppression that is continually produced and reproduced. The interlocking forces of racism, heterosexism, xenophobia, anti-semitism, classism, and other forms of oppression and sources of resistance are marginalized at best. The hierarchical and unequal relations between women and their impact on our relationships are dismissed as potentially divisive. Women's differential access to privilege and power is also left out and unaddressed. Of course, it is going to be mostly privileged women who are going to agree with this emerging framework. Socially privileged women are not forced to deal with other women's power and control over our lives nor with multiple sources of oppression.

Responsive listening skills are helpful here as well. It would mean that feminists listen to women's stories without appropriating them for an already existing agenda and framework. It would mean that we listen to stories in all their complexity and multidimensionality, and this would become the groundwork for our theories and activism. Bearing witness to the stories of those who are different from ourselves means we must not assimilate the stories into our own stories, and at the same time, we must not distance the stories as if they were not connected to our own. I strive to listen now in a way that does not deny differences, but rather explores the differences between and among us. As feminists of color have argued for years, feminists can acknowledge, recognize, and learn from our differences—the differences in our social and political identities, locations, and contexts and the impact these have on our experiences and responses to violence.[12] When we pay attention to the *differences* among women, we create a much more detailed picture of the interpretation and effects of sexual violence on all women. The common problems of self-blame, shame, fear, and trust, for instance, are infused with culture, ethnicity, religion, class, and nation. For instance, the differential relationship of white women and women of color to the cultural constructs of virgins and whores produces the need for a different approach to sexual assault. Moreover, issues of family, ethnic, and racial loyalty, central to the silence and complicity which perpetuates sexual violence, are different depending on the specific configurations of racism, classism, homophobia, xenophobia, among other systems of oppression in particular historical contexts. For instance, the differential relationship of women of color and white women, especially white middle-class women, to the police state is central to our different perspectives on the criminal justice system and its role in ending violence against women. Feminists of color have been at the forefront of offering multilayered analyses of interlocking op-pressions and violence against women; for instance, some exemplary studies illu-minating the intricate contexts in which African-American women experience violence are Beth Richie's *Compelled to Crime*, Traci C. West's *Wounds of the Spirit: Black Women, Violence and Resistance Ethics*, Charlotte Pierce-Baker's *Surviving the Silence: Black Women's Stories of Rape*, and Melba Wilson's *Crossing the Boundary: Black Women Survive Incest*.[13]

While it is essential for white feminists to recognize differences and to incorporate the differences into our feminist scholarship, advocacy, and activism, we must *not* conceptualize "difference" as an aspect of "other women." In research that does address race and class within women's studies research, for instance, white middle-class heterosexual women's experience is defined implicitly as the normative and universal experience of women. In feminist analysis of violence against women, when issues of racial identity and the impact of racism are discussed, they are mostly in terms of the lives of women of color. Race, class, sexual orientation, and religion are mostly absent when discussing the experiences of white women, especially white, middle-class, heterosexual, Christian women. This group of women remains at the center of the generic discourse on violence against women as normative and unmarked. One response to this has been to acknowledge that the ideas are based on white, middle-class, heterosexual, Christian women's experiences.

While this is one step in the right direction, such an approach does not address the unequal *relationships* between us that account for these differences; nor does it account for the ways that white and middle-class and Christian and heterosexual privilege shapes particular women's experiences. As a white middle-class Catholic-raised lesbian woman, I am learning to articulate the racial and class dimensions of my own stories and how my unearned privileges benefit me often at the expense of women who do not have these unearned privileges. Roman suggests that white middle-class heterosexual feminists must go much further than simply naming our identity categories. She writes, "We will need to locate ourselves *within* these relations, going beyond the usual confessions (e.g., 'I am a white, middle-class, heterosexual feminist') that function as little more than disclaimers of privilege."[14] Given the hierarchical nature of a white supremacist capitalist patriarchy,[15] women exist in hierarchical relation to one another, and our lives are connected through these hierarchies. The level of my consumption, for instance, is related to the level of someone else's exploited labor; and the differences that I may construct between myself and the women doing this "exploited labor" may simply be reflections of a neocolonial relationship, not a relationship of connected sisterhood. Similarly, given that white femininity has been defined along the lines of virginity and passivity, my experiences of violence become markers of deviance to a privileged norm, a norm that is not available to women of color whose lives are circumscribed through controlling images of sexual promiscuity.[16] As Michelle Fine writes, "whiteness and 'color' are therefore not merely created in parallel, but are fundamentally relational and need to be studied as a system."[17] In speaking out about experiences of sexual violence, we must outline the contexts in which women are differentially located. We must note how our locations vis-à-vis social hierarchies and controlling images shape the differentiated responses of mainstream social institutions (media, criminal justice, healthcare, education) to women's experiences of sexual violence.

I am instructed by Roman's argument that as white teachers and students we must begin to locate ourselves "*in* the stories of structural racism." She continues:

> We (who occupy racially privileged positions) have much to learn about how to work with white students to transform their (our) desire to be included in the narratives of racial oppression as its disadvantaged victims into a willingness to be included in narratives which fully account for the daily ways we (whites) benefit from *conferred* racial privilege as well as from our complicity in the often invisible institutional and structural workings of racism.[18]

Roman offers a method for white and/or middle-class and/or heterosexual women to recognize the ways in which we are oppressed and privileged, and to analyze how this privilege is relational to oppression. This is an important lesson. I have to rethink again my own process of dealing with the violence and oppression in my life. As a privileged, white middle-class feminist and lesbian, I often saw my experiences through the lens of oppression, not privilege. At the same time, I recognized the lie of individuality and the limitations of an exclusive focus on gender when friends with less unearned privilege would compare their lives to mine. Often, the explanatory factors for the differences in addressing the abuse and violence in our lives were indicators of my race and class privilege, and not indicators of personal differences. The differences are also reflective of the limits of mainstream feminist organizations in addressing the interlocking structural systems that impact the experience of and response to violence. As someone who seeks support from many feminist organizations as a survivor, educator, and activist, I mostly feel welcomed. I have had the unearned benefit of not having to experience racism or classism from women in these organizations (although I did experience heterosexism and homophobia). This has created a relationship to the women's movement that is mostly positive and optimistic, and yet they are not shared by many because of experiences of mistreatment, exclusion, and marginalization based in interlocking systems of oppression and privilege that operate within these organizations.

If feminists assume shared victimization, they don't have to address unequal power as well as responsibility for acting in oppressive ways toward each other. Lorde asks, "What woman here is so enamored of her own oppression that she cannot see her heelprint upon another woman's face? What woman's terms of op-pression have become precious and necessary to her as a ticket into the fold of the righteous, away from the cold winds of self-scrutiny?"[19] Such scrutiny and responsi-bility are essential in a feminist movement grounded in equality and social justice.

RECOGNIZING SYSTEMIC WHITE PRIVILEGE

Feminists must acknowledge systems of privilege as well as oppression in women's lives, and develop strategies that disrupt both. Within a framework of shared vic-timization, the tendency is to see women as individuals who operate within similar structures. This framework allows an allegiance to an individualism that inhibits collective and collaborative strategies against multiple structural inequalities. The social system of capitalism, built on a bootstraps ideology of individual contribu-tion and merit, impacts the feminist struggle against violence as much as any other social grouping. While women's stories are understood as gendered, beyond gen-der they are often viewed as individual and idiosyncratic, while loosely connected to an environment shaped by multiple systems of oppression. Beyond a gendered lens, women's stories often remain anecdotal, and the underlying conditions of privilege and discrimination grounded in race, class, sexual orientation, nation, re-ligion, ableism, among other structural systems, remain muted and invisible, while still entrenched.

Among white feminists, a major result of white privilege is an assumption that "we" are all women who are impacted by gender, and an assumption that race, class, sexual and other social structures are less important. It is the belief in indi-viduality and meritocracy within an assumed homogeneous class of women. As the saying goes, if you work hard enough, you will succeed in whatever you set out to do within the women's movement—be this healing from rape, working in Women's Studies, or organizing against domestic violence. As Scheurich de-scribes, "Among Whites, the idea that each person is largely the source or origin of herself or himself, that is, individualism, is considered a natural facet of life. . . . This belief, then, is deeply infused in White judgments about the way life works. For example, if a person does 'well' in life, it is seen as being largely due to her or his own individual choices; if she or he does 'badly' in life, it is also largely due to her or his choices."[20] In "Wonderbreading of our Country," the author states, "All else being equal, it pays to be white. We will be accepted, acknowl-edged, and given the benefit of the doubt."[21] While white, middle-class feminists recognize the lie of individualism and meritocracy in terms of gender inequality, we have been less willing to recognize the impact of race, class, religious, and na-tional hierarchies and unequal power. In particular, many white feminists seem re-sistant to examining the forces of whiteness, white privilege, and white supremacy in the development of our identities, experiences, and perspectives, both within and outside of the contemporary women's movement.

In "North American Tunnel Vision," Adrienne Rich writes eloquently about the dangerous consequences of an unexamined whiteness among white feminists for the development of a broad-based social justice movement. She writes:

> I had for a long time been struggling along with other white feminists, with the meanings of white identity in a racist society and how an unexamined white perspective leads to dangerous ignorance, heart-numbing indifference, and complacency.[22]

Rich's points are centrally important to consider in feminist efforts against discrimination and violence, especially as organizations become more institutionally connected to state and corporate interests. For instance, white feminists perpetuate a dangerous ignorance when we do not analyze institutionalized white privilege in the institutions we build and work within, including feminist social services, public policy institutions, feminist grassroots organizations, and women's studies programs. As a white middle-class lesbian feminist in academia, I could simply celebrate the increased numbers of women faculty and students in women's studies, and the increased numbers of tenured women faculty and women in higher academic administration. I could analyze these increases as evidence of achievement in changing the male-dominant structure of the university and as evidence that women are faring well. While these achievements are worthy of celebration, they are limited to a narrow group of privileged white middle-class professional women and they have been in part produced through white privilege as well as resistance to white male dominance. In general, in my experience, many Women's Studies programs continue to be white, middle-class dominant in faculty, students, and curriculum. Institutionalized racism, classism, and homophobia continue to shape programs and the experiences of women of color, lesbians, and working-class women within them, as faculty, staff, and students. The possibilities for moving up in the system have been limited to faculty and to those women in higher administration; many women continue to experience the "sticky floor" problem of being stuck in dead-end positions within the university as clerical workers, food workers, and support staff. The achievements, then, are connected to white and professional class privilege, as much as they are a result of women's resistance to white male dominance.

The pathways in my life in the women's movement as in academia are shaped by gender restrictions and violence, as well as white middle-class privilege. The benefits I receive from within the women's movement and in Women's Studies are connected to unearned white middle-class privilege. For instance, I am often given the status of expert because of my academic profession. My analysis, based in part on my experience, is seen as generalizable and normative, rather than narrow and specific. In my work in Women's Studies and in feminist organizations, I do not face racism or classism or xenophobia. My abilities to survive and to thrive despite the oppression and violence I have experienced is due to privilege as much as it is to my own individual efforts in the women's movement. As Scheurich suggests in relation to social status, "Although each individual is to some extent different, and thus there is some contribution that is due to an individual's particular constellation of skills and abilities, the rewards each person receives are to a considerable extent an effect of the inequitable distribution of resources and power by race, class, and gender."[23]

If I am not aware of how white and middle-class privilege shapes my experience, I can remain willfully ignorant about institutionalized racism and classism, which leads to "heart-numbing indifference" to the plight of women with less unearned privileges. This indifference operates when socially privileged women like myself refuse to listen, believe, and respect the perspectives of women of color, with regard to discrimination because they do not match our experiences of these same institutions. If I use my experience at DePaul University, for instance, as a white middle-class lesbian as *the normative experience* of women and of lesbians, I am indifferent to the ongoing practices of racial and class discrimination. Privilege allows me the opportunity to discount the significance of stories about race and class discrimination in women's lives by classifying them as individual, isolated examples that are associated with the women themselves, not with structural inequality. I have seen this happen time and again within women's studies programs. This willful ignorance and social indifference leave white women's unequal power and privilege intact and uninterrogated and in turn leave women of color, who may be seeking alliances, with no validation or support. An important antiracist strategy for those with unearned privileges is to recognize that our experiential perceptions of organizations are linked to social privilege within these organizations. We must seek out the perspectives of women with less unearned privilege before we make judgments about issues of equality and justice.

Ignorance and indifference create a complacency with regard to the state of our social institutions. This is a white, middle-class complacency borne from privilege that serves as a barrier to collective struggle for social justice and equality. The antiracist question for me is how to mitigate ignorance, indifference, and complacency with regard to oppressive and privileging practices within the organizations of which I am a part. One strategy suggested by many before me is to make visible the operations of social privilege.

INTERROGATING "WHITENESS"/WHITE PRIVILEGE

In this country, white supremacy is an orchestrated system of power that works collaboratively with systems of patriarchy, capitalism, and imperialism. bell hooks in *Talking Back* suggests we use the term white supremacy, rather than racism, when defining the overarching system.[24] For me, the focus on white supremacy forces us to look at the ways that whites benefit from racial exclusion, discrimination, and violence and accumulate social power and privilege.

Antiracist efforts would do well to analyze white attitudes, behaviors, and practices in terms of how they bolster the accumulation of privilege in social and institutional contexts, rather than to solely focus on the impact of social discrimination on people of color. Too often, white feminists think working against racism exclusively means "helping" women of color, as if the problem of racism was "their problem."[25] By embracing a "helping" mentality, the underlying structure of white supremacy is bolstered. A "helping" dynamic keeps white people in power. bell hooks illuminates this dynamic as it played itself out among progressive whites in the 1960s. She suggests that they often responded positively to images of black suffering while they balked at images of black strength and power. She argues that the images of black suffering do not challenge whites to interrogate white privilege and power; instead, the consumption of these images by whites reinforces their feelings of superiority. She writes, "The image of blacks as victims had an accepted place in the consciousness of every white person; it was the image of black folks as equals, as self-determining that had no place—that could evoke no sympathetic response."[26] Thus, she argues, "Those white Americans who are eager to live in a society that promotes and rewards racial equality must be willing to surrender outmoded perceptions of black neediness that socialize them to feel comfortable with us only when they are in a superior, caretaking role."

Organizing against white supremacy means that we analyze, target, and challenge white privilege and disrupt and dismantle structures, ideas, and practices that bolster whiteness as superior. The refocusing of antiracist efforts toward white-dominant institutions leads to an interrogation of white supremacist identities and practices. For instance, whites must recognize that the construct of race does not only apply to people of color. Rather, it is important to recognize that all identities in this society are raced and that all of us are impacted by systems of oppression and privilege. Along these lines, Scheurich suggests, "We Whites need to study and report how being White affects our thinking, our behaviors, our attitudes, and our decisions from the micro, personal level to the macro, social level."[27] For myself, I label myself as "white" and interrogate the ways that constructions of race and dynamics of racism and white privilege shape my experiences. I seek to explore and to teach about the cumulative advantage accrued to white people, including white feminists in the women's movement. Rather than exclusively focusing on individual prejudice and/or on the impact of racism on people of color, I analyze how white people's attitudes, behaviors, and actions operate in relational dynamics of unequal social relations. As Michelle Fine describes her shift to "witnessing whiteness," she writes:

> With the raw nerve of reflection and the need for better racial thinking, I avert my gaze from the 'inequities' produced through 'colors' (where my work has lingered for so long) and turn, instead, to the 'merit' that accumulates within the hue of 'whiteness'. . . . I find myself trying to understand how whiteness accrues privilege and status; gets itself surrounded by protective pillows of resources and/or benefits of the doubt; how whiteness repels gossip and voyeurism and instead demands dignity.[28]

In the last ten years, some white privileged antiracist scholars and activists have begun focusing on white privilege. A proliferation of books, educational trainings, and activist groups exist now, and the practice of "interrogating whiteness" is gaining momentum. Given this, there are potential liabilities to a focus on whiteness if it is not consistently linked with a critical antiracist politics addressing institutional and structural change.

DISRUPTING INSTITUTIONALIZED PRACTICES OF RACISM AND WHITE SUPREMACY

The strategies of analyzing the contextual features of women's lives are not sufficient if they do not translate into action. Attention to difference, for instance, has not meant, necessarily, active challenges to white power and institutionalized racism in the programs, organizations, and strategies used to address violence against women. The entrenchment of racism is not simply an intellectual ignorance about women's differentiated and yet connected lives. It is the production and reproduction of power, an active resistance to change, and a will to protect existing power within white dominant organizations.

When I was growing up, I thought of racism as primarily a matter of individual prejudice, and only secondarily a function of power. Prejudice, I thought, was about ignorance and lack of information, even though I noticed that whenever I challenged racism by providing informational facts, I always faced a steel wall of resistance. I grew up with racism; I disagreed with it and challenged it and yet it was embedded in my mind and body. It often dictated the path of my life—my ideas and perspectives, my friends, my social networks, and my involvement in feminist organizing. Yet I attempted to challenge it when it surfaced in my family, among my friends and social networks, and in the schools and churches I attended. My strategy as an adolescent and young adult, however, was to be critical of individual prejudice, without a clear understanding of social power. Through my involvement in feminist and socialist politics in college, I began to develop an analysis of social and institutional power. Recognizing that racism is a system of power means that challenging racism cannot be limited to expanding white women's awareness. Challenging racist practices must involve confronting inequality in relationships and in organizations. Institutionalized racism in predominantly white organizations, including feminist groups, in all of its complex renderings, is ultimately about power and control—it's not just about ignorance, it's not just about conscious and unconscious attitudes and beliefs, and it's not just about cultural differences.

When I became involved in the feminist movement, I did not think I would encounter racism. Along with other white feminists, I assumed that feminists would be against racism and that our goal was to eventually become "nonracist." When I read *This Bridge*, *Women, Race and Class,* and *Ain't I a Woman*, I realized the danger of this assumption. Racism is much more than individual prejudice, and much more than overt bigotry. Upon reading the works of women of color and listening to the stories of my friends, I began to rethink my life and the feminist organizations, classes, and events in which I had been involved. I began to recognize the multiple and varied mechanisms of exclusion, silencing, judgment, and discrimination. I entered feminist conversations, classes, and meetings differently and began to listen from a new perspective. It was through this new lens that the concept of "institutionalized racism" became concrete to me. The National Institute Against Prejudice and Violence explains that institutionalized racism,

> Consists of *standard* organizational practices and norms that *incidentally* but inevitably perpetuate inequality, that is, restrict opportunities. . . . As a pattern of organizational behavior, institutional discrimination does not require that people maintaining the organization be prejudiced. The discrimination occurs as an outcome of the everyday behavior of the organization in pursuit of its goals.[29]

Institutionalized racism accounts for the failures in feminist groups organizing against violence against women.

Within many feminist antiviolence organizations, white middle-class women tend to be in the numerical majority, tend to take control over resources, and, because of skin and class privilege, tend to feel that their analysis and vision are representative of all women. These tendencies have led to narrow agendas and perspectives that are promoted by white middle-class women as if they were universally agreed upon. This practice, borne in social privilege, serves to marginalize, alienate, and often exclude women of color and their interests, concerns, and perspectives, as well as those of lesbians, working-class and poor women, among others. The power imbalances within many mainstream organizations reproduce the power of the white middle-classes. For instance, while many give lip service to wanting women of color in our organizations, white, middle-class feminists often are resistant to accepting the leadership of women of color. I've known many women of color who have worked in predominantly white feminist organizations. A good number have left in frustration due to feeling marginalized and excluded from leadership, and a good many continue to work while they are frustrated with the ongoing practices of racism and white privilege. In the following, I offer a few examples; they are by no means comprehensive, and yet from my experience they are common. One pattern in feminist antiviolence organizations is to hire women of color to do "outreach" and then to make it difficult for them to do the work. In a number of situations, women of color outreach workers have met with much resistance when they have tried to change the outreach agenda or strategies based on their knowledge of their own communities. In some cases, women have met with skepticism and mistrust in their abilities, and in some cases, women were fired. Sometimes when women of color are hired into predominantly white organizations, they are singled out as *the* woman of color. Sometimes a dynamic is set up where white women tend to talk with them only about *race* issues, but not include them in general conversations. When these same women try to incorporate concepts of culture and/or racism more substantially into the programming, they have been met with resistance. Sometimes, women of color shelter workers find that they are the ones with the nightshifts, while the white women are the ones with day shifts. Others tell me that while most women of color are doing much of the direct service work, most white middle-class women are moving into leadership positions.

White middle-class control and unequal power in feminist organizations are largely responsible for the failures in multiracial feminist organizing. The only solution to this is for white and middle-class women to give up exclusive control and power and to work collaboratively with others to create structures with shared leadership and shared power. We must create democratic structures that allow for multiple perspectives. Unfortunately, many white feminists opt for control rather than openness, refusing to acknowledge control prevents real change from occurring. These dynamics must change if white feminists expect to work with women of color as peers and equals. Leadership, power, and control must be shared and distributed, not owned. Building into organizational structures methods to share power and leadership would inevitably change the substance of feminist agendas and strategies.

Within the arena of domestic violence, for instance, white feminist leaders continue to look to the criminal justice system to enforce the agenda against violence without addressing the ways this system has been used to harass and unfairly criminalize women and men of color. Given the consistent critical analysis by feminist scholars and activists, feminists must seriously address in policy and practice the racism and classism integral to the criminal justice system. The refusal to consider the racism contributes to its perpetuation. Feminists of color continue to explore and negotiate the complexities of these issues for violence against women of color, while many white feminists continue to ignore the problems and act as if there is no other way to seriously prevent the perpetuation of domestic violence. The solution, as feminists of color continually argue, is not a question of either/or—either address racism in the system and ignore domestic violence, or address domestic violence and ignore racism. Feminists of color argue that we must address racism in the criminal justice system while making it more accountable to survivors/victims of domestic violence. As feminists move into the twenty-first century, feminists of color must be at the center of redefining and revisioning feminist perspectives, strategies, organizations, and visions.

Moreover, white feminists must consistently acknowledge the significant contributions of women of color to the progressive feminist movement's ideas, strategies, and visions. The feminist movement in this country has benefited enormously from the wisdom, activism, courage, and commitment of women of color. The multivaried perspectives and visions under the broad rubric of feminism, including the practical activist strategies toward equality and justice within the movement, are directly connected to the contributions of feminists of color. In my own experience, it has been feminists of color who have pushed me to expand my analysis, to be inclusive of more women, to challenge my own prejudices, stereotypes, and misconceptions about women different from myself, and to recognize and own my privilege and power. It's white power and unacknowledged privilege that inhibit coalition and collaboration across borders and that diminishes the breadth and strength of the feminist women's movements in this country and in the world.

WHITE ANTIRACIST FEMINIST ACTIVISM

In an effort to refocus antiracist activism toward white communities, some white antiracist feminists have created specific consciousness-raising and study groups as well as action groups to challenge white racist practices in the women's movement. I have participated in a number of these efforts. One of my better experiences was in the early 1990s, when I lived in Boston, with a group of white antiracist feminists called "White Women against Racism and Violence against Women." We initially formed this group as part of a multiracial effort to address violence against women of color in Boston. The effort was initiated by women in a community organization in Roxbury, a predominantly African-American neighborhood in Boston, in response to the brutal murder of a young African-American woman, Kimberly Rae Harbor. Women across the city were horrified by the murder and the appalling lack of media attention and police response to her death. After a series of vigils and community meetings held in Roxbury, white women began to outnumber the women of color. Organizers from the community began to feel that the overwhelming presence of white women was diminishing the efforts to involve the local community. They asked interested white women to refocus our energy to address white-dominant communities and institutions, who were not responsive to violence against women of color.

This antiracist white women's group began to engage in a variety of activities oriented toward white people. We wrote letters to white dominant newspapers challenging racial bias; for instance, we wrote a letter to the *Boston Globe* asking that violence against working-class, poor, and/or women of color receive at least as much media attention as that given to the murder of Mary Jo Frug, a white middle-class law professor at Harvard University. We attended demonstrations and marches with our banner, "No More Terror" that publicized the need for white feminists to fight racism. We distributed leaflets at marches to end violence that highlighted the connections between racism and violence against women. The leaflets also provided suggestions for individual and group actions to address racism. We spoke to feminist groups that were mostly composed of white women about developing an antiracist agenda and worked with them to create antiracist and inclusive strategies in their organizing efforts. In addition to our public efforts, we exchanged information and strategies to address racism and white privilege in our interpersonal and intimate relationships, in our workplaces, in our social groups, and in our feminist organizations. What I learned in this group was that antiracism must be a practice; it must involve action, not just reflection. Through this process, I found more ways to speak out, to protest, to educate, and to practice antiracism in all parts of my life. The process of learning about and acting against racism is ongoing. Since this group, I have participated in other antiracist study groups, including one in Chicago called Queer White Allies Against Racism. Through such groups, white feminists like myself learn to take more responsibility with regard to white privilege, and to take more actions against institutionalized racism. The groups contribute to a sustained antiracist feminist practice that refuses personal ignorance and complacency borne from unearned and unrecognized white privilege and power.

ALLIANCES AND SOLIDARITY: THE BASIS FOR COMMUNITY

In recognizing white middle-class privilege, I no longer assume that sisterhood is powerful and I no longer believe that unity can be created by focusing on women's common oppression. Instead I follow the wisdom of bell hooks who encourages women to bond on the basis of political solidarity rather than shared victimization.[30] In other words, solidarity is created through a shared commitment to struggle for social justice. In the words of Aurora Morales:

> Solidarity is not a matter of altruism. Solidarity comes from the inability to tolerate the affront to our own integrity of passive or active collaboration in the oppression of others, and from the deep recognition of our most expansive self-interest. From the recognition that, like it or not, our liberation is bound up with that of every other being on the planet, and that politically, spiritually, in our heart of hearts we know anything else is unaffordable.[31]

NOTES

1   IF NOT NOW, WHEN?

1. Andrea Dworkin attributes the phrase "atrocity work" to Robin Morgan. Dworkin defines this work as "the morbid side of the women's movement. I deal with the shit, the real shit." Dworkin, *Letters From a War Zone* (New York: E. P. Dutton, 1988), 133.

2. Dworkin, *Letters From a War Zone*, 1988, 133.

3. Emilie Buchwald, et al., *Transforming a Rape Culture* (Milkweed Editions, 1995); Violence Against Women, Bureau of Justice Statistics, U.S. Department of Justice. 202-307-0784 (January 30, 1994); for more recent statistics, visit Department of Justice's Bureau of Justice Statistics at http://www.ojp.usdoj.gov/bjs/.

4. Claire M. Renzetti, *Violent Betrayal: Partner Abuse in Lesbian Relationships* (Beverly Hills, CA: Sage, 1992); Claire M. Renzetti and Charles Harvey Miley, eds., *Violence in Gay and Lesbian Domestic Partnerships* (New York: Haworth Press,1996).

5. U.S. Department of Justice, Office of Justice Programs NEWS, http://www.pmewswire.com/cgi-bin/micro_stories.pl?ACCT=117401&TICK=OJP&STORY=/

6. Amber Coverdale Sumrall and Dena Taylor, eds., *Sexual Harassment: Women Speak Out* (Freedom, CA: Crossing Press, 1992); Gregory Herek and Kevin Berrill, eds., *Hate Crimes: Confronting Violence Against Lesbians and Gay Men* (Beverly Hills, CA: Sage, 1991); Mari J. Matsuda, Charles Lawrence, Richard Delgado, and Kimberlé Crenshaw, *Words that Wound: Critical Race Theory, Assaultive Speech, and the First Amendment* (Westview, 1992); Laura Lederer and Richard Delgado, eds., *The Price We Pay: The Case Against Racist Speech, Hate Propaganda, and Pornography* (New York: Hill and Wang, 1995).

7. Steven A. Holmes, "With More Women in Prison, Sexual Abuse by Guards Becomes a Troubling Trend," *New York Times* (December 27, 1996), A10.

8. Cherríe Moraga, "What Does it Take?" *Loving in the War Years* (Boston: South End Press, 1983).

9. Moraga, 1983.

10. Judith Herman, *Trauma and Recovery: The Aftermath of Violence from Domestic Abuse to Political Terror* (New York: Basic Books, 1992).

11. Liz Kelly, *Surviving Sexual Violence* (Minneapolis: University of Minnesota Press, 1988).

12. See Linda Gordon, *Heroes of Their Own Lives: The Politics and History of Family Violence* (New York: Viking, 1988).

13. For example, Kelly, *Surviving Sexual Violence*, 1988; Diana E. H. Russell, *Sexual Exploitation: Rape, Child Sexual Abuse, and Workplace Harassment* (Beverly Hills, CA:

Sage, 1984); Elizabeth A. Stanko, *Intimate Intrusions: Women's Experience of Male Violence* (Boston: Routledge and Kegan Paul,1985).

14. Dworkin, *Letters From a War Zone*, 1988; Judith Herman, *Father-Daughter Incest* (Cambridge: Harvard University Press, 1981); idem, *Trauma and Recovery*, 1992; Del Martin, *Battered Wives* (New York: Pocket Books, 1976); Beth Richie, *Compelled to Crime: The Gender Entrapment of Battered Black Women* (New York: Routledge, 1996); Susan Schechter, *Women and Male Violence: The Visions and Struggles of the Battered Women's Movement* (Boston: South End Press, 1982); Evelyn White, *Chain Chain Change: For Black Women Dealing with Physical and Emotional Abuse* (Seattle, WA: Seal Press 1985); idem, ed., *The Black Women's Health Book* (Seattle: Seal Press, 1990).

15. New York Radical Feminists, eds., *Rape: The First Sourcebook for Women* (New York: New American Library, 1974); Susan Griffin, *Rape: The Politics of Consciousness* (San Francisco: Harper and Row, 1986); Herek and Berrill, *Hate Crimes*, 1992; Catherine MacKinnon, *Sexual Harassment of Working Women: A Case of Sex Discrimination* (New Haven: Yale University Press, 1979); idem, *Feminism Unmodified* (Cambridge: Harvard University Press, 1987); Amber Coverdale Sumrall and Dena Taylor, eds., *Sexual Harassment: Women Speak Out* (Freedom, CA: Crossing Press, 1992).

16. Gloria Anzaldúa, *Borderlands/La Frontera: The New Mestiza* (San Francisco: Spinsters/Aunt Lute, 1987); Antonia Castañeda, "Sexual Violence in the Politics and Policies of Conquest," *Building with Our Hands: New Directions in Chicana Studies*, eds., Adela de la Torre and Beatriz M. Pesquera (Berkeley: University of California Press, 1993).

17. Louise Armstrong, *Kiss Daddy Goodnight: A Speak Out on Incest* (New York: Hawthorne Press, 1978); Toni McNaron and Yarrow Morgan, eds., *Voices in the Night: Writings by Women Survivors of Child Sexual Abuse* (Minneapolis: Cleis Press, 1982); Queer Press Collective, eds., *Loving in Fear: An Anthology of Lesbian and Gay Survivors of Childhood Sexual Abuse* (Toronto: Queer Press Non-Profit Community Publishing of Toronto, 1991); Diana E. H. Russell, *The Secret Trauma: Incest in the Lives of Girls and Women* (New York: Basic Books, 1986).

18. Kathleen Barry, *Female Sexual Slavery* (New York: Prentice Hall, 1979); idem, *The Prostitution of Sexuality* (New York: New York University Press, 1995); Kathleen Barry, Charlotte Bunch, and Shirley Castley, *International Feminism: Networking Against Female Sexual Slavery* (New York: International Women's Tribune Center, 1984); Andrea Dworkin, *Pornography: Men Possessing Women* (New York: Perigee, 1989); Laura Lederer, ed., *Take Back the Night: Women and Pornography* (New York: William Morrow, 1980); Diana E. H. Russell, *Making Violence Sexy: Feminist Views on Pornography* (New York: Teachers College Press, 1993).

19. Kelly, *Surviving Sexual Violence*, 1988; Richie, *Compelled to Crime*, 1996; Mimi H. Silbert and Ayala M. Pines, "Pornography and Sexual Abuse of Women," *Sex Roles* 10 (1984); White, *The Black Women's Health Book*, 1990.

20. Aurora Levins Morales, *Medicine Stories: History, Culture and the Politics of In-*

tegrity (Boston: South End Press, 1998), 17.

21. Nancy A. Matthews, *Confronting Rape: The Feminist Anti-Rape Movement and the State* (New York: Routledge, 1994).

22. bell hooks, *Ain't I a Woman: Black Women and Feminism* (Boston: South End Press, 1981); idem., *Feminist Theory: From Margin to Center* (Boston: South End Press, 1984); Angela Davis, *Women, Race and Class* (New York: Random House, 1981).

23. See hooks, 1981, 1984; Angela Davis, *Women, Race and Class*, 1981; Kimberlé Crenshaw, "Mapping the Margins: Intersectionality, Identity Politics and Violence," *The Public Nature of Private Violence*, eds., Martha Albertson and Roxanne Mykitiuk (New York: Routledge, 1994); Inés Hernandez-Avila, "In Praise of Insubordination, or What Makes a Good Woman go Bad?" *Transforming a Rape Culture*, eds., Buchwald, Fletcher, and Roth (Milkweed Editions, 1995).

24. Patricia Hill Collins, *Black Feminist Thought* (New York: Routledge, 1990), 222.

25. Collins, *Black Feminist Thought*, 226.

26. Morales, *Medicine Stories*, 123.

27. Antonia Castañeda, "History and the Politics of Violence Against Women," *Living Chicana Theory*, ed., Carla Trujillo (Berkeley: Third Woman Press, 1998); Andy Smith, "Christian Conquest and the Sexual Colonization of Native Women," *Violence Against Women and Children: A Christian Theological Sourcebook*, eds., Carol J. Adams and Marie M. Fortune (New York: Continuum, 1995).

28. Lucie Cheng Hirata, "Free, Indentured, Enslaved: Chinese Prostitutes in Nine-teenth-Century America," *Signs* 5:1 (1979), 4.

29. Peter Kwan, "Invention, Inversion and Intervention: The Oriental Woman in *The World of Suzie Wong, M. Butterfly*, and *The Adventures of Priscilla, Queen of the Desert*," *Asian Law Journal* 5:1 (May 1998), 99–137.

30. hooks, *Ain't I a Woman*, 1981; idem., *Feminist Theory*,1984; Davis, *Women, Race and Class*, 1981; Jennifer Wriggins, "Rape, Racism and the Law," *Harvard Women's Law Journal* 6, no. 1(Spring 1983); Darlene Clark Hine, "Rape and the Inner Lives of Black Women in the Middle West," *Signs* (Summer 1989).

31. Joan Nestle, ed., *The Persistent Desire: A Femme-Butch Reader* (Boston: Alyson Publications, 1992); Leslie Feinberg, *Stone Butch Blues* (Ithaca: Firebrand Books, 1993); Herek and Berrill, *Hate Crimes*, 1992.

32. Susan Estrich, *Real Rape* (Cambridge, MA: Harvard University Press, 1987); Morrison Torrey, "When Will We Be Believed? Rape Myths and the Idea of a Fair Trial in Rape Prosecutions," *U.C. Davis Law Review* 24, no. 4 (Summer 1991).

33. Castañeda, "History and the Politics of Violence Against Women," 1998, 317.

34. Castañeda, 1998, 313.

35. See Davis, 1981; Alison Edwards, *Rape, Racism and the White Women's Movement: An Answer to Susan Brownmiller* (Chicago: Sojourner Truth Organization, n.d.).

36. Davis, 1981; hooks, *Ain't I a Woman*, 1981; Barbara Omolade, "Black Women,

Black Men, and Tawana Brawley—The Shared Condition," *Harvard Women's Law Journal* Vol. 12 (1989), 11–23; Patricia Williams, *The Alchemy of Race and Rights* (Cambridge, MA: Harvard University Press, 1991), 169–78.

37. Jennifer Wriggins, "Rape, Racism and the Law," *Harvard Women's Law Journal* 6 (1983): 103–141.

38. Susan Estrich, *Real Rape*, 1987; and Micaela di Leonardo, "White Lies, Black Myths: Rape, Race, and the Black 'Underclass,'" *The Gender Sexuality Reader*, eds. Roger N. Lancaster and Micaela di Leonardo (New York: Routledge, 1997), 53–68.

39. See Peggy Reeves Sanday, *Fraternity Gang Rape: Sex, Brotherhood, and Privilege on Campus* (New York: New York University Press, 1990).

40. T. Denean Sharpley-Whiting, "When a Black Woman Cries Rape: Discourses of Unrapeability, Intraracial Sexual Violence, and the *State of Indiana v. Michael Gerald Tyson*," *Spoils of War*, eds., T. Denean Sharpley-Whiting and Renee T. White (New York: Rowman and Littleton, 1997), 53.

41. Sharpley-Whiting, 1997.

42. Davis, *Women, Race and Class*, 1981.

43. Rhea V. Almeida, "Unexamined Assumptions and Service Delivery Systems: Feminist Theory and Racial Exclusions," *Journal of Feminist Family Therapy* 5:1 (1993), 6.

44. See Theresa Funicello, *Tyranny of Kindness: Dismantling the Welfare System to End Poverty in America* (New York: The Atlantic Monthly Press).

45. Uma Narayan, *Dislocating Cultures: Identities, Traditions, and Third World Feminism* (New York: Routledge, 1997).

46. See Hernandez-Avila, "In Praise of Insubordination," 1995.

47. bell hooks, *Killing Rage: Ending Racism* (Boston: South End Press, 1995).

48. Morales, *Medicine Stories*, 1998, 122.

49. Antonia Castañeda, "History and Politics of Violence Against Women," 1998, 318.

50. Mari Matsuda, *Where is Your Body: And other Essays on Race Gender and the Law* (Boston: Beacon Press, 1996), 64–65.

51. Leslie G. Roman, "White is a Color! White Defensiveness, Postmodernism, and Anti-racist Pedagogy," *Race, Identity and Representation in Education*, eds., Cameron McCarthy and Warren Chrichlow (New York: Routledge, 1993). 74.

52. Barbara Smith and Beverly Smith, "Across the Kitchen Table, A Sister-to-Sister Dialogue," *This Bridge Called My Back: Writing by Radical Women of Color*, eds., Cherríe Moraga and Gloria Anzaldúa (Watertown, MA: Persephone Press, 1981), 126.

53. Cherríe Moraga, "La Guera," *This Bridge Called My Back: Writings by Radical Women of Color*, eds., Cherríe Moraga and Gloria Anzaldúa (Watertown, MA: Persephone Press, 1981), 29.

54. Moraga, "LaGuera," 1981, 30.

55. Dworkin, *Letters From a War Zone*, 1988, 170.

56. Moraga, "La Guera," 1981, 30.

57. Moraga, "LaGuera," 1981, 32.

58. bell hooks, *Talking Back: Thinking Feminist/Thinking Black* (Boston: South End Press, 1989).

59. hooks, *Talking Back*, 1989, 87–88.

60. hooks, *Talking Back*, 1989, 88.

61. hooks, *Talking Back*, 1989, 89.

62. hooks, *Talking Back*, 1989.

63. Dorothy Allison, *Two or Three Things I Know For Sure* (New York: Dutton Press, 1995), 71–72.

64. hooks, *Talking Back*, 1989.

65. hooks, *Talking Back*, 1989, 33.

66. Dorothy Allison, "Survival Is the Least of My Desires," *Skin*, 1994, 209.

67. Allison, "Survival Is the Least of My Desires," 1994, 213.

2   LESBIANS, PROSTITUTES, AND MURDER

1. This chapter was originally published in *Feminism, Media and the Law*, eds. Martha A. Fineman and Martha T. McCluskey (New York: Oxford University Press, 1997), 249–66.

2. In this chapter, I use the phrase "women working in prostitution" rather than "prostitutes" whenever possible because I do not want to participate in the objectification process that I observe in mass-media accounts of "prostitutes," which renders the women themselves invisible and does not necessarily reflect how the women define themselves.

3. Joan Nestle, *Restricted Country* (Ithaca, New York: Firebrand Books, 1987), 158.

4. Ibid.

5. George Gerbner, "Violence and Terror in and by the Media," in *Media, Crisis and Democracy*, eds., Raboy and Dagenais (Beverly Hills, CA: Sage, 1992).

6. George Gerbner and Larry Gross, "Living with Television: The Violence Profile," *Journal of Communication* 26, no. 2 (1976): 181.

7. Kimberlé Crenshaw, "Race, Gender, and Sexual Harassment," *Southern California Law* 65 (1992); Patricia Hill Collins, *Black Feminist Thought* (New York: Routledge, 1990).

8. Jane Caputi, *The Age of Sex Crime* (Bowling Green, Kentucky: Bowling Green State University Popular Press, 1987); Deborah Cameron and Elizabeth Frazer, *The Lust to Kill: A Feminist Investigation of Sexual Murder* (New York: New York University Press, 1987).

9. Angela Davis, *Women, Race and Class* (New York: Random House, 1981); Ann Russo, "If Not Now, When: Fighting Violence Against Women" Part I, *Sojourner* (November 1991); Crenshaw, "Race, Gender, and Sexual Harassment," 1992.

10. Patricia Williams, *The Alchemy of Race and Rights* (Cambridge, MA: Harvard University Press, 1991); Ann Russo, "Feminist Thoughts on the Stuart Case," *Sojourner* 17, no. 3 (February 1990); idem, "If Not Now, When," 1991; Crenshaw, "Race, Gender, and Sexual Harassment," 1992.

11. Russo, "If Not Now, When," 1991; Crenshaw "Race Gender and Sexual Harrassment," 1992.

12. Jack Hampton, a Texas state district court judge, who gave "a killer of two gay men a 30 year sentence instead of life in prison after remarking that the men wouldn't have been killed 'if they hadn't been cruising the streets picking up teenage boys'" [Gary Boulard, "The Anti-Twinkie Defense," *The Advocate* (June 14, 1994)].

13. *Newsweek*, June 21, 1993.

14. Gregory Herek and Kevin Berrill, eds., *Hate Crimes: Confronting Violence Against Lesbians and Gay Men* (Princeton, NJ: Princeton University Press, 1992), 90.

15. Sean P. Murphy, "2 Women from Mass. Slain in Caribbean," *Boston Globe* 1, no. 1 (December 1998); Peggy Hernandez, "Youth Held in Island Killing Reportedly Suspect in Thefts," *Boston Globe* 2, no. 44 (December 1988); "Scotland Yard Helps Probe 2 Watertown Women's Deaths," *Boston Globe* 3, no. 30 (December 1988).

16. Kay Loncope, "Area Lesbians Share Sadness, Fear After Couple's Slaying," *Boston Globe* 4, no. 1 (December 1988).

17. Ibid.

18. Carlton Smith and Thomas Guillen, *The Search for the Green River Killer* (New York: Onyx, 1991).

19. Herek and Berrill, *Hate Crimes*, 1992.

20. Jon Auerbach, "Study: Killings of Gays More Brutal," *Boston Globe* 21, no. 18 (December 1994).

21. Victoria Brownworth, "An Unreported Crisis," *The Advocate* (November 5, 1991), 50.

22. Herek and Berrill, *Hate Crimes*, 1992; Ann Russo, "Loving Dangerously," *Review of Hate Crimes: Violence Against Lesbians and Gay Men*, eds., Gregory Herek and Kevin Berrill, *Women's Review of Books* (October 1992).

23. Toni Locy and Brian McGory, "Woman Alleges Officer Forced Sex," *Boston Globe* 30, no. 1 (April 1994).

24. "Statement of WHISPER Action Group Members," *WHISPER* VI: 1–2 (Winter/Spring 1992): 3.

25. Caputi, *The Age of Sex Crime*, 1987; Cameron and Frazer, *Lust to Kill*, 1987.

26. Margaret A. Baldwin, "Prostitution and Feminist Discourses of Law Reform," *Yale Journal of Law and Feminism* 5, no. 1 (1992): 87–88.

27. Caputi quotes Jack Levin and James Alan Fox in the discussion of a particular serial killer and the number of women he killed: "We will never know for certain, because the majority of them would have been prostitutes whose disappearance may not have been reported. Some may have ended up among the many "Jane Does in the Los Angeles County morgue" (Caputi, *The Age of Sex Crime*, 1987, 224); See Baldwin, "Prostitution and Feminist Discourses," 1992.

28. Phyllis Chesler, "A Woman's Right to Self Defense: The Case of Aileen Carol

Wuornos," *St. John's Law Review* 66, no. 4 (1993): 946.

29. Baldwin, "Prostitution and Feminist Discourses," 1992, 88.

30. Caputi, *The Age of Sex Crime*, 1987, 117.

31. Combahee River Collective, "Twelve Black Women: Why Did They Die?" *Fight Back: Feminist Resistance to Male Violence*, eds., Frédérique Delacoste and Felice Newman (Minneapolis, Minnesota: Cleis Press, 1981), 68.

32. Elizabeth Sisco, "Forum I: Women Who Kill," *Critical Condition: Women on the Edge of Violence*, ed., Amy Scholder (San Francisco: City Lights Books, 1993), 43.

33. Smith and Guillen, "Green River Killer," 1991.

34. Caputi, *Age of Sex Crime*, 1987, 94.

35. Sisco, "Women Who Kill," 1993, 44.

36. Quoted in Baldwin, "Prostitution and Feminist Discourses," 1992, 87.

37. Sisco, "Women Who Kill," 1993, 42.

38. John Ellement and Efrain Hernandez Jr., "8 Teen-Agers Charged in Rape, Killing of Dorchester Woman," *Boston Globe* 20, no. 1 (November 1990).

39. John Ellement, Sean P. Murphy, Adrian Walker, and Michael Rezendes, "Police Defend Low-Profile Handling of Franklin Field Murder; Critics say Community Should Have Been Warned," *Boston Globe* 21, no.1 (November 1990).

40. Sally Jacobs and Anthony Flint, "The Enigma of Charles Stuart," *Boston Globe*, January 28, 1990.

41. See, for example, Alexander Reid, Peggy Hernandez, and Phyllis Coons, "Cambridge Police Have a Knife, No Motive in Professor's Murder," *Boston Globe* 6, no. 1 (April 1991); Anthony Flint, "Motive Still Unknown in Law Professor's Slaying," *Boston Globe* 8, no. 19 (April 1991).

42. Dolly Smith, "Cambridge Meeting Addresses Street Crime," *Boston Globe* 19, no. 68 (January 1991).

43. Mathew Brelis and Anthony Flint, "An Accomplished Life, A Brutal Death," *Boston Globe* 14, no. 1 (April 1991).

44. Quoted in John Bankston, "Florida Shocked by Case of Lesbian Accused of Serial Murders," *The Advocate* 577 (May 21, 1991), 50.

45. Quoted in Combahee River Collective, "Twelve Black Women," 1981, 68.

46. Rachel West, "U.S. PROStitutes Collective," *Sex Work: Writings by Women in the Sex Industry*, eds., Frédérique Delacoste and Priscilla Alexander (San Francisco: Cleis Press, 1988), 284.

47. Victoria Brownworth, "An Unreported Crisis," *The Advocate* June 14, 1991, 33–38.

48. Ibid.

49. See also Kimberlé Crenshaw, "Mapping the Margins: Intersectionality, Identity Politics, and Violence Against Women of Color," *The Public Nature of Private Violence*, eds., Martha Fineman and Roxanne Mykitiuk (New York: Routledge, 1994).

50. In general, the generic term "women" continues to be used to refer to centers, orga-

nizations, and projects which are predominantly lesbian. For instance, the "women's" music festivals, in Michigan, California, East Coast tend to be predominantly lesbian-initiated and organized, but the festivals are not called "lesbian."

51. Suzanne Pharr, *Homophobia: A Weapon of Sexism* (Inverness, CA: Chardon Press, 1988), 25.

52. Crenshaw, "Mapping the Margins," 1994.

53. Russo, "Loving Dangerously," 1992.

54. Kerry Lobel, ed., *Naming the Violence: Speaking Out About Lesbian Battering* (Seattle, WA: Seal Press, 1986)

55. Beatrice von Schulthess, "Violence in the Streets: Anti-Lesbian Assault and Harassment in San Francisco," in *Hate Crimes: Confronting Violence Against Lesbians and Gay Men*, 1992.

56. von Schulthess, "Violence in the Streets," 1992.

57. Joan Nestle, *A Persistent Desire* (Boston: Alyson Publications, 1992); Leslie Feinberg, *Stone Butch Blues* (Ithaca, NY: Firebrand Books, 1993).

58. Baldwin, "Prostitution and Feminist Discourses," 1992, 81.

59. Ibid., 67.

60. Lynda Hart, *Fatal Women: Lesbian Sexuality and the Mark of Aggression* (Princeton, NJ: Princeton University Press, 1994).

61. Feinberg, *Stone Butch Blues*, 1993; Nestle, *A Persistent Desire*, 1992; Elizabeth Kennedy and Madeline Davis, *Boots of Leather, Slippers of Gold: The History of a Lesbian Community* (New York: Penguin, 1993).

62. Hart, *Fatal Women*, 1994, 9.

63. Ibid., 12.

64. Quoted in Leslie Ernst, Cathy Greenblatt, and Susan McWhinney, "(Ain't) Natural History," *Critical Condition: Women on the Edge of Violence*, ed., Amy Scholder (San Francisco: City Light Books, 1993), 53.

65. Candice Skrapec, "The Female Serial Killer: An Evolving Criminality," *Moving Targets: Women, Murder, and Representation*, ed., Helen Birch (Berkeley: University of California Press, 1994), 243–44.

66. Quoted in Susan Edmiston, "The First Woman Serial Killer?" *Glamour* (September 1991) 325.

67. Ibid., 324.

68. James Kunen, Meg Grant, Cindy Dampier, and Sara Gay Damman, "Florida Cops Say Seven Men Met Death on the Highway When They Picked up Accused Serial Killer Aileen Wuornos," *People*, February 25, 1991, 46.

69. See Victoria Brownworth, "Crime and Punishment: Are the Rules of Law Different for Lesbians Charged with Crimes?" *Deneuve* (February 1995).

70. Quoted in Edmiston, "Woman Serial Killer?" 1991, 325.

71. Quoted in Mark MacNamara, "Kiss and Tell," *Vanity Fair* (September 1991), 96.

72. Quoted in Ibid., 100.

73. Smith and Guillen, *Green River Killer*, 1991, 118.

74. Quoted in Chris Lavin, "Jury Urges Death for Wuornos," *St. Petersburg Times,* January 31, 1992.

75. Phyllis Chesler, "Sex, Death and the Double Standard," *On the Issues* (Summer 1992), 30–31.

76. Moore was never implicated in any of the killings, presumably because she helped get Wuornos to confess to her own involvement. This is despite some evidence that Moore helped Wuornos, at least once, clean out and abandon a car that belonged to one of the men killed.

77. In this movie, on the other hand, the violence is attributed to her past abuse: The encounters with the men she killed are portrayed as triggering flashbacks to earlier abuse and trauma which induce her to kill.

78. Ronald Smothers, "Woman Is Arrested in Series of Killings in Florida," *New York Times,* January 18, 1991.

79. Quoted in Edmiston, "Woman Serial Killer?" 1991, 324.

80. Quoted in MacNamara, "Kiss and Tell," 1991, 98.

81. Quoted in Kunen, Grant, Dampier, and Damman, "Cops Say Seven," 1991, 46.

82. Chesler, "Woman's Right to Self Defense," 956.

83. Ibid., 958.

84. Chesler, "Woman's Right to Self Defense," 1993.

85. Lavin, "Jury Urges Death," 1992.

86. Skrapec, "Female Serial Killer," 1994.

87. Hart, *Fatal Women*, 1994.

88. Melanie Kaye/Kantrowitz, *The Issue is Power: Essays on Women, Jews, Violence and Resistance* (San Francisco: Aunt Lute Books, 1991).

89. Ibid.

90. Bankston, "Florida Shocked by Case," 1991, 50–51.

91. Donald Suggs, "Did the Media Exploit the 'Lesbian Serial Killer Story?'" *Advocate,* March 10, 1992, 98.

92. Ibid.

93. Again, this stands in stark contrast to men's violence against women which often is considered legitimate except for violence by men of color against white middle-class women. I am struck by the contrast in the understanding granted to men who are serial killers versus that given to women who kill men who have abused them.

94. Hart labels this strategy as the one feminists were using, and while you can see hints of this in Chesler's essays about Wuornos, you can also see a clear defense of Wuornos, as in the concluding line to Chesler's article in *On the Issues*, where she says that Wuornos is turning the question, "Well, [being raped, beaten, robbed, arrested and killed] is part of the job, why doesn't she get out?" around to "If men don't want to be killed, they should stay

away from prostitutes—or at least stop degrading and assaulting them" ("Sex, Death and the Double Standard," 1992, 31); Hart, *Fatal Women*, 1994, 151.

95. Hart, *Fatal Women*, 1994, 152.

96. Wuornos initially tried to appeal the seven murder convictions against her. The Florida Supreme Court rejected four of these appeals in early October 1994. For more information, check out the website www.prisonactivist.org/pubs/crossroad/6.3/wuornos.html. From news reports, it seems that Aileen Wuornos is no longer seeking an appeal.

97. You can see the contradictions in such reasoning in Chesler's own recognition of the problem of an "insanity" defense; she writes, "I am not saying that Wuornos did not kill anyone, nor am I saying she is sane—merely that a strategic use of the insanity plea might have saved her from the death sentence. It is still justifiable—even for a seriously traumatized woman—to kill in self-defense and Wuornos's claim of self-defense against a violent john is plausible" (Chesler, "Sex, Death and the Double Standard," 1992, 31).

98. Quoted in Ibid.

99. Hart, *Fatal Women*, 1994.

100. Ibid., 141.

101. Melanie Kaye, "Women and Violence," *Fight Back: Feminist Resistance to Male Violence*, eds., Frédérique Delacoste and Felice Newman (Minneapolis: Cleis Press, 1981), 163.

102. Judith Halberstam, "Imagined Violence/Queer Violence," *Social Text* (Winter, 1993).

103. Ibid., 199.

104. June Jordan, "Poem About My Rights" *Passion: New Poems* (Boston: Beacon Press, 1980).

3   LESBIAN AND BISEXUAL WOMEN'S BATTERING

1. See Pam Elliott, "Shattering Illusions: Same-sex Domestic Violence," *Violence in Gay and Lesbian Partnerships*, eds., Claire M. Renzetti and Charles Harvey Miley (New York: Haworth Press, 1996); Claire M. Renzetti, *Violent Betrayal: Partner Abuse in Lesbian Relationships* (Beverly Hills, CA: Sage, 1992).

2. Elliot, "Shattering Illusions," 1996.

3. See Charlene Allen and Beth Leventhal, "History, Culture, and Identity: What Makes GLBT Battering Different," *Same-sex Domestic Violence: Strategies for Change,* eds., Beth Leventhal and Sandra E. Lundy (Thousand Oaks, CA: Sage Publications, 1999), 75–76.

4. Sandra E. Lundy, "Equal Protection/ Equal Safety: Representing Victims of Same-Sex Partner Abuse in Court," *Same-sex Domestic Violence: Strategies for Change,* 1999; Evan Fray-Witzer, "Twice Abused: Same-Sex Domestic Violence and the Law," *Same-sex Domestic Violence: Strategies for Change,* 1999.

5. Claire M. Renzetti, "The Poverty of Services for Battered Lesbians," *Violence in Gay and Lesbian Domestic Partnerships*, 1996.

6. Allen and Leventhal, "History, Culture and Identity," 1999, 77.

7. Steve Friess, "Behind Closed Doors," *The Advocate* (December 9, 1997), 4.

8. Elliott, "Shattering Illusions," 1996, 7.

9. Matthiu Mendieta, "Hidden Bruises," *The Advocate* (November 23, 1999), 24.

10. Charlene Waldron, "Lesbians of Color and the Domestic Violence Movement," *Violence in Gay and Lesbian Domestic Partnerships*, 1996; Juan M. Méndez, "Serving Gays and Lesbians of Color Who are Survivors of Domestic Violence," *Violence in Gay and Lesbian Domestic Partnerships*, 1996.

11. Beth Leventhal and Sandra E. Lundy, eds., *Same-sex Domestic Violence: Strategies for Change,* 1999.

12. Kimberlé Crenshaw, "Mapping the Margins: Intersectionality, Identity Politics, and Violence Against Women of Color," *Stanford Law Review* 43 (July 1991).

13. Michele Bograd, "Feminist Perspectives on Wife Abuse: An Introduction," *Feminist Perspectives on Wife Abuse*, eds., Kersti Yllö and Michele Bograd (Newbury Park, CA: Sage, 1990), 14.

14. Gregory Herek, "The Social Context of Hate Crimes: Notes on Cultural Heterosexism," *Hate Crimes: Confronting Violence Against Lesbians and Gay Men*, eds.. Gregory Herek and Kevin Berrill (Beverly Hill, CA: Sage, 1992), 89–104.

15. Suzanne Pharr, *Homophobia: A Weapon of Sexism* (Inverness, CA.: Chardon Press, 1988).

16. Leslie Feinberg, *Stone Butch Blues* (Ithaca, NY: Firebrand Books, 1993); Joan Nestle, ed., *The Persistent Desire: A Femme-Butch Reader* (Boston: Alyson Publications, 1992).

17. Daphne Scholinski with Jane Meredith Adams, *The Last Time I Wore A Dress* (New York: Riverhead Books, 1997).

18. Gregory Herek and Kevin Berrill, *Hate Crimes: Confronting Violence Against Lesbians and Gay Men*, 1992.

19. See Herek and Berrill, *Hate Crimes*, 1992; Ann Russo, "Necessary Voices: A Battered Lesbian Fights for Recognition," Chapter 7, this volume.

20. Victoria Brownworth, "An Unreported Crisis," *The Advocate* (November 5, 1991), 50.

21. Brownworth, "An Unreported Crisis," 1991.

22. Brownworth, "An Unreported Crisis," 1991.

23. Lacey M. Sloan and Nora S. Gustavsson, *Violence and Social Injustice Against Lesbian, Gay and Bisexual People* (New York: Harrington Park Press, 1998).

24. Barbara Hart, "Lesbian Battering: An Examination," *Naming the Violence: Speaking Out About Lesbian Battering*, ed., Kerry Lobel (Seattle, WA: Seal Press, 1986), 173–77.

25. Allen and Leventhal, "History, Culture, and Identity," 1999, 81.

26. Hart, "Lesbian Battering," 1986, 175.

27. Munia, "Hurting Our Own: The Ugly Truth about Same Sex Domestic Violence," *Trikone* (July 31, 1998), 15.

28. Kerry Lobel, ed., *Naming the Violence: Speaking Out about Lesbian Battering* (Seattle, WA: Seal Press, 1986); Renzetti, *Violent Betrayal*, 1992.

29. Lobel, *Naming the Violence*, 1986; Ann Russo, "If Not Now, When: Fighting Violence Against Women," Part I and II, *Sojourner* 17, no. 3 (November 1991) and 17, no. 4 (December 1991); idem, "A Battered Lesbian Fights," 1992; Sandra E. Lundy, "Abuse That Dare Not Speak Its Name: Assisting Victims of Lesbians and Gay Domestic Violence in Massachusetts," *New England Law Review* 28 (1994).

30. Munia, "Hurting Our Own: The Ugly Truth about Same Sex Domestic Violence," *Trikone Magazine* 13 (July 31, 1998), 15.

31. Munia, "Hurting Our Own," 1998.

32. Tonja Santos, "Woman-to-Woman Battering on College Campuses," *Same-sex Domestic Violence: Strategies for Change*, 1999, 149.

33. D. Island and P. Letelier, *Men Who Beat the Men Who Love Them* (New York: Harrington Park Press, 1991).

34. Elliott, "Shattering Illusions," 1996, 3.

35. Lobel, *Naming the Violence*, 1986; Sandra E. Lundy, "Abuse that Dare Not Speak its Name, 1994; Russo, "Necessary Voices: A Battered Lesbian Fights for Recognition," Chapter 7, this volume.

36. See Suzanne Pharr, *Homophobia: A Weapon of Sexism* (Inverness, CA: Chardon Press, 1988).

37. Patricia Hill Collins, *Black Feminist Thought: Knowledge, Consciousness, and the Politics of Empowerment* (New York: Routledge, 1990); Crenshaw, "Mapping the Margins," 1991.

38. Collins, *Black Feminist Thought*, 1990.

39. Pharr, *Homophobia: A Weapon of Sexism*, 1988, 65.

40. Steven J. Onken, "Conceptualizing Violence Against Gay, Lesbian, Bisexual, Intersexual, and Transgender People," *Violence and Social Injustice Against Lesbian, Gay and Bisexual People*, eds., Lacey M. Sloan and Nora S. Gustavsson (New York: Harrington Park Press, 1998), 19.

41. Rhea Almeida, Rosemary Woods, Theresa Messineo, Roberto J. Font, and Chris Heer, "Violence in the Lives of the Racially and Sexually Different: A Public and Private Dilemma," *Expansions of Feminist Family Theory through Diversity*, ed., Rhea V. Almeida (New York: Haworth Press, 1994), 103.

42. Gallagher, 1995; Singer and Deschamps, 1994.

43. Onken, "Conceptualizing Violence Against Gay, Lesbian, Bisexual, Intersexual, and Transgendered People," 1998, 19.

44. Nora S. Gustavsson and Ann E. MacEachron, "Violence and Lesbian and Gay Youth," *Violence and Social Injustice Against Lesbian, Gay and Bisexual People*, 1998, 43.

45. Gustavsson and MacEachron, "Violence and Lesbian and Gay Youth," 1998, 45.

46. Michael Scarce, "Male-on-Male Rape," *Just Sex*, eds., Jodi Gold and Susan Villari

(New York: Rowman and Littlefield, 2000), 41.

47. Anthony R. D'Augelli, "Lesbian and Gay Male Undergraduates' Experiences of Harassment and Fear on Campus," *Journal of Interpersonal Violence* 7:3 (September 1992), 383–95.

48. Almeida et al., "Violence Against the . . . ," 1994, 109.

49. Fray-Witzer, "Twice Abused," 1999.

50. Angela West, "Prosecutorial Activism: Confronting Heterosexism in a Lesbian Battering Case," *Harvard Women's Law Journal* 15 (1992), 269.

51. Allen and Leventhal, "History, Culture, and Identity," 1999, 79–80.

52. Dorie Gilbert Martinez, "Mujer, Latina, Lesbiana—Notes on the Multidimensionality of Economic and Sociopolitical Injustice," *Violence and Social Injustice Against Lesbian, Gay and Bisexual People*, 1998.

53. Martinez, "Mujer, Latina, Lesbiana," 1998.

54. Martinez, "Mujer, Latina, Lesbiana," 1998, 101–102.

55. Claire M. Renzetti and Charles Harvey Miley, *Violence in Gay and Lesbian Domestic Partnerships*, 1996; Leventhal and Lundy, eds., *Same-sex Domestic Violence*, 1999.

56. Leventhal and Lundy, eds., *Same-sex Domestic Violence*, 1999.

57. Martha Lucía García, "A 'New Kind' of Battered Woman: Challenges for the Movement," *Same-sex Domestic Violence: Strategies for Change,* 1999, 170.

58. García, "A 'New Kind' of Battered Woman," 1999, 167.

59. Munia, "Hurting Our Own," 1998.

60. "Necessary Voices: A Battered Lesbian Fights for Recognition," Chapter 7, this volume.

61. Sarah Sulis, "Battered Bisexual Women," *Same-sex Domestic Violence: Strategies for Change,* 1999.

62. Gustavsson and MacEachron, "Violence and Lesbian and Gay Youth," 1998, 47.

63. Melanie Kaye/Kantrowitz, *The Issue is Power: Essays on Women, Jews, Violence and Resistance* (San Francisco: Aunt Lute Books, 1992).

64. Kaye/Kantrowitz, *The Issue is Power*, 1992, 37.

65. Liz Kelly, *Surviving Sexual Violence* (Minneapolis: University of Minnesota Press, 1988), 20.

66. bell hooks, *Feminist Theory: From Margin to Center* (Boston: South End Press, 1984).

4 PORNOGRAPHY'S STORIES

1. Andrea Dworkin, *Letters From a War Zone* (New York: E.P. Dutton, 1988); idem, *Pornography: Men Possessing Women* (New York: E.P. Dutton, 1989); Catherine Itzin, *Pornography: Women, Violence, and Civil Liberties* (London: Oxford University Press, 1992).

2. Dworkin, *Letters From a War Zone*, 1988, 265.

3. R. Betterton, *Looking On: Images of Femininity in the Visual Arts and Media* (London: Pandora, 1987); Susan Cole, *Pornography and the Sex Crisis* (Toronto: Amanita Enterprises, 1989); Gail Dines and Jean M. Humez, eds., *Gender, Race and Class in Media* (Beverly Hills, CA: Sage Publications, 1995); Gail Dines, Robert Jensen, and Ann Russo, *Pornography:The Production and Consumption of Inequality* (New York: Routledge, 1998); Andrea Dworkin, *Woman Hating* (New York: Dutton, 1974); idem, *Pornography*, 1989; Susan Faludi, *Backlash: The Undeclared War against American Women* (New York: Crown, 1991); bell hooks, *Yearning: Race, Gender, and Cultural Politics* (Boston: South End Press, 1990); idem, *Black Looks: Race and Representation* (Boston: South End Press, 1992).

4. Tracey Gardner, "Racism in Pornography and the Women's Movement," *Take Back the Night*, ed., Laura Lederer (New York: William Morrow and Company, 1980); Dworkin, *Pornography*, 1989.

5. Gardner, "Racism in Pornography," 1980, 105–106.

6. For instance, in a survey of Minnesota residents, 50 percent of a statistical sample agreed with the statement that "in the majority of rapes, the victim was promiscuous or had a bad reputation," and that the majority of rapes were reported only because "the woman was trying to get back at the man she was angry with or was trying to cover up an illegitimate pregnancy." This information comes from Martha Burt, "Cultural Myths and Supports for Rape," *Journal of Personality and Social Psychology*, 38 (1980), and was reported by Margaret Baldwin, "The Sexuality of Inequality: The Minneapolis Pornography Ordinance," *Law and Inequality* 2 (August 1984): 635–36.

7. Dworkin, "Why Pornography Matters to Feminists," *Letters from a War Zone*, 1988, 205.

8. Margaret Baldwin, "The Sexuality of Inequality," 1984, 640.

9. See Andrea Dworkin, *Letters from a War Zone*, 1988.

10. Laura Lederer, ed., *Take Back The Night: Women and Pornography* (New York: William Morrow, 1980); Diana E.H. Russell, *Against Pornography: The Evidence of Harm* (Berkeley, CA: Russell Publications, 1993); Diana E.H. Russell, ed., *Making Violence Sexy: Feminist Views on Pornography* (New York: Teachers College Press, 1993); Catharine MacKinnon and Andrea Dworkin, *In Harm's Way: The Pornography Civil Rights Hearings* (Cambridge, MA: Harvard University Press, 1997); Frédérique Delacoste and Felice Newman, eds., *Fight Back: Women's Resistance to Male Violence* (Minneapolis, MN: Cleis Press, 1981).

11. Andrea Dworkin and Catharine MacKinnon, *Pornography and Civil Rights: A New Day for Women's Equality* (Minneapolis, MN: Organizing Against Pornography, 1988); Laura Lederer and Richard Delgado, *The Price We Pay: The Case Against Racist Speech, Hate Propaganda, and Pornography* (New York: Hill and Wang, 1995); Andrea Dworkin, *Letters from a War Zone*, 1988.

12. Dworkin, *Pornography*, 1989; Dworkin, *Letters from a War Zone*, 1988; MacKin-

non, *Only Words*, 1993; Itzin, *Pornography*, 1992.

13. Luisah Teish, "A Quiet Subversion," *Take Back the Night*, ed., Laura Lederer (New York: William Morrow, 1980), 117.

14. Dorchen Leidholdt, "Where Porn Meets Fascism," *WIN* (15 March 1983); Diane E.H. Russell, *Making Violence Sexy: Feminist Views on Pornography* (New York: Teachers College Press, 1993); Itzin, *Pornography*, 1992.

15. Catharine MacKinnon, *Toward a Feminist Theory of the State* (Cambridge, MA: Harvard University Press, 1989), 199–200.

16. Maryviolet Burns, *When the Speaking Profits Us: Violence in the Lives of Women of Color* (Seattle, WA: Center for the Prevention of Sexual and Domestic Violence, 1986); Loretta Ross, "Third World Women and Rape," *Aegis* (Summer 1982); Amott and Matthieu, *Race, Gender and Work* (Boston: South End Press, 1991); Patricia Hill Collins, *Black Feminist Thought* (New York: Routledge, 1990); Sonia Shah, *Dragon Ladies: Asian American Feminists* (Boston: South End Press, 1997).

17. Gardner, "Racism in Pornography," 1980, 113.

18. Gardner, "Racism in Pornography," 1980, 113.

19. Alice Walker, "Coming Apart," *Take Back the Night*, ed., Laura Lederer (New York: William Morrow and Company, 1980), 95–104.

20. Patricia Hill Collins, *Black Feminist Thought*, 1990, 170–71.

21. Quoted from Roberto Santiago, "Sex, Lust and Videotapes: How Pornography Affects Black Couples," *Essence* (November 1990): 64.

22. Santiago, "Sex, Lust and Videotapes," 1990.

23. Gail Dines-Levy, "Pornography: The Propaganda of Misogyny," *The Community Church News*, Community Church of Boston, Massachusetts. Text of an address given on November 29, 1987.

24. Dorchen Leidholdt, "Where Porn Meets Fascism," 1983, 19.

25. Dworkin, "Women Lawyers and Pornography (1980)," *Letters from a War Zone* (New York: E.P. Dutton 1988), 240.

26. See Patricia Hill Collins, *Black Feminist Thought* (New York: Routledge, 1990).

27. Andrea Dworkin, *Pornography: Men Possessing Women* (New York: G. P. Putnam, 1989), 216.

28. Dworkin, *Pornography*, 1989, 216–17.

29. See Patricia Hill Collins, *Black Feminist Thought*, 1990, 168–73. Elena Featherston, "On Becoming a Dangerous Woman," *Sexual Harassment: Women Speak Out*, eds., Amber Sumrall and Dena Taylor (Crossing Press, 1992), 71–77.

30. See Angela Davis, *Women, Race and Class* (New York: Random House, 1981); Jennifer Wriggins, "Rape, Racism, and the Law," *Harvard Women's Law Journal* (Spring 1983): 103–41; or bell hooks, *Ain't I a Woman* (Boston: South End Press, 1981).

31. MacKinnon, "Francis Biddle's Sister," *Feminism Unmodified* (Cambridge, MA: Harvard University Press, 1987), 171–72.

32. Dworkin, *Pornography*, 1989; Itzin, *Pornography*, 1992; Laura Lederer and Richard Delgado, *The Price We Pay: The Case Against Racist Speech, Hate Propaganda, and Pornography* (New York: Hill and Wang, 1995).

33. The eroticization of youth and age/power differences are also common to gay male pornography.

34. Ann Burgess, *Child Pornography and Sex Rings* (Lexington, MA: D.C. Heath and Co., 1984); Tim Tate, "The Child Pornography Industry: International Trade in Child Sexual Abuse," *Pornography*, ed., Itzin, 1992.

35. In an article by Rich Snowden that appeared in *Aegis*, he discusses his work with incest/child sexual abuse offenders who often claimed that the young girls initiated the sexual activity. The men often claimed that the young girls were the ones with the power.

36. "Court Overturns Cartoonist's Sex Convictions," *San Jose Mercury News*, February 27, 1992.

37. Gail Dines-Levy, "Pornography: The Propaganda of Misogyny—III," *The Community Church News*, Community Church of Boston (May 1988).

38. From Don Feder, "Kid Porn in Mainstream Mags," *Boston Herald*, June 6, 1988.

39. *Pornography and Sexual Violence: Evidence of the Links* (London: Everywoman Press, 1988). Reprint of the Public Hearings to Add Pornography as Discrimination Against Women, 12–13 December 1983, in Minneapolis, Minnesota; see also Michele Eliott, "Images of Childern in the Media," *Pornography*, ed., Itzin, 1992.

40. Gail Dines-Levy, "Pornography: The Propaganda of Misogyny," *Community Church News*, Community Church of Boston. Lecture given in March 1988.

41. Information from "Incest and Pornography," *WAVPM News Page* IV.2 (February 1980): 1–3. Interview with Rich Snowden (founding member of Men Against Sexist Violence in San Francisco). He also mentions an article in *Playboy's Forum* by Wardell Pomeroy which proclaims the positive outcomes of father/daughter incest.

42. Collins, *Black Feminist Thought*, 1990, 169.

43. Gardner, "Racism in Pornography," 1980, 105–106, 108.

44. These pornographic books were found for sale at the *Video Expo* on Boylston Street in Boston, Massachusetts, in the mid-1990s.

45. This same criminal justice system has virtually left white men immune from prosecution for the rape of all women, particularly women of color, and men of color immune from prosecution for the rape of women of their racial communities. Gardner argues that one cannot overlook the fact that over 2,000 Black men were lynched from 1889 to 1899, and over 50 percent of them were charged with rape or attempted rape of white women. The rape charge continued to be used by the media as an overriding justification of lynching through the first half of the century. See also Angela Davis, *Women, Race and Class* (New York: Random House, 1981), 172–201; Jennifer Wriggins, "Rape, Racism, and the Law," *Harvard Women's Law Journal* 6.1 (Spring 1983): 103–41.

46. Quoted by Gardner, "Racism in Pornography," 1980, 110–11.

47. Dworkin, *Pornography*, 1989, 155–56.

48. Dworkin, *Pornography*, 1989.

49. Dworkin, *Pornography*, 1989, 156.

50. Dworkin, *Pornography*, 1989, 156–57.

51. Osanka and Johann, *Sourcebook on Pornography*, 56.

52. Dorchen Leidholdt, "Where Porn Meets Fascism," 1983, 20.

53. Dworkin, *Pornography*, 1989, 147. See her whole discussion 143–47.

54. See for instance, Saundra Pollock Sturdevant and Brenda Stoltzfus, *Let the Good Times Roll: Prostitution and the U.S. Military in Asia* (New York: The New Press, 1992); Than-dam Truong, *Sex, Money and Morality: Prostitution and Tourism in Southeast Asia* (London: Zed Books, 1990); Yayori Matsui, "Why I Oppose Kisaeng Tours," *International Feminism: Networking Against Female Sexual Slavery*, eds., Kathleen Barry, Charlotte Bunch, and Shirley Castley (New York: International Women's Tribune Center, Inc., 1984), 64–72; Venny Villapando, "The Business of Selling Mail-Order Brides," *Making Waves: An Anthology of Writings By and About Asian American Women*, ed., Asian Women United of California (Boston: Beacon Press, 1989), 318–26.

55. Other examples of the use of pornography in generating racism include: in Bangladesh, pornographic movies were shown in Pakistan among the camps during the war in 1971, when hundreds of thousands of Bengali women were being systematically raped by Pakistani troops. In the U.S., pornography focused on Asian women during the war in Vietnam [from Marty Langelan, "The Political Economy of Pornography," *Aegis* (Autumn 1981): 14].

56. See Varda Burstyn, ed., *Women Against Censorship* (Douglas and McIntyre, 1985).

57. Brief Amici Curiae of Feminist Anti-Censorship Taskforce in support of Plaintiffs. *American Booksellers v. Hudnut*. U.S. Circuit Court of Appeals (7th Circuit). Docket No. 84-3147. April 8, 1985. Page 37.

58. Deirdre English, "The Politics of Pornography," *Mother Jones* (April 1980), 48.

59. See Samois, ed., *Coming to Power* (Boston: Alyson Publications, 1981).

60. "Incest and other Sexual Taboos: A Dialogue Between Men and Women," *Out/look* No. 6 (Fall, 1989), 51–57.

61. "What It Means to Be Colored Me," *Out/look* (Summer 1990), 2.

62. Audre Lorde, "Sadomasochism: Not About Condemnation," *A Burst of Light* (Ithaca, NY: Firebrand Books, 1988), 14.

63. Julie Maya Stoil, "Radical Visionary for Justice," Interview with Andrea Dworkin, *Woman of Power* (Winter/Spring,1986), 77.

64. Dworkin, *Pornography*, 1989, 146. Here Dworkin draws a parallel between the denial of sexual violence and the denial of the torture and slaughter of Jews in Nazi Germany. In both cases the victims are characterized as passive, compliant, complicit. She writes: "The importance of the two specifics—Jew and women—resides in the resonating power of sexual memory. It is her image—hiding, running, captive, dead—that evokes the sexual tri-

umph of the sadist. She is his sexual memory and he lives in all men. But this memory is not recognized as a sexual fact, nor is it acknowledged as male desire: it is too horrible. Instead, she wants it, they all do. The Jews went voluntarily to the ovens. . . " (146).

5   LESBIAN PORN STORIES

1. This is a revised version of "Lesbian Pornography: Discourse of Inequality and/or Resistance," *Cultural Performances: Proceedings of the Third Berkeley Women and Language Conference*, eds., Mary Bucholtz, A.C. Liang, Laurel A. Sutton, and Caitlin Hines (Berkeley Women and Language Group, 1994).

2. Varda Burstyn, ed., *Women Against Censorship* (Toronto: Douglas and McIntyre, 1985); FACT, ed., *Caught Looking: Feminism, Pornography and Censorship* (New York, 1986); Pamela C. Gibson and Roma Gibson, eds., *Dirty Looks: Women, Pornography, Power* (bfi Publishing, 1993); Nadine Strossen, *Defending Pornography* (New York: Scribner, 1995).

3. Pat Califia, "Among Us, Against Us: The New Puritans [1980]," *Public Sex: The Culture of Radical Sex* (Pittsburgh, PA: Cleis Press, 1994), 113–14.

4. Califia, "Among Us," 118.

5. Cindy Jenefsky and Diane Helene Miller, "Phallic Intrusion: Girl-Girl Sex in *Penthouse*," *Women's Studies International Forum* 21:4 (1998), 375–85.

6. Lisa Henderson, "Lesbian Pornography," *Women and Language* 14, no. 1 (March 1991).

7. Jill Dolan, "Practicing Cultural Disruptions: Gay and Lesbian Representation and Sexuality," *Critical Theory and Performance*, eds., Janelle G. Reinelt and Joseph R. Roach (Ann Arbor: University of Michigan Press, 1992), 272.

8. Jenny Kitzinger and Cecilia Kitzinger, "'Doing It': Representations of Lesbian Sex," *Outright*, ed., Gabriele Griffin (London: Pluto Press, 1993).

9. Essex Hemphill, "Does Your Mama Know About Me? Does She Know Just Who I Am?" *Gay Community News* (25–31 March 1990), 8, 11.

10. "What It Means to Be Colored Me," *Out/look* (Summer 1990), 9.

11. Lisa Henderson, "Lesbian Pornography: Cultural Transgression and Sexual Demystification," *Women and Language* 14, no. 1 (March 1991), 3.

12. Henderson, 1991.

13. Andrea Dworkin, *Letters from a War Zone* (New York: Dutton, 1988), 266–67.

14. The following claims are based on an analysis of sixteen issues of *On Our Backs* from 1991 and 1992, one of the most popular lesbian pornography publications. The publishers report in 1992 that the magazine has a circulation of about 10,000.

15. Red Jordan Arobateau "Cum E–Z," *On Our Backs* (November/December 1991), 28.

16. Arobateau, "Cum E–Z," 38.

17. Arobateau, "Cum E–Z," 39.

18. Arobateau, "Cum E–Z," 40.

19. Jan Richman, *On Our Backs* (March/April 1991), 28.

20. Katherine Davis, Introduction, *Coming To Power*, ed., Samois (Boston: Alyson, 1982), 8–9.

21. Davis, Introduction, *Coming To Power*, 12–13. Specific essays in *Coming to Power* that address feminism and s/m include: Johanna Reinholdt, "From S/M, Feminism, and Issues of Consent" (80–85); Gayle Rubin, "The Leather Menace: Comments on Politics and S/M" (192–227); and Pat Califia, "A Personal View of the History of the Lesbian S/M Community and Movement in San Francisco" (243–87).

22. Robin Ruth Linden, Introduction, *Against Sadomasochism*, ed., Linden et al. (Palo Alto: CA: Frog in the Well Press, 1982), 4.

23. Andrea Dworkin, "Women Lawyers and Pornography (1980)," *Letters from a War Zone* (New York: Dutton, 1988), 241.

24. Some controversy exists over the breadth of the definition of sexual sadomasochism. See Chrystos, *In Her I Am* (Vancouver, B.C.: Press Gang Publishers, 1993), 83–88, for a helpful contribution to the conversation.

25. Pat Califia, *Sapphistry: The Book of Lesbian Sexuality* (Tallahassee, FL: Naiad Press, 1980), 118.

26. Califia, *Sapphistry*, 1980, 124.

27. Ann Wertheim, "Daddy's Little Girl," *On Our Backs* (May/June 1991), 40.

28. Wertheim, "Daddy's Little Girl," 1991, 40.

29. Mickey Warnock, "Arizona's Most Wanted," *On Our Backs* (July/August 1991), 44.

30. Anna Svahn, "The Strength of Trees," *On Our Backs* (March/April 1992), 29.

31. Anna Conchita Senos, "The Shower," *On Our Backs* (July/August 1991), 42.

32. Abs Bennett, "Mistress of Iron," *On Our Backs* (July/August 1992).

33. Ann Wertheim, "Daddy's Little Girl," 1991, 41.

34. Anna Svahn, "The Strength of Trees," 1992, 40.

35. Svahn, "The Strength of Trees," 1992.

36. Diviana Ingravallo, "Ex-Catholics Do It Better," *On Our Backs* (January/February 1991), 28, 32.

37. Califia, *Sapphistry*, 1980, 64.

38. Kerry Lobel, ed., *Naming the Violence: Speaking Out About Lesbian Battering* (Seattle: Seal Press, 1986).

39. Bennett, "Mistress of Iron," 1992, 39.

40. Dominique Dagmarr, "April Showers," *On Our Backs* (March/April 1991), 45.

41. Anna Conchita Senos, "The Shower," *On Our Backs* (July/August 1991), 42.

42. Pamela Pratt, "Dress Codes," *On Our Backs* (November/December 1991), 32.

43. Kathleen Bear Johnston, "Dressing Room Encounters," *On Our Backs* (March/April 1992), 32.

44. Anna Conchita Senos, "The Shower," 1991, 42.

45. Kathleen Bear Johnston, "Dressing Room Encounters," *On Our Backs* (March/April 1992), 30.

46. Anna Conchita Senos, "The Shower," 1991, 42.

47. Abs Bennett, "Mistress of Iron," 1992, 38.

48. Kathleen Bear Johnston, "Dressing Room Encounters," 1992, 32.

49. Jenny Kitzinger and Cecilia Kitzinger, "'Doing it': Representations of Lesbian Sex," *Outright:Lesbianism and Popular Culture*, ed., Gabriele Griffin (London: Pluto Press, 1993), 15.

50. Kitzinger and Kitzinger, "'Doing it': Representations of Lesbian Sex," 1993, 25.

6 SEXUAL CONFLICTS AND CONTRADICTIONS

1. An earlier version of this chapter, "'Feeding People in All Our Hungers'" appeared in *Pornography: The Production and Consumption of Inequality* (New York: Routledge, 1998).

2. Andrea Dworkin, *Woman Hating* (New York: E.P. Dutton, 1974); idem, *Our Blood: Prophecies and Discourses on Sexual Politics* (New York: Harper and Row, 1976); idem, *Letters From a War Zone* (New York: E. P. Dutton, 1988); idem, *Pornography: Men Possessing Women* (New York: Dutton, 1989).

3. Audre Lorde, *Sister Outsider* (Ithaca, NY: Firebrand Books, 1984); idem, *A Burst of Light* (Ithaca, NY: Firebrand Books, 1988).

4. Kathleen Barry, *Female Sexual Slavery* (New York: Prentice-Hall, 1979).

5. bell hooks, *Feminist Theory: From Margin to Center* (Boston: South End Press, 1984); idem, *Talking Back: Thinking Feminist, Thinking Black* (Boston: South End Press, 1989).

6. Catharine MacKinnon, *Feminism Unmodified* (Cambridge, MA: Harvard University Press, 1987).

7. Dorothy Allison, *Skin: Talking About Sex, Class and Literature* (Ithaca, NY: Firebrand Books, 1994); idem, *Two or Three Things I Know for Sure* (New York: Penguin Books, 1995).

8. Chrystos, *Dream On* (Vancouver: Press Gang Publishers, 1991); idem, *In Her I Am* (Vancouver: Press Gang Publishers, 1993).

9. Amber Hollibaugh, *My Dangerous Desires* (Durham: Duke University Press, 2000).

10. Cherríe Moraga, *Loving in the War Years* (Boston: South End Press, 1983); idem, *The Last Generation* (Boston: South End Press, 1993).

11. Joan Nestle, *A Restricted Country* (Ithaca, NY: Firebrand Books, 1987); idem, *A Persistent Desire: A Femme-Butch Reader* (Boston: Alyson, 1992).

12. Allison, *Skin: Talking About Sex, Class and Literature*, 112.

13. Liz Kelly, *Surviving Sexual Violence* (Minneapolis: University of Minnesota Press, 1988); Wendy Maltz and Beverly Holman, *Incest and Sexuality: A Guide to Understanding and Healing* (Lexington, MA: Lexington Books, 1987).

14. MacKinnon, "Sex and Violence: A Perspective (1981)," *Feminism Unmodified* (Cambridge, MA: Harvard University Press, 1987) 86–87.

15. MacKinnon, *Toward a Feminist Theory of the State* (Cambridge, MA: Harvard University Press), 127–28.

16. Andrea Dworkin, "Against the Male Flood: Censorship, Pornography and Equality (1985)," *Letters from a War Zone* (New York: E.P. Dutton, 1988), 265.

17. Carole Vance and Ann Snitow, "Toward a Conversation About Sex in Feminism: A Modest Proposal," *Signs* 10.1 (Autumn 1984): 130.

18. Gayle Rubin, "Thinking Sex: Notes for a Radical Theory of the Politics of Sexuality," *Pleasure and Danger*, ed., Carole S. Vance (London: Pandora Press, 1984), 275.

19. Rubin, "Thinking Sex," 1984, 308.

20. Rubin, "Thinking Sex," 281.

21. Lisa Duggan, Nan Hunter, and Carole Vance, "False Promises," in *Women Against Censorship*, ed., Varda Burstyn (Vancouver, BC: Douglas and McIntyre, 1985), 142–43.

22. Ann Snitow, quoted in "Porn: Liberation or Oppression?" *oob* (May 1983): 14.

23. Paula Webster, "Pornography and Pleasure," *Heresies* No. 12 (1981), 48–51.

24. Webster, "The Forbidden: Eroticism and Taboo," *Pleasure and Danger* 393.

25. Duggan, Hunter, and Vance, "False Promises: Feminist Antipornography Legislation," 145.

26. Webster, "Pornography and Pleasure" 50.

27. Webster, "Pornography and Pleasure" 49.

28. Lisa Orlando, "Bad Girls and 'Good' Politics," *Voice Literary Supplement* (December 1982): 1, 16. Orlando believes that a woman's position on pornography is ultimately dependent upon whether one emerged from childhood as a "good girl" or "bad girl." For herself, she suggests that "as a bad girl, I can't help viewing the feminist antiporn movement as a bunch of good girls on the rampage. . ." (16).

29. Webster, "Pornography and Pleasure" 35.

30. Langelan, *Aegis* (Autumn 1981): 12–13.

31. Florence Rush, *The Best Kept Secret* (Englewood Cliffs, NJ: Prentice-Hall, 1980).

32. Andrea Dworkin, Interview with Elizabeth Wilson, *Feminist Review* (June 1982), 24.

33. MacKinnon points out that the ideology of sexology, sexual liberation, and pornography is basically derived from "neo-Freudian derepression theory" which suggests that women's resistance to sexual liberation comes from sexual repression. She argues on the contrary that women's sexuality has not been repressed in the Freudian sense; "We have experienced deadening and silence and subordination. Men have eroticized the idea that their sexuality has been denied, but their sexuality has been nothing but expressed and expressed and expressed. Sexual liberation, from this perspective, looks like a male rationalization for forcing sex on women" (from MacKinnon, *Feminism Unmodified*, 1987, 144).

34. Dworkin, *Letters from a War Zone*, 1988, 127.

35. Allison, *Skin*, 1994, 117–18.

36. Allison, *Skin*, 1994, 213.

37. Allison, *Skin*, 1994, 116–117.

38. Dworkin, *Letters from a War Zone*, 1988, 127.

7   NECESSARY VOICES

1. This chapter was originally published as "A Battered Lesbian Fights for Recognition," in *Sojourner* 17:9 (May 1992):14, 16–17.

2. Only two of the Framingham Eight had their sentences commuted.

3. At the time this was written, up until today, the shelter for battered women in this area is not open to lesbians and bisexual women.

8   WHITE MEN CAN'T KILL?

1. Aishah Shahidah Simmons, "Creating a Sacred Space of Our Own," *Just Sex* (New York: Rowman and Littlefield, 2000), 53.

2. African American Women in Defense of Ourselves, in *Still Lifting, Still Climbing*, ed., Kimberly Springer (New York: New York University Press, 1999), 42–43.

3. Michelle Fine, "Witnessing Whiteness," *Off White: Readings on Race, Power, and Society*, eds., Michelle Fine, Lois Weiss, Linda C. Powell, and L. Mun Wong (New York: Routledge, 1997).

4. Elly Bulkin and Becky W. Thompson, "The Spectacle of Race in the O.J. Simpson Case," *Sojourner* 20: 1 (September 1994), 9.

5. Barbara Schulman, "Toward a Constructive White Antiracist Feminist Response to Racism and Domestic Violence," *Sojourner* (November 1995), 7.

6. Aaronette M. White, "Talking Black, Talking Feminist: Gendered Micromobilization Processes in a Collective Protest Against Rape," in *Still Lifting, Still Climbing*, ed., Kimberly Springer (New York: New York University Press, 1999), 189–218.

7. Ann Russo, "Feminist Thoughts on the Stuart Case," *Sojourner* (February 1990).

8. See, for instance, T. Denean Sharpley-Whiting, "When a Black Woman Cries Rape: Discourses of Unrapeability, Intraracial Sexual Violence, and *the State of Indiana v. Michael Gerard Tyson*," in *Spoils of War: Women of Color, Cultures, and Revolutions*, eds., T. Denean Sharpley-Whiting and Renée T. White (New York: Rowman and Littlefield, 1997), 45–58.

9. Peggy Hernandez, "A Victim of Violence is Laid to Final Rest," *Boston Globe* (October 29, 1989), 1.

10. Katheryn K. Russell, *The Color of Crime* (New York: New York University Press, 1998).

11. Jody Miller and Peter Levin, "The Caucasian Evasion: Victims, Exceptions, and Defenders of the Faith," in *Images of Color, Images of Crime*, eds., Coramae Richey Mann

and Marjorie S. Zatz (Los Angeles, CA: Roxbury Publishing Company, 1998), 220.

12. U.S. Department of Justice Release, January 30, 1994, from the Bureau of Justice Statistics, National Crime Victimization Survey Report, "Violence Against Women" (NCJ-145325).

13. bell hooks, *Killing Rage, Ending Racism* (New York: Owl Books, 1995).

14. Christopher B. Daly, "Pregnant Woman's Murder Shakes Boston's Image," *Washington Post* (November 1, 1983), A3.

15. Angela Davis, "Rape, Racism, and the Myth of the Black Rapist," *Women, Race, and Class* (New York: Random House, 1981).

16. Kirk A. Johnson, "Media Images of Boston's Black Community," *Trotter Institute Review* 4:1 (Spring 1990), 10–15.

17. Lillian Smith, *Killers of the Dream* (New York: W.W. Norton, 1949); Trudier Harris, comp., *Selected Works of Ida B. Wells-Barnett* (New York: Oxford University Press, 1991).

18. Larry Martz, Mark Starr, and Todd Barrett, "A Murderous Hoax," *Newsweek* (January 22, 1990), 16.

19. Sally Jacobs, "Stuart Reportedly Bought $10,000 Policy on his Wife," *Boston Globe* (February 1, 1990), 1.

20. Russell, *The Color of Crime*, 115.

21. Ibid.

22. Marian Meyers, "News of Battering," *Journal of Communication* (Spring 1994), 59; quoting G. Finn, "Taking Gender into Account in the 'Theatre of Terror': Violence, Media, and the Maintenance of Male Dominance," *Canadian Journal of Women and the Law* 3(2), 381.

23. Fred Bruning, "The Race Factor in a Brutal Killing," *Maclean's* (February 5, 1990), 11.

24. Martz, Starr, and Barrett, "A Murderous Hoax," 1990.

25. Sally Jacobs and Anthony Flint, "The Enigma of Charles Stuart," *Boston Globe* (January 28, 1990).

26. Jacobs and Flint, "The Enigma of Charles Stuart."

27. For instance, in the New Bedford, Massachusetts serial killings of the 80s, the news reports emphasized that the women murdered were involved in drugs and in prostitution. The media stories often imply that the women's murders are inevitable and that the women involved are more expendable than "other" women (i.e., white middle-class married women). See Ann Russo, "Lesbians, Prostitutes, and Murder," Chapter 2, this volume.

28. "The Killing of Carol Stuart." *The Economist* (January 13, 1990), 31.

29. Jonathon Alter and Mark Starr, with Todd Barrett and Kate Robins, "Race and Hype in a Divided City," *Newsweek* (January 22, 1990).

30. Russell, *The Color of Crime*, 1998, 114.

31. Farai Chideya, *Don't Believe the Hype: Fighting Cultural Misinformation about African-Americans* (New York: Plume, 1995), 190.

32. Ibid.

33. Alter and Starr, "Race and Hype," 1990.

34. Chideya, *Don't Believe the Hype*, 1995, 193.

35. Ibid., 193–97.

36. Russell, *The Color of Crime*, 1998, 117; see also Miriam H. Ruttenberg, "A Feminist Critique of Mandatory Arrest: An Analysis of Race and Gender in Domestic Violence Policy," *American University Journal of Gender and the Law* 2:17 (1994), 171–97.

37. Chideya, 200, 201.

38. Alter and Starr, "Race and Hype," 1990.

39. Russell, *The Color of Crime*, 1998, 84.

40. Ibid., 44.

41. Nancy Berns, "'My Problem and How I Solved It': Domestic Violence in Women's Magazines," *The Sociological Quarterly* (Winter 1999). She notes that in her survey of women's magazines, a very few articles (8 out of 111) focused on social and cultural context as a source of violence; for instance, during the media coverage of Simpson's case, one article in *Redbook* addressed athletes and wife abuse.

42. Evan Thomas, "Day and Night," *Newsweek* (August 29, 1994), 43.

43. Ibid.

44. Suzanne Schindehette, "The Man with Two Faces," *People Magazine* (July 4, 1994), 39.

45. Thomas, "Day and Night," 1994, 43.

46. Schindehette, 1994, 35.

47. Ibid.

48. Thomas, "Day and Night," 1994, 43.

49. Rachel Jones, "Striving for Success Doesn't Make Us 'White,'" *Boston Globe* (September 6, 1994), 11.

50. Elly Bulkin and Becky W. Thompson, "The Spectacle of Race in O.J. Simpson's Cast," *Sojourner* (September 1994).

51. Ann Ducille, "The Unbearable Darkness of Being: 'Fresh' Thoughts on Race, Sex, and the Simpsons," *Birth of a Nation'Hood*, eds., Toni Morrison and Claudia Brodsky Lacour (New York: Pantheon, 1997), 303.

52. "Ten Risk Factors," *Newsweek* (July 4, 1994), 29.

53. Michele Ingrassia and Melinda Beck, "Patterns of Abuse," *Newsweek* (July 4, 1994), 29.

54. Uma Narayan, *Dislocating Cultures* (New York: Routledge, 1997).

55. Ibid., 117.

56. Elizabeth Mehren, "Boston Area Shaken by Slayings Involving Doctors," *Los Angeles Times* (July 22, 2000), 13.

57. Kay Lazar, "Deadly Docs—3 Accused Shared Power, Privilege," *Boston Herald* (July 23, 2000), 1.

58. Barbara Schulman, "Toward a Constructive White Antiracist Feminist Response to Racism and Domestic Violence," *Sojourner* (November 1995), 7.

9 TAKING BACK OUR LIVES

1. Aurora Levins Morales, *Medicine Stories: History, Culture and the Politics of Integrity* (Boston, MA: South End Press, 1998), 16.

2. Jodi Gold and Susan Villari, eds., *Just Sex* (New York: Rowman and Littlefield, 2000).

3. Janelle White, "Because Violence is a Weapon of Oppression, Antirape Must Mean Antioppression," *Just Sex*, 2000, 167–80; Aishah Shahidah Simmons, "Creating a Space of Our Own," *Just Sex*, 2000, 47–58.

4. Janelle White, "Because Violence is a Weapon of Oppression, Antirape Must Mean Antioppression," *Just Sex*, 2000, 171.

5. White, "Because Violence is a Weapon of Oppression," 2000, 168.

6. White, "Because Violence is a Weapon of Oppression," 2000, 168.

7. Lily D. McNair and Helen A. Neville, "African-American Women Survivors of Sexual Assault: The Intersection of Race and Class," *Women and Therapy* 18:3/4 (1996), 107.

8. Anthony R. D'Augelli, "Lesbian and Gay Male Undergraduate Experiences of Harassment and Fear on Campus," *Journal of Interpersonal Violence* 7:3 (September 1992), 383–95.

9. Shamita Dasgupta, "Women's Realities: Defining Violence Against Women by Immigration, Race, and Class."

10. Katie Koestner, "The Perfect Rape Victim," *Just Sex*, 2000, 33.

11. Kathy Miriam, "Illusions of Postfeminism," *Just Sex*, 2000, 100.

12. Katie Gibbs refers to Katherine Gibbs Business School.

10 THE STRUGGLE FOR INTEGRITY IN AN UNJUST WORLD

1. Andrea Dworkin, *Letters from a War Zone* (New York: Dutton, 1988).

2. Jill Freedman and Gene Combs, *Narrative Therapy: The Social Construction of Preferred Realities* (New York: Norton, 1996), 77.

3. Aurora Levins Morales, *Medicine Stories: History, Culture and the Politics of Integrity* (Boston: South End Press, 1998), 4.

4. It took many years for me to name my father's sexual abuse. It was only through the deaths of my parents that I began to directly address it. In contrast, I had periods as a young adult when I would recall and relive the sexual abuse by a male neighbor. It was when I came into contact with feminist literature about sexual abuse in the late 70s and early 80s that I first told anyone about the sexual abuse of this neighbor. From there, it took another eight years, and my mother's death, before I felt confident to name my father in

the memories that came as flashbacks and nightmares. Despite the concrete memories, it continues to be difficult to say that sexual assault is what my father did to me.

5. Tish Langlois, *Fault Lines: Incest, Sexuality, and Catholic Family Culture* (Toronto: Second Story Press, 1997), 13.

6. Amber Coverdale Sumrall and Patrice Vecchione, *Catholic Girls* (New York: Plume, 1992), 3.

7. Langlois, *Fault Lines*, 1997, 122.

8. Langlois, *Fault Lines*, 1997, 129.

9. Adrienne Rich, *On Lies Secrets and Silence* (New York: Norton, 1979), 190.

10. I am drawing from the work of Dorothy Smith as she is used to frame the work of Tish Langlois (1997). As described by Langlois (1997, p. 64), "Ruling ideology creates a disjuncture, a 'line of fault,' because what women *actually* do within the dominant order is not always what it is in our *interest* to do. The line of fault becomes visible when women realize that the categories defined by men are 'a forced set of categories into which we must stuff the awkward and resistant actualities of our worlds.'"

11. Langlois, *Fault Lines*, 1997, 126.

12. Langlois, *Fault Lines*, 1997, 115.

13. Langlois, *Fault Lines*, 1997.

14. Mary Daly, *The Church and the Second Sex* (1974); Gena Corea, *The Hidden Malpractice: How American Medicine Mistreats Women* (Jove/HBJ, 1977).

15. Morales, *Medicine Stories*, 1998, 13.

16. Langlois, *Fault Lines*, 1997, 105–106.

17. Here I am speaking to my parents' explosive tempers and outrages, my father's control and dominance, and not the sexual abuse which I had not named directly.

18. Dorothy Allison, *Two or Three Things I Know for Sure* (New York: Penguin Books, 1995), 70–71.

19. Allison, *Two or Three Things*, 1995, 44.

20. Dorothy Allison, *Skin: Talking About Sex, Class and Literature* (Ithaca, NY: Firebrand Books, 1994).

21. Susan Estrich, *Real Rape* (Cambridge, MA: Harvard University Press, 1987).

22. Audre Lorde, *The Cancer Journals* (San Francisco: Sinsters/Aunt Lute, 1980), 13.

23. Julia Cameron, *The Artist's Way* (New York: Putnam, 1992).

24. Morales, *Medicine Stories*, 1998, 127.

25. Dworkin, *Letters From a War Zone*, 1988.

11   A FEMINIST PRACTICE OF ANTIRACISM

1. Barbara Smith, "Racism and Women's Studies," *The Truth That Never Hurts* (New Brunswick, NJ: Rutgers University Press, 1998), 96.

2. Cherríe Moraga and Gloria Anzaldúa, eds., *This Bridge Called My Back: Writings*

by Radical Women of Color (Watertown, MA: Persephone Press, 1981); Angela Davis, *Women, Race and Class* (New York: Random House, 1981); bell hooks, *Ain't I a Woman?* (Boston: South End Press, 1981); and Gloria Joseph and Jill Lewis, *Common Differences: Conflicts in Black and White Feminist Perspectives* (New York: Doubleday, 1981).

3. Leslie G. Roman, "White is a Color! White Defensiveness, Postmodernism, and Anti-racist Pedagogy," *Race, Identity and Representation*, eds., Cameron McCarthy and Warren Chrichlow (New York: Routledge, 1993), 79.

4. Audre Lorde, *Sister Outsider* (Freedom, CA: Crossing Press, 1984), 124.

5. "Wonderbreading of the Country," 20.

6. Terrence Crowley, "This lie of entitlement—my privilege to describe the reality of women—gives a rape culture its life. . . . When this lie is disallowed, the rape culture is challenged at its foundation. If I go on to name that lie, if I break ranks with the patriarchy by acknowledging that I cannot know the reality of those subordinated by the system of values that entitles me, that system is no longer seamless; its existence is endangered."("The Lie of Entitlement," *Transforming a Rape Culture*, 1995.)

7. Audre Lorde, *Sister Outsider*, 1984, 124.

8. Ibid., 130.

9. Barbara Smith, "Between a Rock and a Hard Place," *Yours in Struggle*, Elly Bulkin, Minnie Bruce Pratt, and Barbara Smith (Brooklyn, NY: Long Haul Press, 1984), 77.

10. Jennifer Simpson, "Identifying Race Privilege: From One White to Another," *Open Hands*, 11, no. 2 (Fall, 1995), 11.

11. Aurora Levins Morales, *Medicine Stories: History, Culture and the Politics of Integrity* (Boston, MA: South End Press, 1998), 114.

12. See, for instance, bell hooks, *Ain't I a Woman*, 1981; Gloria Joseph and Jill Lewis, *Common Differences: Conflicts in Black and White Feminist Perspectives*, 1981; Audre Lorde, *Sister Outsider*, 1984; Cherríe Moraga, *Loving in the War Years* (Boston: South End Press, 1983), among many others.

13. Beth Richie, *Compelled to Crime: The Gendered Entrapment of Battered Black Women* (New York: Routledge, 1996); Traci C. West, *Wounds of the Spirit: Black Women, Violence, and Resistance Ethics* (New York: New York University Press, 1999); Charlotte Pierce-Baker, *Surviving the Silence: Black Women's Stories of Rape* (New York: Norton, 1998); Melba Wilson, *Crossing the Boundary: Black Women Survive Incest* (Seattle, WA: Seal Press, 1994).

14. Roman, 77–78.

15. bell hooks uses this phrase throughout her work and I find it very useful and compelling.

16. Patricia Hill Collins, *Black Feminist Thought* (1990).

17. Michelle Fine, "Witnessing Whiteness," *Off White: Readings on Race, Power and Society* , eds., Michelle Fine, Lois Weis, Linda C. Powell, and L. Mun Wong (New York: Routledge, 1997), 58.

254 TAKING BACK OUR LIVES

18. Roman, 84.

19. Lorde, *Sister Outsider*, 1984, 132.

20. James Joseph Scheurich, "Toward a White Discourse on White Racism," *Educational Researcher* (November 1993), 6–7.

21. "Wonderbreading of our Country," 29.

22. Adrienne Rich, "North American Tunnel Vision," *Blood, Bread, and Poetry* (New York: W.W. Norton, 1986).

23. Scheurich, "Toward a White Discourse on White Racism," 1993, 7.

24. bell hooks, *Talking Back* (Boston: South End Press, 1989).

25. hooks, *Talking Back*, 1989, 54.

26. hooks, *Talking Back*, 1989, 59.

27. Scheurich, "Toward a White Discourse on White Racism," 1993, 9.

28. Fine, "Witnessing Whiteness," 1997, 57.

29. *Campus Ethnoviolence...and the Policy Options* (Washington, D.C.: National Institute Against Prejudice and Violence, 1990).

30. bell hooks, *Killing Rage* (Boston: South End Press, 1995), 51.

31. Morales, *Medicine Stories*, 1998, 125.

PERMISSIONS

INDEX